EBERLY LIBRARY
WAYNESBURG
COLLEGE

Waynesburg, Pennsylvania

in memory of

Margaret Gross Turja
Class of 1932
presented by

Reverend and Mrs.
Arthur W. Turja

823   F459Zbe

Henry Fielding at Work

Magistrate, Businessman, Writer

Lance Bertelsen

palgrave

First published 2000 by
PALGRAVE™
175 Fifth Avenue, New York, N.Y. 10010 and
Houndmills, Basingstoke, Hampshire, England RG21 6XS
Companies and representatives throughout the world.

PALGRAVE™ is the new global publishing imprint of St. Martin's Press LLC Scholarly and Reference Division and Palgrave Publishers Ltd (formerly Macmillan Press Ltd).

ISBN 0-312-23336-1 hardback

Library of Congress Cataloging-in-Publication Data

Bertelsen, Lance.
    Henry Fielding at work : magistrate, businessman, writer / Lance Bertelsen.
        p.   cm.
    Includes bibliographical references and index.
    ISBN 0-312-23336-1
        1. Fielding, Henry, 1707–1754.   2. Authors, English—18th century—Biography.   3. Justices of the peace—England—Biography.   4. Businessmen—Great Britain—Biography.   I. Title.
PR3456.B47   2000
823'.5—dc21
[B]   00–0369907

A catalogue record for this book is available from the British Library.

Design by Letra Libre, Inc.

First published: September, 2000
10   9   8   7   6   5   4   3   2   1

For Mattias and Elin,
my pride and joy,
and Denise,
my love

Contents

Acknowledgments

As scholar, writer, and friend, Denise Sechelski reminded me daily that clarity and entertainment are not inimical to the writing of literary history. The prose of the third-floor set—Rumrich's force, Rebhorn's grace, and Whigham's originality—provided impressive variations on that theme. Jim Garrison helped as only an eighteenth-century colleague and chairman can. Tom Lockwood remains the most generous scholar I know. Clem Hawes's enthusiasm worked, I think, in mysterious ways. Sue Heinzelman lent insights into eighteenth-century legal narrative. Discussions with George Boulukos, Scarlett Bowen, and Jenneken VanKeppel expanded my thinking. James Thompson offered valuable suggestions toward strengthening an early version of chapter 1 that appeared in *Eighteenth-Century Studies*. The staffs of the British Library, the Humanities Research Center, and the Huntington Library were efficient and cheerful. And a Dean's Fellowship from the College of Liberal Arts at the University of Texas provided useful time off. Finally, thanks again mom and dad.

Introduction

Fielding's Last Offices

No useful Talent in the Society will be idle, nor will any Man long want a Seller and Purchaser of what he is desirous either to purchase or dispose of; whereas at present many a Man is Starving, while in the Possession of Talents, which would be highly serviceable to others, who could and would well reward him.

—*A Plan of the Universal Register-Office,* 1751

On Tuesday last William Neal was committed to Prison by Justice Fielding, for stealing several iron Rails, the property of Sir Francis Head: as was Christopher Emners, for picking the Pocket of Mr. Rolte of a silk Handkerchief; and John Marsh on an Indictment of wilful and corrupt Perjury. The same Day one Thomas Halwyn, charged Catherine his Wife, and Benjamin and Samuel, two young Lads, her Sons by a former Husband, with beating him.

—*The Covent-Garden Journal,* 1752

Henry Fielding's last offices were in Bow Street and the Strand. In Bow Street Fielding served as magistrate for Westminster and Middlesex from November 1748 to May 1754, a period during which he interrogated thousands of people—thieves, prostitutes, vagrants, carousers, receivers of stolen goods, con artists, embezzlers, wife beaters, husband beaters, rapists, and murderers—to determine whether alleged lawbreakers should be released, chastised from the bench, or committed to prison to await trial.[1] At the same time, several blocks away at the Universal Register Office in the Strand, Fielding's half-brother John, various

clerks, and sometimes Henry Fielding himself made similar kinds of judgments on the truthfulness of presumably law-abiding clients—clergy,
landowners, teachers, craftsmen, apprentices, and especially servants—who
sought to register property, services, or themselves for sale, rent, or employment. In January 1752, to link and advertise the two institutions, the
journalist Henry Fielding launched *The Covent-Garden Journal*, a periodical that served simultaneously to report and comment on the cases brought
before Justice Fielding, to promote the Universal Register Office, and to
provide readers with news, entertainment, and social commentary.

As a magistrate, businessman, and writer, Fielding was in a singular position to textualize eighteenth-century English cultural conditions and
materially to author the text of his society. As a writer, Fielding theorized
the necessity of employment, fictionalized the behavior of working and
nonworking people, moralized on the proliferation of criminals and prostitutes, and promoted journalistic, commercial, and legal causes; as a magistrate and businessman, Fielding advertised, controlled, and profited from
judicial, commercial, and literary institutions that had real power to affect
the lives of his fellow citizens. Not only did he extol employment, he co-
owned an employment agency. Not only did he deplore prostitution, he
"saved" prostitutes. Not only did he commit fictional criminals to paper,
he committed actual criminals to prison. And he could and did commit
actual criminals to prison and paper simultaneously. The growth of scholarly interest in the interaction of eighteenth-century textual production,
commerce, and the law suggests that more particular attention should be
paid to Fielding's unique incorporation of magistracy, entrepreneurship,
and professional writing.[2] For Fielding, such incorporation seemed natural. For the scholar, it offers a case study in the textual, psychological, and
material negotiations linking eighteenth-century cultural practices, as well
as a lived embodiment of such negotiations in the experience of one of the
premier writers of the period.

Until now, Fielding's overlapping activities as writer, magistrate, and
businessman have been approached in two ways. Literary studies have
tended to parcel them into comparative groupings—law and the novel, for
example—for the purpose of constructing broader critical syntheses.[3] Biographical approaches have treated them in a more integrated and personal
manner, but with a tendency toward the cursory and the laudatory. In his
comprehensive biography, for example, Martin Battestin has written that
Fielding "from the beginning of his magistracy . . . understood the value
of advertising his office, not merely from the mercenary motive of increasing his business, but for public-spirited reasons. In this way he alerted
the citizenry to the nature and prevalency of the evils that plagued society: moreover, by publishing descriptions of criminals and stolen goods . . .

he attempted to check the spreading epidemic."[4] Fielding would have certainly agreed with this characterization—since he invented it—but it does little to probe the more intricate relationships between public spirit and mercenary motivations, between descriptions of criminals and journalistic entertainment, which seem to cry out for critical attention. Similarly, Battestin appraises *The Covent-Garden Journal* as "a vehicle for promoting the Universal Register Office and for keeping the public apprised of Fielding's activities and concerns at Bow Street, . . . coloured throughout by the graver moral purpose that characterizes all Fielding's writings of these last years."[5] Again one must wonder what additional ethical colorations might emerge from a close examination of an entertainment journal authored by a sitting magistrate and dedicated simultaneously to amusement, business, and court reporting. Although both John Bender and Peter Linebaugh have provided some critical counterbalance by suggesting that a predilection for surveillance and control deeply informs Fielding's literary and legal activities, no study has yet addressed the more subjective and commercial motivations related to the entertainment dimension of *The Covent-Garden Journal,* which may have affected Fielding's practice as magistrate and author during this period.[6]

For its part, the Universal Register Office has largely been portrayed as a quaint enterprise, offering "the combined services of an employment agency, a financial institution, a real estate agency, a curiosity shop, and a travel bureau."[7] Pat Rogers whimsically calls it "a kind of Universal Aunts"; Peter Linebaugh, more matter-of-factly, describes it as a "labour exchange where employers might examine prospective servants and study their character references."[8] Bertrand Goldgar's edition of *A Plan of the Universal Register-Office* judiciously contextualizes the institution but without probing the more complicated and potentially darker elements of its practice. And Battestin writes with some enthusiasm that "'Noble' is perhaps not too grand a word for this business."[9] Needless to say, little effort has been made to reconstruct the sensations or procedures of the register office—the atmosphere, emotions, motives, and rules affecting its proprietors and clients—nor has the relationship of these goings-on to Fielding's more well-documented practice at the magistrate's office been fully examined. For the majority of twentieth-century critics, biographers, and historians, the remarkable intersection of Fielding's activities in Bow Street, in business, and in the literary journal that brought his two offices together has remained a topic of vague but generally positive interest, eliciting performance evaluations ranging from exemplary to, at least, good-intentioned.[10]

Yet, despite the seeming verdict of history, Fielding's contemporaries were quick to point out what they felt were the deeply mixed motivations of his practice. They charged that the episodes from Bow Street reported in *The Covent-Garden Journal* functioned chiefly as sordid entertainments, that the journal itself was primarily a vehicle that brought together law and sensationalism to promote Fielding's business and personal interests, and that Fielding's hypocrisy in the journal was the literary embodiment of his corruption on the bench: charges central to the paper wars that swirled around Fielding during the last years of his life. While no one was to repeat Fielding's conjunction of magistrate and journalist, his combining of the business of the register office and commercial journalism quickly inspired imitators: during the 1750s and 1760s at least two other register offices sponsored papers as a form of advertisement.[11] As in Fielding's case, such utilitarian relationships produced texts not only concerned with advertising innovative institutions and their offerings, but dedicated to providing a paying readership with news and entertainment. The definition (or redefinition) of social, economic, and literary value was central to such cultural work; but so was, rather more surreptitiously, the creation (or evolution) of complexly articulated innuendoes and evasions that simultaneously abetted and mystified the material impact of such activity.[12] Such commercial emulation engendered not only parallel texts and proceedings, but also sparked fierce competition that boiled over into accusations and counteraccusations, parodies and satires, offering heretofore unexploited points of entry to the ethically complex world of the register offices and the culture they served.

The dialogue between moral ambition and skeptical analysis that complicates Fielding's reputation in his later years makes a richly contextualized reading of the contemporary texts of the magistrate's court and the register office (beyond the fact that both institutions survive only as texts) central to our understanding of the work of those offices and the personal and cultural matrixes from which Fielding's later writings emerged. As will become evident, Fielding's lifelong experience in Grub Street—as writer, advertiser, entertainer, impresario, and scrambling ne'er-do-well—deeply influenced his practice as a magistrate and a businessman.[13] The role played by advertising and entertainment receives extensive attention in this study, not least because the primary record of both the Bow Street Magistrate's Office and the Universal Register Office is contained in advertisements, squibs, journals, and pamphlets that were intended chiefly to entertain. Although social tracts such as *An Enquiry into the Causes of Late Increase of Robbers* and *A Proposal for Making an Effectual Provision for the Poor* have much to tell us about Fielding's thought on social problems (and, as such, have been extensively analyzed by others), they have far less to tell us about his daily practice and ethical negotiations as magistrate, businessman, and professional writer than do, I think, *The Covent-Garden Journal, Amelia, A*

Clear State of the Case of Elizabeth Canning, The Journal of a Voyage to Lisbon, and the paper wars that framed, enveloped, and determined them.

My objective is to expand, through the reading of both central and marginal texts, our understanding of Fielding's practice as magistrate, businessman, and writer and, in turn, to illuminate the ways Fielding's experience in those capacities affected the conception, form, and articulation of his final literary works. To do so entails the very difficult reconstruction of Fielding's affective and ethical relationship to his clientele—an endeavor that posits not only a deep encroachment of personal and subjective considerations into "public" pronouncements and decisions, but emphasizes the degree to which more traditional models of social relations continued to influence institutions and behavioral patterns of seemingly the most objectified and "modern" kind.[14] Such a strategy necessarily relies on biographical as well as literary material and seeks biographical as well as literary insights.[15] Indeed, the mixed interests that characterize Fielding's later career often provide not only a crucial context for understanding his final works, but an all-too-human microcosm of the personalized interactions of law, commerce, and literary production that characterize mid-eighteenth-century England: interactions, it seems to me, too often neglected in more thematically oriented studies of mid-century cultural practice.

Such a project necessarily engages less explored corners of Fielding's experience. I have approached Fielding's work in Bow Street, for example, through the tabulation and close study of Fielding's clientele as reported in the Covent Garden columns of *The Covent-Garden Journal* in an attempt to test larger or more impressionistic historical generalizations concerning his judicial practice. Among literary scholars, Fielding's later works have recently received a good deal of attention as examples of the interaction of law and fictional narrative at mid-century. Most famously, John Bender has proposed that Fielding's participation in a legal system moving away from "personal operators" (who "improvised freely," were "physically demonstrative" and "vocally present") toward the "impersonality of written rules, regulations, and procedures" bears "an ideologically profound relationship" to "increased transparency of narration in his novels."[16] Alexander Welsh has linked the mid-eighteenth-century inclination to prefer circumstantial evidence in criminal trials to concurrent changes in literary narrative (in Fielding's case, *Tom Jones*).[17] John Zomchick has argued that *Amelia* contributes to the social and fictional construction of the "juridical subject."[18] And numerous critics have discussed Fielding's social and legal writings in an attempt to draw (or complicate) generic distinctions between fictional and nonfictional narrative.[19] But none have looked very closely at the descriptions of Fielding's magisterial practice in *The Covent-Garden Journal,*

nor asked what effect his divided interest in his clients as legal and potential journalistic subjects may have had on his authorial and judicial behavior. Nor, beyond myriad readings of the opening scenes at Justice
Thrasher's and the closing ones at the good justice's, has the study of Fielding's actual (as opposed to theoretical) legal experience had much impact
on critical readings of *Amelia*.

Similarly, with the exception of Goldgar's fine introduction to *A Plan
of the Universal Register-Office,* discussions of the Register Office, when they
occur at all, have tended to flatten that ambiguous institution into cartoon-
like simplicity: a "noble" scheme, "a kind of Universal Aunts," or, more
negatively yet closer to the mark, a "labour exchange where employers
might examine prospective servants and study their character references."[20]
It was certainly all of that, but more—and more complexly. For, like the
Bow Street Magistrate's Office, the Universal Register Office was a site
pervaded by Fielding's training in publicity and entertainment—and, less
explicitly, in authority and vice—and, as such, structured, operated, and
often advertised as catering not only to those who were interested in securing or providing employment, but those who were simply *interested:* the
"curious," the oglers, the readers of newspapers and journals, the visitors to
the shows of London—including the legal one in Bow Street and the entrepreneurial one in the Strand. In seeking to market his clientele as entertainments as well as social or moral entities, Fielding suggests something
about his own characteristic way of engaging the world as a place where
interest as "curiosity" and interest as "useful connection" (or "influence")
habitually overlap—indeed, where the latter often seems a function of the
former.

This conflation of interests informs my subsequent approach to *Amelia:*
an approach that subordinates the usual focus on female virtue to a discussion of the dynamics of personal influence and desire. The Fielding
brothers' idealized institution of rational referral—the Universal Register
Office—is proposed as the absent (or, more accurately, expurgated) presence at the center of the novel, a still point of objectified clientage that anchors a relentless fictional enactment of two more traditional and
excruciatingly subjective forms of interest: influence trading and the marketing of flesh. In this light, Amelia herself, Fielding's "favourite child,"
emerges as less a wholly innocent paragon and more an adept in the game
of interest—one willing to offer a taste of her personal charms to the interested in order to obtain their "interest" on behalf of her husband. Such
innocence as she possesses, I argue, functions in much the same way as
Fielding's (and perhaps humanity's) own: it is a convenient and sometimes
necessary blindness to the true motivations of others, and an ability to construct and perhaps believe a euphemized version of one's own self-inter-

ested behavior. The identification of this personalized dynamic in Fielding's life and fiction opens the way to a larger discussion of the continuing importance of interest and connection at mid-century, as "modern" practices and institutions are infiltrated and distorted by older forms of personal clientage and exploitation.

In partial contrast to the ethical complexities of *Amelia,* the Elizabeth Canning case—Fielding's last and most selfless exercise in legal journalism—is then examined as a phenomenon that simultaneously reviews and partially overturns the attitudes toward Grub Street, servants, evidence, interest, innocence, and prostitution that have emerged in the previous chapters. My reading of Fielding's *A Clear State of the Case of Elizabeth Canning* emphasizes the pamphlet's significance as part of a media (rather than strictly legal) event and attempts to integrate that event into the rich rhetorical context provided most immediately by the Fielding-Hill paper war and more broadly by the long-standing cultural and symbolic presuppositions associated with commercial literary production.

The process of recuperating or recasting Grub Street foundations that begins in *Elizabeth Canning* continues at a manic pace in Fielding's posthumously published *The Journal of a Voyage to Lisbon*—a work I approach not primarily as a review of Fielding's attitudes on English law and society, but as a resurrection of popular, trangressive literary forms and motifs that radically relativizes the legal and social content of his final observations and provides a disconcertingly ironized context, cast off from the proprieties of magistracy, from which to look back at the more mystified and mystifying elements of his last offices.

Several segments of the study offer new historical information. An original tabulation of Fielding's Bow Street clientele and their activities, as recorded in the Covent Garden columns between January 3 and November 24, 1752, forms the foundation of my analysis of Fielding's ethical and rhetorical performances on the bench and in *The Covent-Garden Journal.* The reconstruction and analysis of the work of register offices is based on a fragmentary and often fugitive textual record consisting mainly of proposals, puffs, advertisements, and satires. Henry Fielding's *A Plan of the Universal Register-Office,* skillfully edited and introduced by Bertrand Goldgar, is a central document, as are various attacks and counterattacks, ads and counter ads, generated by competition between the Universal Register Office and Philip D'Halluin's Public Register Office, the proposal for which is reprinted for the first time in Appendix II. I have focused particularly on servants in my analysis of the material and textual practices of the Universal Register Office (and similar register offices) because the Fieldings' attitudes toward their service clientele seem so closely to parallel Henry Fielding's legal estimation of his Bow Street clientele and indeed his editorial attitude toward the population at large. Understandably, Fielding's competitors in business and in print sought to exploit—allegorically or straightforwardly—what they perceived to be the more compromised or corrupted elements of his legal, journalistic, and business practices; rather than being summarily dismissed, as they often are by Fielding scholars, such competing texts have been read closely, seriously, and skeptically for what they may suggest about the day-to-day operation of the institutions with which Fielding was associated.

Eighty years ago, Wilbur Cross remarked that in "Fielding's work appear all kinds of women"—a statement that could well apply to this study.[21] Here, the prominence of women derives not so much from design as from circumstance: the most elaborate reports from Bow Street deal with prostitution and domestic violence; the register offices' most visible clients are maid servants; the titular hero of Fielding's last novel is a woman; the victim and villain of his most intriguing and media-saturated legal case are Elizabeth Canning and Mary Squires. The Fielding that emerges from the study is unquestionably a man fascinated with "all kinds of women," and engaged in various legal, literary, economic, emotional, and sexual transactions with them. Angela Smallwood has written that "an active debate about the social position of women, and about sexual difference and gender roles in eighteenth-century society, forms a major theme running through the whole of Henry Fielding's creative writing," and her work on that theme has done much to counter Fielding's reputation among early feminist critics as a "misogynist monster."[22] But neither Smallwood's study nor Jill Campbell's examination of the relationship of sexual ambiguity and political instability in Fielding's works have addressed Fielding's official and literary interactions with women in his roles as magistrate and register office proprietor.[23] In this, as in other ways, Fielding's performance in his last offices seems a subject worthy of serious examination.

Finally, it has been my intention not only to shed light on Fielding's later career, but to work through his activities toward a revised understanding of the interaction of law, commerce, and professional writing at mid-century, one that takes more seriously into account the personal and affective dimension of such interactions than have, I think, critical approaches based primarily on economic, legal, and rhetorical models. Filtered through the individual agent, the relationship of eighteenth-century literature and commerce (or literature and law) emerges more as a series of nuanced and "messily contingent" human responses to the historical moment than a set of neat teleological analogies.[24] As we return again to the recognition that the separation of "public" and "private" spheres in the eighteenth century is generally less consistent and predictable than Habermasian terminology would suggest, the farrago of personal subjectivity and

public reflection that marks Fielding's later career offers a compelling subject of study.[25] Henry Fielding was an intricate, contradictory, and exas-
perating man; he was also the only writer of the eighteenth century to
incorporate in his own person the intersection of legal procedure, commercial interest, and literary production that has so engaged recent students
of the period. My hope is that *Henry Fielding at Work* will not only provide
new insights into what Claude Rawson has called "the intellectual and
emotional oscillations of a many-sided man," but will suggest a more hu-
manized critical approach to the cultural history of eighteenth-century
England.[26]

Chapter 1

Judicial and Journalistic
Representation in Bow Street

Henry Fielding took the oaths for the Westminster magistracy on October 25, 1748; on November 2 he began holding court in the famous house in Bow Street, Covent Garden, formerly occupied by the magistrate Thomas DeVeil. The following January 12—primarily for economic reasons and with significant help from the Duke of Bedford—he added the Middlesex County magistracy to his appointments.[1] Fielding was a "court JP"—a specially appointed urban magistrate with a heavier workload and correspondingly higher level of government financial support and judicial power than his gentleman-amateur counterparts in the country.[2] Martin Battestin has called Fielding's office "among the most cheerless and despicable in the kingdom," one that daily brought him face-to-face with "a horrid parade of thieves and cheats, robbers and murderers, rapists and sodomites; many who reveled in cruelty, who battered women and ravished children"[3]—a description that may be usefully compared with the partial record of the Bow Street Magistrate's office presented below.

Within a month of setting up as magistrate for Westminster, Fielding began intermittently sending reports of his cases to the daily newspapers. During December 1748, 17 such cases appeared in print, establishing a pattern of publication that would continue throughout Fielding's tenure on the bench.[4] Three years later, in January 1752, Fielding launched *The Covent-Garden Journal,* a twice-weekly paper that ran reports from the Bow Street Magistrate's Office in nearly every issue and greatly increased the amount of printed intelligence about his court. These journal and newspaper reports provide the primary sources of firsthand information about Fielding's activities in Bow Street.[5] They have been approached by scholars in varying ways. Legal historians have extensively mined them for examples of magisterial practice, but have paid very little attention to their rhetorical texture or to their function as entertainments and advertisements.[6] Social historians and Fielding's biographers have tended to emphasize the more sensational cases and important administrative innovations. Thus the development of the Bow Street runners has been recounted again and again. Fielding's own description of his campaign in the winter of 1753 "to demolish the then reigning gangs, and to put the civil policy into such order, that no such gangs should ever be able, for the future, to form themselves into bodies, or at least to remain any time formidable to the public" has often been cited as an example of his self-sacrifice in the cause of justice.[7] The personal and political ramifications of Fielding's role in the famous Bosavern Penlez case have been widely discussed, with predictably contentious results.[8] And Fielding's involvement in the extraordinary narrative and continuing mystery of Elizabeth Canning's alleged kidnapping has fascinated scholars and amateurs for centuries.

As yet, however, no effort has been made to tabulate the number and variety of clients and cases that would have come before Fielding in the course of his everyday work as magistrate, nor to examine critically the written record of his performance on the bench. The first part of this chapter attempts, through a tabulation based on the court reportage in *The Covent-Garden Journal,* to suggest such a profile of Fielding's clientele and to offer answers to three fairly simple questions: Who were these people? What did they do? And with what frequency? The second part of the chapter addresses the more difficult issue of Fielding's relations, as justice and journalist, with his clientele and audience.

I

To address issues of eighteenth-century crime and punishment at all is to venture into contentious historical ground. Since the publication of *Albion's Fatal Tree* in 1975, there has been a growing scholarly interest in the lives and activities of the "criminal" underclass of eighteenth-century London, an interest that achieved something like celebrity status in 1992 with the publication of Peter Linebaugh's *The London Hanged.* In his introduction, Linebaugh provides a controversial overview of the development of the subdiscipline between 1975 and 1992—one that suggests that the work of historians not sharing his political or topical orientations (those interested in law and the police, for example) essentially skews our view of crime in the period: "What subsequent discussion [after 1975] gained in methodological sophistication and breadth of contributions, it lost in conceptual timidity and the narrow rejection of the historical imagination, as the history of crime was increasingly transformed into the history of administration or 'the machinery of justice.'"[9] Although Linebaugh's confrontational tone is probably a response to Joanna Innes's and John Styles's equally contentious statement that criminality "has recently ceased to be the focus of the most innovative work in the field" and that there are "good reasons why research in this field should have stalled,"[10] this is nevertheless a difficult sentence to interpret. Can Linebaugh be suggesting that studies of laws, courts, and administrative mechanisms (by his own admission, the growth industries of eighteenth-century England) are irrelevant to understanding the period? Or that any such study, to be valid, must necessarily include a sympathetic bond and advocacy relationship with the accused? Given the overwhelming injustice inherent in his topic—the killing of human beings for small infractions against property—it is unfortunate that Linebaugh's insistently polemical stance often has the effect of dampening (at least in this reader) the moral outrage it is intended to sustain. For Linebaugh dehumanizes the police, the juries, the judges, the middling sort, and the elites in precisely the way he accuses those groups of dehumanizing the poor they would hang.[11] While Linebaugh's rich statistical and sociological material makes his a significant book in any case, his admitted ideological bias leads not only to exaggeration of tone and interpretation but, for the literary historian or historian of the press, parochial reduction and sometimes outright inaccuracy.

The treatment of the Fielding brothers is a case in point. The Fieldings, Linebaugh tells us, founded "*The Public Advertizer*" [sic] and the Universal Register Office as "a police venture" to provide "information on the servant labour market" and "systematically" to collect "information about stolen property and the recovery of stolen goods."[12] This sounds sufficiently sinister in the Orwellian mode. But *The Public Advertiser* was in fact a modified continuation of *The General Advertiser,* Henry Woodfall's 18-year-old, 12-column daily paper, which had intermittently run criminal material from Fielding for several years; it even continued to number its issues from the 18-year-old *General Advertiser*—the issue of March 3, 1753, for example, is No. 5724.[13] And although *The Public Advertiser* at its inception (December 1, 1752) did promise to carry regularly Fielding's announcements soliciting information on robberies, burglaries, thefts, and stolen goods, these announcements in the event ran prominently beneath the masthead for little more than three months, disappearing on March 10, 1753, and thereafter appearing only intermittently either beneath the masthead or in the advertising columns of the paper. Even at their most obtrusive, Fielding's announcements took up at best 1/20th of a paper concerned primarily with advertising the theater, books, medicines, and movable property (usually eight or more columns), with the remaining columns devoted to ship news, foreign news, London news, stocks, essays, and belle lettres—hardly a "police venture."[14]

The paper for which such a claim might more plausibly be made is *The Covent-Garden Journal,* written almost exclusively by Fielding, published from his and his half-brother's brokerage, The Universal Register Office, and carrying regular reports from Bow Street under the heading "Covent Garden." Appearing in every issue from January 3 through June 27 and somewhat less frequently thereafter, these reports represent the most regular and consistent record of Fielding's work as a justice.[15] Flanked by advertisements and news and edited with an eye toward entertainment value, the "Covent Garden" columns, however, do not demonstrate the comprehensiveness or accuracy one would expect to find in official legal records. Persons and crimes are not consistently noted or described; quantitative generalizations cloud statistical vistas. Nevertheless, the columns do contain a collection of over 500 people (accused, victims, witnesses, law officers, charity cases) who came before the court and are significant indicators of the kinds of cases Fielding would have dealt with on a daily basis. The Alpha and Criminal Activity tables in Appendix I tabulate this clientele for the first time, alphabetically listing all of the people and cases that appeared in *The Covent-Garden Journal* from January 3 to November 24, 1752.

Allowing for vague or conglomerate references (see below), the cases reported in the Covent Garden columns for most of 1752 break down like this: abusing and assaulting a master (1); accessory to murder (1); acting (3 conglomerate entries covering groups of amateur actors: prentices, milliners, etc.); assault (10); assisting a breakout (1); attempted murder (1); bigamy (1); breaking the chariot of a noble (1); breaking the peace (3 individualized entries; several conglomerate references); burglary (6); chance-medley (1); cheating & defrauding (4); domestic violence (9); embezzlement (4); enticing to murder (1); exercising trade on the Lord's Day (3); exposing the body of an abortive child (1); felonies (10); forgery (1); fraud (1); gaming (1 conglomerate entry—"thirty idle Persons, all of them Apprentices, Journeymen and Gentlemans Servants, and all in the high Road to Ruin"); housebreaking (2); idle & disorderly (37 individual entries; several conglomerate entries); insulting a noble (1); keeping a bawdy house (2); kidnapping (1); murder (6); perjury (2); poisoning (1); prison break out (1); prostitution (13); rape (5); receiving stolen items (5); returned from transportation (2); riding upon a dray (1); robbery (12); sodomitical practices (1); swindling (1); theft (147); threatening murder (1); uttering counterfeit money (3); vagabond (2).[16] It is immediately evident that the most sensational crime, murder, appears only six times—thus putting into perspective the highly unusual event of "five different murders, all committed within the space of one week, by different gangs of street robbers" that provoked Fielding's famous campaign against gangs in 1753.[17] In 1752, the most common crimes by a wide margin are disorderly conduct and theft.

The cases were recorded by Fielding's law clerk, Joshua Brogden, and sometimes editorialized upon by Fielding himself. The roles played by each in the production of the Covent Garden columns is a difficult question. My sense is that Brogden kept the basic record, supplied qualitative assessments from time to time, and probably made editorial decisions about which cases in omnibus listings were interesting enough to warrant slightly expanded descriptions. Fielding clearly had final editorial control as well as the opportunity to rewrite episodes that particularly interested him. It is hard to imagine that any representation that finally appeared in print would not have reflected his views. In the largest sense, then, Henry Fielding is the author—in the traditional sense of "the one who inspired the whole enterprise"—if not necessarily always the writer of the columns.[18]

The columns contain few notable people. Charles Macklin (presumably the actor) appears as a victim in one of the very last columns (November 17) having had his pocket picked of a silk handkerchief by one Francis Dust. John Hill (writer of the "Inspector" columns and Fielding's sometime journalistic enemy) appears in the column of January 10 as both victim and witness in a case involving armed robbery.[19] And the "Right Hon. the Secretary of War" (Henry Fox) appears as a victim of poultry theft—of all things—in the column of March 23. As a historical record, then, the Covent Garden columns are made up primarily of the mishaps of people nobody has heard of and about whom nobody cares. Yet they represent, I would argue, a significant nonfiction source of information about the everyday lives of the underclasses at the middle of the eighteenth century; especially so because many of the crimes recorded in them were not serious enough to go to trial and thus (perhaps) find their way into the *Old Bailey Sessions Papers*.

Of these less serious crimes, the rather loose category of "idle & disorderly" (closely related to "breaking the peace") is particularly interesting for what it tells us about Brogden's reporting habits and their effect on the statistical evaluation of the columns. Variously called "idle, loose & disorderly," "idle & lewd," "idle & dissolute," "idle & disorderly," and "idleness" (all of which I have standardized as "idle & disorderly"), it comprises 37 individual cases and four conglomerate references. If this seems rather small for a pleasure and entertainment district like Covent Garden, the reason soon becomes clear: Brogden was simply not interested in consistently listing the names of those accused of so ubiquitous a crime. Only in the early columns for January 24 and 26 does he individually identify all of the idle persons hauled before Fielding. By January 31, such persons are mentioned only as conglomerate statistics—e.g., "Twenty to Bridewell, as idle and disorderly Persons." And after February 3 even mention of such large groups becomes rare. Moreover, related crimes such as prostitution and domestic violence are not described as "idle and disorderly," although clearly they are part of the nonlarcenous mischief with which Fielding had to deal regularly. The early frequency of collective "idle & disorderly" notices and other crimes against the peace seem to indicate that vagrant and unruly people, not felons, made up the highest percentage of Fielding's clientele.[20]

The Covent Garden columns are more specific about direct crimes against property, which account for 167 of the individualized cases recorded by Brogden.[21] It is important to remember that the legal distinctions defining crimes against property and their potential penalties were significant in the eighteenth century: robbery, for example, "always involved the direct confrontation of victim and offender"; burglary was considered extremely serious because it involved the "breaking into a house while the inhabitants were asleep and defenseless"; housebreaking designated entering a house during the daylight hours and could be considered more or less serious depending upon whether "there was someone at home who was 'put in fear.'"[22] Moreover, in the nonviolent cases that I have simply called "theft," there were elaborate legal distinctions defining a variety of nonclergyable larcenies (theft from a house, theft from a shop, pickpocketing, sheep-stealing, etc.), as well as designating simple grand larceny or petty larceny depending upon the kinds of things stolen, the place where the theft occurred, and the overall value of the theft.[23]

Such distinctions were of great importance to Fielding, who devoted almost an entire Covent Garden column (February 24) to lamenting the strict procedural requirements and unfortunate results of English laws pertaining to larceny:

> By the Law of England, as it now stands, if a Larceny be absolutely committed, however slight the Suspicion be against the accused, the Justice of the Peace is obliged in strictness to commit the Party; especially if he have not Sureties for his Appearance to answer the Charge.
>
> Nor will the trifling Value of the Thing stolen, nor any Circumstance of Mitigation justify his discharging the Prisoner. . . .
>
> Thus for a Theft of two-pence or three-pence value, a poor Wretch may lie confined and starving in a Goal near two Months in the Town.

Fielding goes on to list the pernicious effects of such confinement, and it seems likely that in his own dealings with the various categories of larceny he exercised as much latitude as possible under the law. However, because

Brogden does not often list the value of stolen items or distinguish between various levels of larceny, such categories remain extremely vague in the text, and it seems outside my current purpose to attempt to correlate the crimes he reports with the myriad distinctions operative under the law.[24] One distinction can be made however: in the Covent Garden columns all of those accused of robbery, burglary, or housebreaking are men, while almost half (73) of the 147 persons accused of theft are women.

The items most often stolen by both men and women (by number of thefts, not quantities stolen) were wearing apparel (23), handkerchiefs (20), money (19), and quantities of linen (15). The particulars of these larcenies may be found in the Stolen Property table, Appendix I. Sometimes the categories overlapped: George Grayham and Barnard Seers, for example, were accused of stealing "a great Quantity of Linen, Wearing-Apparell, Money, and other Things" (April 13). Other, odder items turn up—large quantities of lead (March 9, April 10, April 27, July 3), carpenter's tools (January 24), Dutch cocks and hens (March 23), burgundy, champagne and other liquors (March 9)—but as a whole Fielding's larcenous clientele seems chiefly to have been made up of people working in what might be called the "small cloth trade."

The Covent Garden columns, then, indicate that the everyday activity of Fielding's court was primarily concerned with idle and disorderly persons and small-time larcenists. The columns contain a remarkable cast of characters, ranging from unrepentent pimps to burned-out bakers in need of charity, but rather than Battestin's "horrid parade" it seems something more like a tragi-comical soap opera—a point Battestin seems to concede when he writes that "the continuing drama in Fielding's courtroom at Bow Street was by no means unrelievedly of the tragic or pathetic kind."[25] But whether tragic, pathetic, or comic, the "continuing drama" at Bow Street was almost always of the *entertaining* kind, and Fielding, trained as an entertainer, writer, and impresario, was indisputably its director. His judicial duty was to preside over what amounted to a daily series of pretrial hearings; his authorial interest was to textualize those hearings in a way that would both entertain his audience and reflect well upon his performance as a court JP, particularly in his role as mediator between the perpetrator and victim, and between the victim and the courts. J. M. Beattie explains that in the eighteenth century the justices of the peace "formed an essential link between the victim and the courts. . . . [I]t was their duty to bring the parties in conflict before them, to take depositions of the complainant and his witnesses, to examine the accused, and to ensure that they appeared at the next sitting of the appropriate court."[26] Moreover as the century proceeded, the role of the magistrate as interpreter expanded so that "the magistrate's examination ceased being simply a means of assembling the best evidence against the prisoner and took on some of the characteristics of a judicial hearing. Magistrates began to feel more obligation to make some assessment of the evidence being presented and to assume more right to dismiss charges when they thought the case too weak to justify a trial."[27] In their expanded role, magistrates could also function as counselors, encouraging the negotiation of extrajudicial settlements between parties—"composing," as Fielding himself described it, "instead of inflaming, the quarrels of porters and beggars (which I blush when I say hath not been universally practised)."[28] In the reports from Bow Street, we find Fielding acting in all of these capacities: interrogator, interpreter, judge, mediator, and, in his editorial commentary and rewrites of the hearings, moralist and entertainer.

The cases in the Covent Garden columns thus offer us not only the best record of Fielding's quotidian docket, but also a unique example of both his judicial and editorial practice: a practice at the crossroads of literary entertainment and legal procedure. To illustrate what can happen at this crossroads, I will address Fielding's handling of two types of crime related to the broad category of "idle and disorderly" but sensational enough to regularly elicit expanded "entertainment style" coverage: prostitution and domestic violence. The prostitute's story and the family feud have, of course, always sold papers, and Fielding would have been particularly sensitive to their "literary" qualities. But more than that they constituted, in ways that many crimes against property did not, circumstantially and emotionally complex situations in which Fielding felt he could exercise to the fullest his skills as a student of human nature, judge, and mediator. Thus Fielding the magistrate often plays an expanded role in such cases, while Fielding the journalist later devotes additional space and care to rhetorically fleshing out the performances. In addressing these cases, I will be asking two questions: what effect did the court cases serving as potential copy for an entertainment periodical have on the shaping—simultaneously journalistic and judicial—of the reportage and perhaps even adjudication of those cases? And what does this infiltration of the literary into the legal tell us about the dynamics of Fielding's court and the personality of the man who presided over it?

II

Henry Fielding had a perceptual and rhetorical problem with prostitutes, one that dates at least from the time of the Penlez case of 1749 when he was accused of actively preventing the destruction of bawdy houses because he was on their payroll (see below).[29] His youthful career as a rake made him particularly susceptible to these kinds of accusations; and he did not help matters when in the Covent Garden column for June 22, 1752, he printed and seemed to endorse the "Meanwell" letter—a letter that attacked Parliament's 1752 anti-prostitution act "for regulating Places of Publick Entertainment, and punishing Persons keeping disorderly Houses"—by listing the ill effects of a ban on prostitution.[30] Fielding was widely thought to be the letter's author, and at the very least he made it quite clear that he was willing to consider its general argument when he composed a headnote describing the letter's origin:

> *The following Letter which was sent to the Justice by an unknown Hand, hath been transmitted to us; and tho' perhaps some Points are carried a little too far, upon the whole I think it a very sensible Performance, and worthy the Attention of the Public.*[31]

Fielding considered the letter important enough to print it in the larger typeface used for his leaders, but it seems to me equally significant that he chose to run it under the Covent Garden heading.[32] In so doing, he emphasized the connection between his journalistic persona, "Sir Alexander Drawcansir" of *The Covent-Garden Journal*—who wrote the headnote and printed the letter—and his alter ego, Justice Fielding of the Covent Garden columns, who originally received the letter and, in the schizophrenic world of the journalistic imagination, passed it on to Drawcansir. Interestingly, neither Goldgar nor Battestin mention the headnote in their discussions of the Meanwell letter, although it must have been a significant factor in confirming public opinion regarding Justice Fielding's lax stance on prostitution.[33]

Faced with the widespread belief that he had authored the letter, Fielding attempted to defend himself in *The Covent-Garden Journal* No. 57 (August 1, 1752), but paradoxically in a leader that reveals a deep affinity for the language of prostitution and perhaps for its practices. Commenting on his newfound popularity in the bawdy houses, Drawcansir writes that "Tom Wilding assures me, that old Sawney is the reigning Toast of all the Ladies at Jenny D—s's, and compliments me much on being an *honest Fellow*, and, as he phrases it, *one of us.*" Then, in a display of prostitute's rhetoric that is perhaps a bit too close for comfort, he notes that "a fair one who signs herself MARI MURRAIN, tells me I am a *hearty Cock,* and declares, with about twenty Oaths, that she is ready to rub down my old Back at any Time without a Present."[34] Despite later passages of vitriolic rhetoric directed against the trade ("as such Prostitutes are the lowest and meanest, so are they the basest, vilest, and wickedest of all Creatures"), Fielding's rebuttal of the Meanwell letter seems to reveal a lurking fascination with the oldest profession—one that, paired with his earlier endorsement of Meanwell, suggests a writer oscillating between outrage and sympathy, humor and lechery.

Such fascinations seem to have been plainly evident to Fielding's readership, for although crime reports from Bow Street occupied at most three columns of the 12-column *Covent-Garden Journal,* they were repeatedly recognized and criticized by contemporary writers as one of the most distinctive features of Fielding's twice-weekly paper. As early as January 1752, for example, a writer for *The Gentleman's Magazine* surmised that Justice Fielding's "chief encouragement" in undertaking *The Covent-Garden Journal* was "the opportunity which his office afforded him of *amusing* his readers with an account of examinations and commitments; the exploits which constables and thief-takers should atchieve by his influence and direction, and the secrets of prostitution which should be discovered by his penetration and sagacity" (my emphasis).[35] Goldgar notes that Fielding's enemies routinely accused him of "outrageous self-advertisement," deploring the fact that Justice should assume, in the words of the *Craftsman* (May 2, 1752), "the Airs of a giggling, prating Wretch."[36] This destabilizing mixture of vice-as-minatory-example and vice-as-titillating-entertainment generates the tonal and ethical ambiguities of the Covent Garden columns.

It is, not surprisingly, a mixture particularly evident in Fielding's judicial and rhetorical treatment of prostitutes. Twelve prostitutes appear in the Covent Garden columns, along with one indeterminate group of nine "loose, idle, and disorderly Persons, and common Night-Walkers" (November 10), but it seems likely that a significant number of women accused of other crimes—particularly "idle & disorderly" conduct—may also have been engaged in the sale of sex. Two of the reports concerning prostitutes are especially elaborate. The first (January 10) concerns the extraction of information from four young women taken from a "notorious Bawdy-House at the Back-side of St. Clements," one of whom particularly caught Fielding's eye:

> One of these Girls, who seemed younger and less abandoned than the rest; was fixed on as a proper Person to give Evidence against the others but could not be prevailed upon that Evening; upon which she was confined separately from the rest; and the next Morning being assured of never becoming again subject to her late severe Task-Master, she revealed all the Secrets of her late Prison-House, Acts of Prostitution, not more proper to be made public, than they are capable, as the Law now stands, of being punished. . . . She was very pretty, under 17 Years of Age, and had been 3 Years by her own Confession upon the Town.

Two weeks later, on January 24, a similar and even more fully articulated episode of this kind appeared. Saunders Welch, the High Constable for Holborn, a fast friend of Fielding's, and a shareholder in the Universal

Register Office, brought in "several lewd Women" who had been apprehended at a house owned by one Philip Church:

> Among the Women taken at this House, was one Mary Parkington, a very beautiful Girl of sixteen Years of Age, who, in her Examination said, That she was the Daughter of one Parkington a Hatter . . . that her Father dying, her Mother married again; that she lived with her said Mother till within these three Weeks; that about three Weeks ago she was seduced by a young Sea-Officer, who left her within a Day or two; that being afraid and ashamed to go Home to her Mother, and having no Money, she was decoyed by a Woman to this Bawdy-House, where she was furnished with Clothes; for which she gave a Note for Five Pounds; that she was there prostituted to several Men for Hire; and all the Money, except a few Shillings, she was obliged to pay over to the Mistress of the House; that since she was in the aforesaid House, her Mother, as she heard, had used great Pains to enquire after her; and that she would have returned to her, if she could, but was kept a Prisoner there, against her Will and Consent, and the Doors always locked, to keep her and other Women within the said House; and sayeth that she was threatened by Church, if she offered to make her Escape, that he would arrest her on that Note of Five Pound, which she had given for Clothes, apparently not worth Ten Shillings. . . .
>
> In the Conclusion, the Justice committed Mr. Church and his man, and four of the Women, and recommended the Care of Mary Brown [Brogden's mistake for "Parkington"?], and another Girl of the same Age, and under the same Circumstances, to a sober and discreet Constable, 'till the next Morning.

Both accounts end with pleas by Fielding advocating the reform of prostitution laws to "put an End to the very exorbitant, and yet growing Evil, the daily Cause of Misery and Ruin of great Numbers of young, thoughtless, helpless, poor Girls, who are as often betrayed, and even forced into Guilt, as they are bribed and allured into it" (January 10); reforms that would make prosecution "so cheap and easy, that the Keepers of these Houses would be at least afraid of committing such dreadful Outrages, and of Driving Youth, Beauty, and Modesty . . . headlong to the Ruin of Body and Soul" (January 24).

Martin Battestin has sympathetically interpreted these episodes as showing Fielding "striving time and again, often beyond what a strict interpretation of the laws would warrant, to temper justice with mercy, and to influence changes in the laws themselves. . . . It is impossible to read these reports without sensing the intolerable fatigue of body, mind, and spirit to which Fielding daily subjected himself at Bow Street—or to read them without admiring . . . his leniency to those he believed had not yet become incorrigible offenders."[37] Bertrand Goldgar, on the other hand, comments on the Parkington case with rather more sensitivity to its literary (or entertainment) dimension: "Fielding's tone here is like that of all those other compassionate, even sentimental, portraits of prostitutes . . . almost commonplace by the early 1750s and invariably revealing the young woman as victim rather than sinner."[38]

Both of these interpretations offer valuable insights into Fielding's judicial and literary practice; both give us an element of the magistrate-author central to his complex character. But it is crucial to remember that Fielding's descriptions of both prostitutes are not merely factual reports (as Battestin seems to believe) nor factual variations on a fictional commonplace (as Goldgar proposes). They are, as the writer for *The Gentleman's Magazine* pointed out, the very self-advertising matrix of Fielding's *Covent-Garden Journal:* episodes intended to exploit "the opportunity which his office afforded him of amusing his readers with an account of examinations and commitments . . . and the secrets of prostitution which should be discovered by his penetration and sagacity."[39] Afforded the opportunity, Fielding amuses his readers by "penetrating" the lives of two young prostitutes; prostitutes whom he constructs as objects for viewing and then sequentially views, interviews, saves, textualizes, and editorializes upon. In the first vignette, a young girl with sexual secrets, secrets that she must be convinced to reveal, "Acts of Prostitution, not . . . proper to be made public," is prepared, probed and eventually split wide-open by a justice who recognizes her as "pretty" and "less abandoned": that is, simultaneously attractive and worth saving. In the second incident, Fielding taps into another young prostitute and extracts even more "secrets": we discover how Mary Parkington was decoyed into the bawdy house and given clothes for which she signed a note effectively enslaving her; we are told "she was there prostituted to several Men for Hire" and forced to pay the proceeds to her captors; we find that, Clarissa-like, she was kept a prisoner with doors always locked. In short, we find in the guise of court reportage brief sensational narratives of a distinctly sexual nature.[40] On the surface both episodes demonstrate Fielding's compassion and concern for the victims, but the rhetorical effect of the texts seems to me potentially to encode a narrative of another kind, one which (adapting Fielding's phrase) "bribes and allures" the reader to reconstruct imaginatively "all the Secrets of her late Prison House, Acts of Prostitution, not . . . proper to be made public" that the justice has discovered about two 16-year-olds—one "very pretty" and the other "very beautiful." Authorized by a magistrate and published in an entertainment journal authored by him, such narratives not only provoke sympathy but also invite the reader to exercise and enjoy textual/sexual power over women, similar to that legally, visually, and verbally enjoyed over prostitutes by Justice Fielding.[41]

While it may be objected that such a reading willfully ignores all of the good Fielding hoped to achieve in his lenient treatment of prostitutes, my intention here is not to debate Fielding's theoretical stance on social and criminal matters but to explore the conflicted and often self-serving elements of his practice, specifically those involving the intersection of the magistracy and the press. In this endeavor, it is instructive to put oneself in the position of the beautiful 16-year-old, and ask why, if Fielding were primarily interested in saving Mary Parkington, he would broadcast her name in print throughout London as having been "prostituted to several Men for Hire"? Such information seems certain to have blasted any hope she might have had that the incident would be forgotten and her former innocence (and presumed marriageability) restored. Occupied with the scintillating details of the story, Fielding seems inadvertently, as he advertised his own humanity, to have mishandled the most human element of the case.

Clearly, pretty prostitutes affected Fielding in complicated ways—a generalization perhaps nowhere more disconcertingly exemplified than in his tendency to valorize beauty as a moral commodity in the world of the court in a way that essentially duplicated its value as a commercial commodity in the world of prostitution. It is in fact verifiable that nowhere in the Covent Garden columns is there a single description of an ugly or even plain prostitute that Fielding determines to be worth saving.[42] Yet a good-looking offender, even caught dead to rights, is usually given the benefit of the doubt. On March 9, for example, "several Persons of ill Fame" were bound over,

> among whom was a young Woman remarkably handsome, genteel, well dressed, and behaved herself with great decency before the Justice: Notwithstanding which Appearance, it was sworn that she had been extremely drunk in the Streets the preceeding [sic] Night, and had picked up the Constable. She expressed however so much Penitence, that the Justice shewed her all the Compassion in his Power.[43]

This was not a naive judgment. No one was more aware of the power of physical beauty than Henry Fielding. In *Tom Jones* he remarked that "perfect Beauty in both Sexes is a more irresistible Object than it is generally thought."[44] In *Amelia* he commented on the "great . . . Advantage of Beauty in Men as well as Women, . . . so sure is this Quality in either Sex of procuring some Regard from the Beholder"; and later seemed almost to anticipate the intersection of the judicial and the personal that seems to have marked his court room practice: "I am firmly persuaded that to withdraw Admiration from exquisite Beauty, or to feel no Delight

in gazing at it, is as impossible as to feel no Warmth from the most scorching Rays of the Sun."[45] Fielding, of course, goes on to recommend running away from beauty's power, but concludes by enthusing "how natural
is the Desire of going thither! and how difficult to quit the lovely
Prospect!" (232).

Such irresistible attraction worked not only ethically but sexually, and
not only in the court room but on the printed page. For in the Covent
Garden columns, valorized beauty, while overtly presented as an ethical
force overriding plain evidence, is simultaneously packaged in a suggestive
rhetoric invoking texts (and sex) far removed from the Bow Street court.
Although pretty prostitutes are described by Fielding in such sympathetic
commonplaces as "young, thoughtless, helpless, poor Girls," the adjectives
of sensibility paradoxically work to evoke the ambiance of Gothic and
Sadean fantasy: these are a particularly attractive kind of corrupted or cor-
ruptible innocents. Fielding's descriptions of young prostitutes suggest that
the intersecting languages of law and sympathy may act textually to provoke the same subversive erotic charge they seek legally to muffle. Appearing in a commercial publication, legal depositions double as
"amusements," with all the voyeuristic and transgressive potential such
mixed motivations imply.

This paradox was not lost on Fielding's contemporaries. Bonnell
Thornton, writing in *Have At You All: or, The Drury-Lane Journal* (a periodical sponsored by Fielding's rival Phillip D'Halluin at the Public Register
Office), seems immediately to have recognized the potentially subversive
effect of Fielding's conflation of magistracy and entertainment. In the first
Covent Garden column (January 3), for example, it had been reported that
one Mary Brown, a servant and witness to a burglary, came before Fielding and "deposed literally as followeth: 'The Bitch came up Stairs as I was
coming down Stairs, and she put her Nose to the Ground; and for that I
says, Ruose, what is the Matter with you; and then I said just so to the
Bitch, if you will go into the Tap Room, I will go with you, and the Bitch
went down Stairs before me . . . and there I saw the Chap behind the
Door, and said what in the Name of God do you do here; and then he fell
upon me, and aimed to strike me in the Head, for he hit me in the Shoulders, and then I run up and called my Master." A week later, playing off
this episode, Thornton (as "Madam Roxana Termagent") mocked and then
parodied Fielding's journalistic practice. "[T]ho' *Drury-Lane* cannot furnish
me with the witty and humorous depositions of blundering servant-girls,"
he wrote, "yet it will supply me with the equally instructive and polite
conversation of the hundreds—To give you a specimen in your own style
and manner":

Drury-lane, Jan. 16

Sunday last MOLL DRAGGLETAIL, alias FOUL-MOUTH, alias FIRE-SHIP, alias STRIP ME NAKED, alias BUNG YOUR EYE, was seiz'd by old ROGER MOUTHWATER the watchman, and carried before Justice SCRIBBLE; being charg'd with an intent to commit fornication, by street-walking in the Strand. As she was dragging along, they discoursed litterally as followeth. 'D-mme, you old rotten son of a b-tch, you lives by us poor girls misfortins, G-d blast ye'—Come along, wool ye, I'll carry ye'—carry me to number hell, you dog; you shan't haul me by G-d.—If you won't come civilly, I'll call my partner,'—'Call and be d-mn'd to ye, I'll have attendance, d-mme, I'll have attendance.'—'Watch, watch! here lay hould on her, do'—'Come along, mistress.'—'G-d d-mn your eyes, your hearts, your liver, your lungs, your lights, your odd joints, your members, &c. &c. &c.[46]

In an exaggerated passage mimicking the subdued subversive energy generated by the Covent Garden columns, the servant becomes a prostitute; the bitch, Ruose, becomes the watchman (an "old rotten son-of-a-bitch" and a "dog"); and Fielding becomes both author and character—the scribbler about justice and Justice Scribble. The passage as a whole emphasizes Fielding's interest in vulgar language and prostitutes and, more importantly, his mystified deployment of both as a means to sell papers. Fielding, of course, was quite aware of the entertainment value of criminal matters and their potentially subversive effect on an audience. In the Covent Garden column of March 27, for example, he attacked public executions at Tyburn as being "not for *the Reformation, but the Diversion of the Populace*"; and he wrote even more pertinently in the leader of June 27 that the gallows were "a great Friend to the Press" and the "whipping Post hath been likewise of eminent Use to the same Purposes": "as the Merchants seem at present to have their Eye chiefly on the Whipping-post for the Advancement of their Manufactures, it is to be hoped Courts of Justice will do all that in them lies, to encourage a Trade of such wonderful Benefit to the Kingdom."[47] Yet if the irony is palpable in the text, in practice Fielding seems to have missed it, for his comments appear in the same issue of *The Covent-Garden Journal* that carries in the Covent Garden columns a report about a "remarkable Charge laid before the Justice" concerning a woman attacked with a cleaver by another woman in men's clothes who turns out to have been solicited to the crime by the first woman's husband: "It appeared that he had had a Child by the prisoner, had lived with her in a State of criminal Conversation two Years. And when this Woman was told in the Prison, that both she and her Lover would be hanged, she cried out in an Agony, *Hang me, hang me,—but Spare him.*" In the issue of June 27, Fielding the

moralist and Fielding the journalist collide head-on: he criticizes the use
of crime and punishment to sell papers, and one page later he indulges in
the practice he has just deplored.

That Fielding was susceptible to such rhetorical and behavioral disloca-
tion is no longer in question. J. Paul Hunter has noted Fielding's ability to
"wrestle central contradictions . . . only to a standoff."[48] Bertrand Goldgar
and Robert Hume have sensitively explored his mixed motivations as an
"opposition" playwright in the 1730s.[49] And Thomas Lockwood's won-
derfully subtle appreciation of Fielding's behavior during the enforcement
of the 1737 Licensing Act reveals a man with an acute sense of the uses of
hypocrisy and no strong aversion to indulging himself in the very practices
he publicly attacks. Lockwood writes of his silence in 1737–38 that "Fielding, though seeming to know what meanness could be disclosed, yet will
do no disclosing, for reasons perhaps not much different from those that
made Sir Robert himself such a lover of the dark. Walpole succeeded in a
bill of theatrical control and censorship which had failed . . . two years before. He found his advantage this time where it would seem most unlikely
to lie, with Fielding and that reckless satirical disadvantage of himself at
Fielding's playhouse, where the unheard-of freedom of representation—
the freedom more even than the politics of the representation—gave color
for once to an unprecedented measure of official control. It seems to me
very probable that Fielding likewise found his real security on this occasion flowing not so much from the direction of the Haymarket as from the
less likely direction of the Treasury office, and that he in common with the
minister—if not also in concert with him—could make private opportunity of public defeat."[50]

If Fielding the playwright could combine public defeat with private
opportunity, so Fielding the justice/journalist could combine public
morality with private exploitation. Certainly Goldgar is correct in assess-
ing Fielding's official attitude toward prostitutes as a socially acceptable if
emotionally antithetical mixture of "budding benevolence" and "traditional moral contempt."[51] And these are the terms in which perhaps even
Fielding himself would have explained it. But it should be recognized that
this formulation represents the polarities of his *public* stance only. What
such a reading neglects, but the Covent Garden columns reveal, is a more
private dialectic played out exclusively within the boundaries of benevolence: one that privileges sexual attraction (as a corrupt form of the benev-
olence-induced "pleasure" theorized by advocates of sensibility?) as the
basis for charitable action. I do not mean to suggest that Fielding publicly
(or even privately) premeditated or advocated such privileging, but that he
habitually acted as if he did. Although Fielding obviously felt better about
saving prostitutes than condemning them, he clearly felt best if they could

be shown to be savable because their attractions of person and demeanor simultaneously excited his unquestionably active (not to say dominating) sexual impulses and provided material that later could be turned to journalistic use. Whether such exploitative behavior is interpreted as despicable or merely human, and whether it contaminates in any meaningful way the potentially salutary effect of his public stance on prostitution, depends upon whether one accepts or rejects the theory Fielding so often demonstrated in his novels: that corruption often lurks at the heart of benevolence, and benevolence sometimes lurks at the heart of corruption.

III

The dialectic of humane and exploitative, official and titillating, that informs Fielding's descriptions of prostitutes in the Covent Garden columns recurs with remarkable vigor in his reporting of domestic violence and rape cases. The majority of these cases are given in great detail and include such literary amenities as first-person dialogue, twists and turns of plot, and surprise endings. Most report bizarre (if not downright deviant) behavior, the kind guaranteed to hold the interest of the "curious" reader. In fact, a summary of the most spectacular cases sounds remarkably like a preview of weekly offerings on today's talk-show circuit: January 10—A woman of 70 says a young man and two female accomplices raped her. But the young man says he and the old woman are married and he can prove it. Then it turns out he's wanted on a robbery charge. He brings in a woman as his alibi, but she turns out to be one of the accomplices. January 24—A husband accuses his wife and her two sons of beating him unmercifully. But the neighbors say she's an honest, hard-working woman whose husband regularly took her money, beat her, and threatened to kill her. What will the justice decide? March 27—A 60-year-old woman is beaten by her niece for having an affair with her husband, but the niece's husband denies it and accuses his wife of beating him every day for two weeks. Who's telling the truth? And what does the pugilistic wife do when the truth comes out? April 27—Two women named Macculloh beat up a third with the same last name. Are they sisters having a quarrel? No! They're all married to the same man![52] May 4—A wife accuses her husband of never having sex with her and of beating her regularly since their marriage. He denies it. The neighbors say he's a peaceful, honest man who sustained a crippling back injury only a day after his marriage. Who's right? Surprise ending!

I record these examples not so much to show that human nature and what sells print products and air time hasn't changed much, but to contextualize the crucial difference between what Fielding did and what a talk-show host does. For Fielding was the presiding justice in a magistrate's court—a man with the authority to arrest, examine, and commit to prison any English citizen. His "talk show" isn't a show: it's a working court room over which he has official judicial power. Yet he records his court room activities, transcribes them into an entertainment column, and publishes them in a journal he writes and edits as an advertising vehicle for a business in which he is a major partner. Although Fielding's court was honest and well-run by the standards of the time, his journalistic practice seems bizarrely analogous to a modern judge ordering his court clerk to videotape the proceedings of a criminal trial, then personally editing them with voice-overs into a twice-weekly television program sponsored by an employment agency he owns.[53]

The kind of rhetorical and ethical complications injected into such reporting by the demands of literary performance are strikingly illustrated in the complete record of the third case adumbrated above: the beating of 60-year-old Elizabeth Bewley by her niece (March 27). Here, unless I am badly mistaken, we find Fielding not only commenting on a case recorded by Brogden, but completely rewriting it in something like the style of *Tom Jones*. The case is introduced as "a Tragi-comical Cause"—a description that is quickly confirmed by the handling of the complainant: "The Aunt, who is about Sixty-year's of Age, brought her Niece of about Twenty-five before the Justice for beating her; which indeed she had done in no perfunctorious Manner, having given the old Gentlewoman two Black-Eyes, and beat out one of her Teeth." While the opening statement is straightforward enough, the following clause launches a vocabulary of amused amazement ("perfunctorious" highlighting "two Black-Eyes, and beat out one of her Teeth") that transforms a badly beaten woman into a kind of cartoon punching bag. The niece, likewise, is portrayed as the stereotypical virago as she confesses, then justifies, the fact: "indeed [she] gloried in it alledging as a full justification, that her Aunt held a criminal Converse with her Husband, which she declared she would not tamely submit to while she had a Drop of Blood left in her Body."

Incest (a theme of some appeal to Fielding) has been added to injury, and the stage is set for the introduction of the principal:

And now the Husband himself came forward, when lo! the very Picture of Shadow, the Woman's Taylor appeared. He seemed hardly to deny his Wife's Accusation, upon which he was asked how he could be guilty of the Sin of Adultery and Incest (which are by the by no Crimes in our Law) without any Temptation: For the Wife, besides being Young was Pretty, whereas the Aunt had not, at least since her Beating, any Remains of Comeliness, when poor Shadow thought proper to deny the more Criminal Part; but confessed the running away from his Wife: In Excuse for which, he declared that she had beat him every Day for a Fortnight together, which Batteries did indeed remain of Record, very legible on his Face.

If this is not Fielding, it is Brogden doing a remarkably fine imitation of him. The voice is the voice of *Tom Jones*—amused, ironic, knowing—not the resigned, perhaps even despondent narrator conventionally associated with the Fielding of *Amelia* and Bow Street. The dramatic "when lo!," the conflated allusion to Falstaff's recruits, the continued use of the name "Shadow" to identify the husband, the double take of "at least since her Beating," and the socially comedic incongruity of a wife beating her husband combine in a literary portrait reminiscent of Partridge's fate after his beating for purported infidelity: "The poor Man, who bore on his Face many and more visible Marks of the Indignation of his Wife, stood in silent Astonishment at this Accusation; which the Reader will, I believe, bear Witness for him, had greatly exceeded the Truth" (90).[54]

Yet Truth sometimes exceeds Accusation—and not even Fielding could have dreamed up the remarkable denouement of this little court room drama. For while negotiations toward an "Accommodation" are being carried on in an outer room, "something happening to provoke the Wife, she fell violently on the supposed Lovers, and laid both her Husband and her Aunt sprawling at her Feet." Fielding is forced by this event to commit the wife, only to have her subsequently bailed by a *"very substantial* House-keeper."[55] When finally the battlefield is cleared, Fielding turns to the husband, whom he admonishes "concerning the horrid Sins charged upon him; but the poor Shadow protested his Innocence, and with great Earnestness, and possibly great Truth, declared, *That he would rather have one Pot of good Beer than all the Women in Europe.*"

This is a memorable performance: funny, knowing, pathetic, surprising, and in the end sympathy-provoking. It elides the hard reality of domestic violence by making it humorous, yet it strikes about the right moral chord with regard to the husband, who seems the victim of an abusive household controlled and contested by two strong-willed women. Besides its literary quality, it is most notable for the way it shifts our interest away from the beaten Elizabeth Bewley, who is never allowed to speak in the first person, and toward "the poor Shadow"—a character we come to know and love. Such sympathetic realignment is also evident in the Halwyn case (January 24) in which "one Thomas Halwyn, charged Catherine his Wife, and Benjamin and Samuel, two young Lads, her Sons by a former Husband, with beating him." This time, however, our sympathies flow from the accusing husband to the accused wife, as the husband's long, absurdly self-conscious

monologue—"she flies upon me like any Dragooness: indeed I shou'd be
Man enough for her, for that Matter, but then there's her two Sons that
take her Part; and so Yesterday, as I was saying, they all fell upon me, and
beat my poor Head to a Mummy, or Jelly, as a Man may say"—exposes his
prevarication even before the neighbors' testimony causes Fielding to jail
him and set his wife and stepsons free.

Such monologues were presumably included by Fielding to give the
readers the flavor of proceedings in the court (a flavor rather less uniform
than Battestin's "cheerless and despicable"), but in them the difficulties of
interpretation arising from the intersection of justice and *jeu* recur. They
are particularly marked in the first case summarized above, the rape of a
70-year-old woman by her supposed husband, John Smith (January 10).
Like the Bewley case, the Smith case involves the liaison of an older
woman with a younger man—a sensational and often comic motif, familiar in novels and plays, certain to raise the interest of the readership. But
the elaboration of such a case for entertainment purposes raises questions
about Fielding's own attitudes toward rape and domestic violence, particularly as in the eighteenth century the more "benign" forms of these activities, wearing the mask of comedy, often flirted with social
acceptability.[56] As with the prostitution cases, such divided social and textual attention invites readings that explore the possibility of divided judicial attention.

The Smith case is even more byzantine in its complete form than
could be conveyed in the summary. It is, as Brogden/Fielding remarks, "a
very remarkable Affair." John Smith, a "young Fellow," is charged with
the rape of a 70-year-old woman he claims is his wife.[57] The woman declares that "she knew not of any Marriage with him, and if there was any,
that it was done without her Consent or even Knowledge, when she was
by some Liquor, the strength of which was unknown to her, intoxicated
and deprived of her Senses." The next day Smith "broke open her House,
came to Bed with her, and asserted the Right of a Husband, and against
her Consent, with the Assistance of two Women, ravished her; after
which he carried off all she was worth, to the value of several Hundred
Pounds." Sensational and perversely comic ingredients abound: sex,
drugs, chronological misalliance, ravishment with the help of other
women. Not surprisingly, rather than reporting summarily the proceedings and their outcome, Fielding reconstructs the longest monologue to
appear in the Covent Garden columns, John Smith's "very oratorical" defense. Graced with irony and satirical sting, a selection of the best of
"Smith's" lines reveals an affinity more perhaps to the Little Haymarket
than to Bow Street:

"[T]his fair Lady being old, had no great Occasion to carry her Interest to the Grave."

"I was married to this fair Lady, with the Expectation of Fortune, and not for Beauty, as you see."

"Upon my Honour, I did as much as I could do as a Husband, did I not, Madam?"

"She is an exorbitant Usurer, and will lend your Worship eighteen Shillings, upon a Note for twenty."

"[I]f I live, or die, I will remember never to marry her any more."

To assert that Fielding "reconstructs" much of this monologue (about a quarter of which appears above) is not to say that the essence of Smith's performance is somehow falsified, but that the author clearly took the time to expand and embellish what at best would have been shorthand notes written by Brogden *currente calamo*. The entertainment value of such an expansion is clear enough; but what is perhaps less evident is the way in which the monologue works to reduce the potential seriousness of Smith's purported crimes by making him seem a comic character caught in a comic marriage. As if to emphasize Fielding's own detachment from the issues of an elderly woman's forced marriage and rape with which the report began, the case takes a sudden turn after the monologue to a completely different charge against John Smith. The new plot centers on Fielding, the cagey judge, ferreting out Smith's commission of a highway robbery: "All this [referring to Smith's oratory], and much more, the Justice had the Patience to hear, upon private Information, that he was suspected of another capital Offence, and that the Witnesses against him were coming. At last arrived Dr. Hill, and his Man; the latter of whom charged the Prisoner with robbing his Master on the 26th of December last, on the Highway." Although Smith counters with a witness, Jane Tate, to provide an alibi, "by a fatal error, on separate Examination, though they agreed in every other Circumstance, they disagreed as to the Day, which they had forgot." In the end, Jane Tate is also identified as "one of the Women charged in the Accusation of Rape; so that, in the Conclusion, Mr. Smith, and his Witness, shared the same Fate, and were committed to several Prisons."

The dramatic arrival of the hack-cum-quack Dr. John Hill (then writing the "Inspector" column for the *London Daily Advertiser*) was fortunate not only for the development of the case but for the development of my argument. For Fielding's extrajudicial dealings with him provide something like a low allegory of the author-cum-justice's tendency to blur the boundary separating Bow Street and Grub Street. In a well-known incident, Fielding seems, during Hill's original deposition on December 28, to have taken the opportunity to propose, in Battestin's words, "that they might make their journals more entertaining by engaging in a little harmless literary horseplay in the context of a 'Paper War.'"[58] Harmless enough, perhaps, until we remember that the person proposing the journalistic collaboration was the justice who would have to deal with Hill's alleged assailants should they be found. Given the circumstances, one has to wonder whether Fielding's involvement with Hill made him extra zealous in suspecting Smith—who was charged with a completely different crime—and too quick to call Hill as a witness. Certainly the evidence must have been doubtful because Smith was later acquitted.[59]

Fielding's approaching a material witness with a literary proposition indicates the kind of perceptual crossed-wiring that typifies his behavior on the bench during this period, a tendency further emphasized by the remarkable inclusion at the end of the Covent Garden column for January 10 of a mock column for January 11 reporting "that a famous Surgeon, who absolutely cured one Mrs. Amelia Booth, of a violent hurt in her Nose, insomuch, that she had scarce a Scar left on it, intends to bring Actions against several ill-meaning and slanderous People, who have reported that the said Lady had no Nose." Here Fielding's own fictional creation migrates to the "real" site of Bow Street (just as, one might add, puffs for the Universal Register Office had migrated to the pages of *Amelia*). Indeed, *Amelia*'s appearance in the Covent Garden columns marks the seed of an idea Fielding brought to fruition two issues later. On January 18, *The Covent-Garden Journal* ran, immediately following the Covent Garden column, the first installment of a new feature reporting Sir Alexander Drawcansir's proceedings at a "Court of Censorial Enquiry"—a fictional court resolved "to hear, and determine, all manner of Causes, which anywise relate to the Republic of Letters."[60] Its chief targets were, predictably, *Amelia*'s and Drawcansir's critics. By the fifth issue of *The Covent-Garden Journal*, then, law was providing the metaphor for judging literary and journalistic practice, while literary and journalistic practice was providing the vehicle for profitably exploiting official legal judgments.

In the Covent Garden columns, Fielding combined what today would be considered, at least in theory, the separate prerogatives of the court and the press. The ethical ambiguity generated by the oscillation of these two conflicting impulses—to record accurately and to entertain or, at a more immediate, performative level, to maintain public judicial power and impartiality while entertaining private literary/emotional subjectivities—sums up the overall impression of Fielding's court as it is preserved in the journalistic record. In emphasizing the interpenetration of such discursive and psychological impulses, I would hope to modify the more binary separation of Fielding's legal and fiction writing epitomized by Arlene

Wilner's insistence that, unlike the fiction, the legal writings are "not 'heteroglossic'"; that Fielding the legal pamphleteer "represents the voice of civil authority" or "resembles the subjective, authoritative justices of the old order, muffling the multiple voices of the complicated case in his own carefully constructed version of a story that he expects to be accepted less in the weight of the evidence than on its appeal to the authority of traditional socio-sexual constructs and accepted views of the relationships among members of various social classes."[61] Such an assessment not only oversimplifies the rhetoric of the "legal" pamphlets that Wilner here addresses, but leads her to the ultimate generalization that "in his fiction Fielding felt he could risk relinquishing to his audience the kinds of autonomy and authority that in Bow Street and back parlors had to be carefully guarded."[62]

My hope has been to show that Fielding did not "guard" his "authority and autonomy" in Bow Street very "carefully" at all when he decided to retail them for threepence in the columns of a twice-weekly entertainment journal. This is not to say that the bombastic Drawcansir persona in his role as "Censor-General" would have been taken unequivocally to represent Fielding's serious views. The allusion to the character from Buckingham's *The Rehearsal* and the essayistic tradition of adopting slightly absurd mouthpieces would have been understood. But there is also in *The Covent-Garden Journal* a secondary character named "Justice Fielding" who seems to admit no such self-deprecating or fictionalizing interpretation and yet whose situation as author and character in a long-running and rhetorically embellished court room drama undercuts what Wilner calls the "voice of civil authority" and exposes the court to ridicule. It is "Justice Fielding's" performance in the Covent-Garden columns, as both author and subject, that produces potentially a breakdown in the authority of the court (one posited by Grub Street's sneering at "Justice Scribble") and unquestionably the imaginative transformation of its clientele into marketable literary products.

Unlike most journalists, Henry Fielding was not only able to imagine and write about but to *control* an institution that had a direct effect on people's lives. Given this power, his intermittent confusion of overt authority and covert transgression could and in some cases did produce material exploitation. While this is not to say that Fielding's motivations in his periodical or his court were consciously exploitative, it is to suggest that they were significantly affected by his simultaneous interest in what was true, what was right, and what would sell. Exploitation from a position of authority was possible, but so was, through an audience's recognition of this exploitation, a backlash that transgressed the very authority Fielding sought to uphold. In other words, Henry Fielding's (conscious or unconscious) transgressions within authority produced countertransgressions of authority that must inform any interpretation of the effects of his writing and activity in the Bow Street Office. Moreover, such a dynamic suggests that, in Fielding's case and perhaps more generally as well, the impulses associated with the "Enlightenment project" or the "great age of 'institutionalizing'"—surveillance, classification, rationalism, the rule of law, commercial calculation—were subject to persistent modification by the older social practices and human desires that, masked by reformist rhetoric, continued to lurk, as they do today, within the aspiration to improve and ameliorate.[63] As we will see, it is a contradictory dynamic vividly manifested in the work of the Universal Register Office.

Chapter 2

The Work of the Register Office

I

In February 1751, Christopher Smart, writing as "Mary Midnight," took credit for predicting the success of an institution opened a year earlier by the half brothers Henry and John Fielding. Noting that her "sedulous Application to the useful Science of Astrology" allowed her to determine "whenever a lucky Coincidence of propitious Symptoms attends the Birth of anything," Midnight wrote that she "foresaw from the favourable Appearances, which attended the Birth of an Office some time since erected opposite *Cecil-street* in the *Strand,* under the Title of the UNIVERSAL REGISTER OFFICE" that such an institution would prosper. Indeed, the Universal, "agreeable to the foreboding of my Art, I find by the general Approbation of the Publick and Countenance of the People of Fashion, to have already in great Measure answer'd, and to be every Day more and more likely to answer its extensive Design, and the Purpose of Publick Good."[1]

The rhetoric of Smart's astrological fiction humorously encodes the structural problem that brought the register office into being, at least as Henry Fielding imagined it. The chancy odds of "a lucky Coincidence of propitious Symptoms" attending "the Birth of anything" dramatizes in the planets the unfortunate state of sublunary economic affairs in which, as Fielding sees it, lucky coincidence too often fails to effect mutually beneficial communication and transaction: "In large and populous Cities, and wide and extended Communities, it is more probable that every human Talent is dispersed somewhere or other among the Members; and consequently every Person who stands in Need of the Talent, might supply his Want if he knew where to find it; but to know this is the Difficulty, and this Difficulty still encreases with the Largeness of the Society."[2] In the rational practice of the register office, however, dependence on luck was to become obsolete, and the missed connections and inefficiencies that characterize more traditional venues for meeting and commerce ("Fairs, Markets, Exchanges") were to be eliminated: "Here the Buyer and the Seller, the Master and the Scholar, the Master and the Apprentice, and the Master and the Servant are sure to meet: Here ingenious Persons of all Kinds will meet with those ready to employ them, and the Curious will be supplied with every thing which it is in the Power of Art to produce."[3]

On the surface, then, the relationship between Smart's tongue-in-cheek prediction in an entertainment journal and Fielding's serious proposal in a prosaic pamphlet seems an inverted one: the midwife's rhetoric of the occult ironically emblematizing all the unpredictability of worldly things that Fielding's orderly practice proposes to rectify. Yet both predict with an air of almost otherworldly infallibility. Midnight assures the success of the Office; while Fielding assures the success of the work of the Office: employer and employee "are sure to meet"; the curious "will be supplied with every thing." Moreover, both imply that the work of their respective institutions will be not only salutary but entertaining. Fielding's phrase, "The Curious will be supplied with *every thing* which it is in the *Power of Art* to produce" (my emphasis), could stand as a motto to Smart's eclectic journal, which advertised itself as "*Containing* all *the* WIT, *and* all *the* HUMOUR, *and* all *the* LEARNING, *and* all *the* JUDGEMENT, *that has* ever been, or ever will be *inserted in* all *the other* Magazine."[4] This odd congruence of universalizing impulses—one serious, the other comic—throws into high relief the ambiguous ambitions of Fielding's project. For as Fielding himself would surely have recognized, there was something in the choice of the term "Universal" itself to designate the scope of the office that threatened to recall both the Duncean lunacy of totalizing projects and the brilliance of Augustan parodic entertainments based upon them. Indeed, Smart himself invoked this relationship in two later squibs in *The Midwife*. On June 29, 1751, Mary Midnight advertised her own plans to open ("at the Sign of the Mop Handle in *Shoe-Lane*") a similar institution:

An Office for the IGNORANT

OR,

A Warehouse of Intelligence

Where Physicians may learn the true Practice of Physic, Divines the true Practice of Piety, and Lawyers the true Practice of Law. In a Word, Fumblers of all Faculties will be corroborated without Loss of Time.[5]

And later still, after the opening of *The Old Woman's Oratory,* Mary Midnight proposed from her "Rostrum" that a "*Thought-Warehouse* or *Opinion-Office,* be erected in the most conspicuous and commodious Part of this City."[6]

The humorous tension between job placement and popular entertainment in these squibs seems to invite a more detailed interrogation of the work of the register office than is usual in Fielding studies. Traditionally, the eclectic advertisements, letters, pamphlets, plays, journals, graphic works, and fictional allusions that together give a sense of the practice and contemporary interpretation of this innovative brokerage have been read almost exclusively from the Fielding brothers' point of view (that is, in such a way as to maximize its praiseworthy and even whimsical elements and ignore its less savory ones).[7] Pat Rogers, for example, writes that the office was "a kind of Universal Aunts": "indeed the latter title may have been partly borrowed from this source (there was, too, an old phrase 'universal maid,' meaning a general servant). The firm was in business as an employment agency and as an estate-management service; it engaged in money-lending, insurance, and all kinds of brokerage. Its advice function extended to travel, which anticipates Thomas Cook in the field of tourism by almost a century. Since it was a hard time to get servants—it always has been—Londoners were particularly glad to use the office for this purpose. It was lucky that nobody had yet invented the newspaper personal column."[8] Battestin takes this view a bit further, remarking that "'Noble' is perhaps not too grand a word for this business. Though his motives doubtless were chiefly commercial rather than altruistic, Fielding believed, however quixotically, that the Universal Register Office would be a panacea to cure the ills of the body politic."[9] Recently, however, Bertrand Goldgar has provided a more dispassionate factual and interpretive foundation for analytical work on the subject, noting, for example, that the *Plan* "is an extended advertisement, not a serious social tract."[10] His findings have provided a basis for the following discussion of the relations between clientele and institution, aid and exploitation, and advertisement and practice at the register office.

The institution was initially theorized in the Fielding brothers' promotional *Plan of the Universal Register-Office,* which appeared on February 21, 1750/51.[11] For a fee (ranging from three-pence to one shilling, depending on the commodity or service in question), the clerks at the Universal would either list or allow the customer to view lists of estates, houses, or lodgings to be sold or rented; places or employments "to be sold, or anywise disposed of"; apprentices who "want Masters" and vice versa; "Masters and Mistresses who teach any Science or Art"; "Partners in Trade"; "All manner of Goods"; "Conveniencies for Travelling"; and most significantly "Servants of all Kinds, such as Riders, Book-keepers, and Journey-men, Stewards and Clerks; Domestic Servants, as House-Stewards, Gentlemen, Valets, Butlers, Cooks, Gardeners, Coachmen, Footmen, Grooms, Postilions, &c. Governesses, Housekeepers, Waiting-maids,

Cook-maids, House-maids, Laundry-maids, dry and wet Nurses, &c &c."[12] The point according to Fielding was to facilitate commerce, employment, and exchange, so that "no useful Talent in the Society will be idle, nor will any Man long want a Seller and Purchaser of what he is desirous either to purchase or dispose of; whereas at present many a Man is Starving, while in the Possession of Talents, which would be highly serviceable to others, who could and would well reward him." The Universal Register Office was to provide "a Place of universal Resort, where all the Members of the Society may communicate all their mutual Wants and Talents to each other. So that no Person may want what another is capable of supplying him with, provided he is able and willing to pay the Price."[13]

The register office, then, was to be a "Place of universal Resort"—a phrase that implies both egalitarian refuge and social mixing, and that seems somehow more appropriate to the Pump Room at Bath than to an employment agency in the Strand. In fact, the connotations of both sites are suggestive of the register office's practice. For at mid-century the register office served not only as a processing center for unemployed urbanites and for country people new to London, but as an entertainment venue as well. Because it promoted itself as a fertile and emotionally charged mixing ground for various disparate elements of society ("a Place of universal Resort, where all the Members of the Society may communicate all their mutual Wants and Talents to each other"), the register office was touted by the Fieldings and others as an interesting place to visit and view. But, paradoxically, such "mixing in the service of business" (or mixing in the business of service) potentially sponsored just the kind of social and generic contamination that had long worried conservative authors and antiluxury theorists. The Fieldings' response to this mixture of pleasures and threats seems to have been to invite participation and spectatorship, but to infuse the register office's fluid environment with a rigid decorum based on inquisition and deference and dedicated to the proposition that all men are not created equal but must be herded by the proprietors into proper roles and relationships.

The kinds of contradictions necessarily attending such a scheme become evident in the first major dispute (besides the Glastonbury Waters controversy)[14] to engage the proprietors of the Universal Register Office—one that precisely points out the potentially revolutionary dangers (from a conservative point of view) inherent in a scheme of universal access and improvement. For what happened was that employment at the Universal Register Office inadvertently sparked the aspirations of a young entrepreneur who then attempted to fulfill the *Plan's* promise "that no Person may want what another is capable of supplying him with, provided he is able and willing to pay the Price." When his overtures were rejected, he, in effect, rejected the deferential behavior the Fieldings required, and a miniature version of class warfare erupted.

The particular episode, involving a young Belgian named Philip D'Halluin who left the Universal Register Office to set up the competing Public Register Office, provides a telling example of how pro-Fielding advocacy has tended to color our view of the activities of the Universal Register Office. A typical redaction—before Goldgar's work—occurs in W. L. Cross's biography and pictures poor John Fielding shocked by the betrayal of "Dullwin" and "amazed at conduct of a stranger he had aided in distress."[15] Battestin, for his part, omits the episode altogether. Again, Goldgar's revisionary account has got the episode right (calling a self-serving letter by John Fielding an "ungenerous piece of chauvinism" and crediting D'Halluin with "somewhat more dignity that John Fielding had been able to muster")[16] and raises issues I would like to look at in more detail here.

On November 4, 1751 John Fielding published a letter in the *London Daily Advertiser* describing how his rival D'Halluin (whom he calls "Dullwin, a Travelling Frenchman") purportedly wheedled his way into the Universal Register Office in order to steal trade secrets:

> Dullwin . . . enter'd his Name on our Books to teach the French Language; nor was there any Neglect on our side to serve him, but the contrary, he being employed by our Means. The more I interested myself in his Service, the more frequent his Visits were: At length he was treated with so much Familiarity, that he was suffered, when the Office was very full, to assist the Clerks in their Duty, which he did with great willingness, and with all the Appearance of Friendship imaginable, which at that time he had put on to conceal the Design which he was meditating to our Disadvantage, being all the while instructing himself in the Method of our Books. About two Months ago he totally disappeared, and in Opposition to those who had been his Friends, has presumed (I think I may use that Expression) to erect a pretended Office, under the Title of the Public Register Office, formed upon our Plan, with this Difference only, that he artfully insinuates to the Public, that he will register all Articles gratis; a Delusion which needs no Comment.[17]

Having set out to impugn "Dullwin's" business ethics, Fielding invokes English xenophobia and class bias, stressing that the proprietors of the Universal are a "Society of Gentlemen" (as opposed to the competition) and asking rhetorically "whether the Ingenuity and Industry of Englishmen to serve their own Country, and themselves, are thus to be plundered of the Rewards of their Labour by the Invasion of a Foreigner." The emphasis throughout the letter is on the Fieldings' condescension in treating

D'Halluin "with so much Familiarity" as to have "suffered" him to help
around the office. The name "Dullwin" (besides being a convenient pun)
alludes, of course, to "Dulness"—*magna mater* of bad writing and shoddy,
low-class commerce. In effect, John Fielding attempts to cast the Public
Register Office as the business equivalent of Grub Street literature, characterized by plagiarism, crassness, dishonesty, and foreignness. It strikes me
that even the names of the two competing institutions seem to reinforce
this contrast: the Fieldings' high-flown (but ambiguous) "universal" contrasting sharply with D'Halluin's quotidian "public."

D'Halluin's version of events predictably contradicts John Fielding's. He
was, he tells us, "born in Brussels," but spent the "greatest Part of his Life
in London, having been bred to business under John Backer, Esq., in
Mark-Lane, a very eminent Merchant . . . who, in Consideration of his
Diligence and Fidelity left him Five hundred Pounds":

> Mr. D'Halluin . . . did apply to Mr. Folding's Register Office; but not find-
> ing the success he expected, he called often, and, by calling became so fa-
> miliar as frequently to make Registries for him in his Books, which he did
> for a considerable time, without the least Gratuity; but at length liking the
> Business and finding, by Mr. Folding's Acknowledgement, that he was sin-
> gularly useful to him, he proposed his being taken in as a Partner, but re-
> ceived several evasive Answers. However, still continuing to expect an
> Eclarissement from him as to that Particular, he at last insisted upon a cate-
> gorical Answer, which proved a Negative."[18]

Having been denied a partnership by Fielding, D'Halluin went into business for himself, opening the Public Register Office with persons who "are
not only Englishmen, but Englishmen who claim this Undertaking as their
own, and whose Fortune, Honesty, and Honour they would think injured
by being compared to . . . Mr. Folding's."

Both Fielding's and D'Halluin's histories tell us more about their respective class positions than about the events at the register office. Fielding's attitude seems to be that D'Halluin, as a social inferior, should have
been happy to help around the office because of the attention paid to him
by his social superiors. D'Halluin, on the other hand, sees himself as an
asset to the business and a potential partner—a well-trained young man on
the rise, who wishes to be taken seriously. When D'Halluin reveals himself
as a potential competitor, Fielding is reduced to name-calling.

The tonal differences engendered by these conflicting viewpoints inform the published "Plans" of the respective register offices as well (see Appendix II). Although the overall concept of D'Halluin's "Plan" differs little
from Henry Fielding's, the rhetorical contrasts are striking, particularly in

the handling of that touchiest of subjects, servants.[19] Henry Fielding exclusively adopts the master's point of view in describing the practice of his
office. Servants will be questioned closely about their background ("Qualification, Age, married or single, whether had the Small Pox, what Place
lived last, and how long; with every Particular of their Characters") and
questioned with a good deal of rigor: "the Public may be assured, that the
utmost Care will be taken to prevent any Imposition; and that none will
be registered in this Office who give the least suspicious Account of themselves, and who have lived in any disreputable Places." The oppressive atmosphere created by this kind of paternalistic, quasi-judicial interrogation
is nicely dramatized in a puffing letter to the *London Daily Advertiser* (June
3, 1751) by one "Z.Z." (probably John Fielding):

> I have never seen a Servant in my Life appear with that Awe and Deference,
> to receive the Commands of a Master, whatever were his Quality, as they
> stood before the Managers of the Office, to give an Account of themselves.
> The Care of the Office, in respect to Servants, will best appear from the fol-
> lowing Questions asked every Servant before their being admitted to be
> registered: What is your Age? Of what Country? Have you had the Small-
> Pox? Are you single or married? Where did you last live? In what Capacity
> did you act? How long did you live there? What was the Reason of your
> leaving that Place? Where did you live before you came to your last Place?
> What was the reason of your quitting that Place? Who will give you a Char-
> acter? . . . The Caution given to the Servants going to Places, by reminding
> them, that their Conduct alone must recommend them to the Patronage of
> that Office, it being designed as an Asylum for the best Servants only, I con-
> fess, gave me a sensible Pleasure."[20]

While Z.Z. might have got a thrill out of this process, the servants probably didn't. There is throughout the description a habitual suspicion and
condescension that must have made a trip to the Universal Register Office an uncomfortable if not degrading experience.[21] That Henry Fielding
shared this prejudice seems evident not only in his fictional portrayals of
servants—from Shamela to Honour to little Betty—but in the way he
seems to relish in *An Enquiry into the Causes of the late Increase of Robbers*
(1751) the laws enacted to force the unemployed poor into service.[22]
Moreover, as if to emphasize the connection between crime, con jobs, and
servants, the final page of that pamphlet contained an advertisement for the
Universal Register Office that began:

> The rude Behaviour and insolence of Servants of all Kinds is become a gen-
> eral Complaint: for which Insolence the Law has given no other Power of
> punishing than by turning them away; and this would be often Punishment

enough, if the Servant could not easily provide himself with another Place:
But here they find no Manner of Difficulty; for many Persons are weak
enough to take Servants without any Character; and if this be insisted on,
there is an ingenious Method in this Town of obtaining as false Character
from one who personates the former Master or Mistress: To obviate all this,
an Office is erected in the Strand, opposite Cecil-Street, where the best Servants in every Capacity are to be heard of; and where the Public may be assured, that no Servant shall ever be register'd, who cannot produce a real
good Character from the last Place in which he or she actually lived.[23]

Of course, one could argue that suspicion and degradation were an accepted part of service; but in that case, the contrasting rhetoric of D'Halluin's "Plan" seems even more remarkable for its open acknowledgment of
the various class positions of his potential clientele and the necessary
diminution of self-worth that the economics of service implies:

Almost every Man, whose Condition is above Servitude, cannot be very
happy without a Servant; and all whose Circumstances oblige them to be Servants, can subsist but poorly without Masters. Now as the Office Registers
Masters of all Ranks, in any Trade or Occupation, and Servants of all Kinds,
from the Steward and Housekeeper to the most inferior Servant of both Sexes
(and these never Register'd but with the same Caution and Care that any
Gentleman would use when he chuses a Servant for himself) it is plain and
evident, that great Benefit and Ease must accrue to both Master and Servant,
by making the Office a Means of giving them reciprocal Information.[24]

D'Halluin (or whoever wrote the "Plan" for him) addresses with some sub-
tlety the emotional and economic tensions of the class structure, beginning
at that point where the lowest master is only barely removed from the servant class. Having announced that servants are servants only because "Circumstances oblige them to be," he then puts their relations with their
masters on a business-like basis: happiness and subsistence determine the
arrangement, not patriarchal right nor underclass duty.[25] D'Halluin even has
the audacity to float the parenthetical clause about registering with "Caution and Care" in such a way that although it refers first to the inferior servants, and then to the upper servants, it is syntactically possible to read it as
referring also to the "Masters of all Ranks" that the office registers.

What we hear in this passage, it seems to me, is the voice of someone
who has been a menial speaking to members of his former class.[26] Servants, by and large, are presented as human beings under certain terms of
employment, not domestic appliances nor irresponsible juveniles. Likewise,
the Public Register Office's newspaper advertisements seem to address an
audience of responsible working people:

> The Servants of all Degrees in this Kingdom are hereby acquainted, that Gentlemen and Ladies of the best Fashion, as well as eminent Merchants and Tradesmen, apply daily to the above Office for Servants; where everyone is registered Gratis . . .
>
> As nothing can be of so great Use to any Servant who applies, as a sufficient Character, those who bring the best Testimonials, and most undoubted Proofs of it, will have the first and greatest Regard shewn them, and all speedy Means taken to establish them according to their Qualifications and Desert.[27]

Unlike the Fieldings, who stress interrogation and the ferreting out of secret transgressions, D'Halluin emphasizes the positive side of the registering process. He addresses the servants first, acquainting them with the possibility of employment. He focuses on the existence of the "best Testimonials." He promises "the first and greatest Regard" to those who best fulfill the office's criteria. Though we cannot assume that D'Halluin's sympathetic advertisements necessarily assured non-exploitative treatment of servants at the Public Register Office, they may have lured clientele away from the Fieldings and had some effect in altering the tone of the Fieldings' textual relationship to their service clientele. For although in the Fieldings' earlier newspaper advertisements servants are almost always fully commodified—"Apprentices and Domestic Servants of every Kind, with most undoubted Recommendations, may be had here"[28]—in later advertisements in *The Covent-Garden Journal,* the Fieldings seem to take a more humanizing line:

> All Servants, whose behaviour has entitled them to a fair Character for their Sobriety, Capacity, and Fidelity, from the Master or Mistress they served last, will always be sure of meeting with Encouragement suitable to their Merit by applying to the Gentlemen of this Office, whose particular Care it will be to fix them in Stations for which they are qualified, and prevent their lying out of Place at their own Expence; a Circumstance too often fatal to both Sexes.[29]

The verbal contrasts evident in the Plans and advertisements of the competing register offices were, not surprisingly, echoed in the journals each eventually sponsored: Fielding's *The Covent-Garden Journal* and Bonnell Thornton's *Have At You All: or, Drury-Lane Journal. The Covent-Garden Journal* was the first to appear and seems in part to have been a response to yet another problem caused by the Fieldings' patronizing attitude toward their competition. In the *Plan,* Henry Fielding had made derogatory remarks about the ineffectiveness of public advertisements. These remarks seem to have provoked *The Daily Advertiser* (in a delicious irony) to refuse the Fieldings' ads altogether.[30] Z.Z., in his letter of June 3, 1751, to *The London Daily Advertiser* (not to be confused with *The Daily Advertiser*), expressed "Surprize and Indignation . . . that the Author of, perhaps, the driest unentertaining Daily Paper [*The Daily Advertiser*], which ever did, or can exist in a sensible City, had suppressed [the Universal Register Office's] Advertisements." Matthew Jenour's *Daily Advertiser* had a larger daily circulation and was a more functionally pure advertiser than any other London newspaper—it ran few leaders, essays, or reviews. As the proprietor of a competing advertising medium, Jenour had something at stake in his dealings with the newly reinvented register office and was probably happy for an excuse to drop the Fieldings' ads. The Fieldings' attitude is more paradoxical: to denigrate the effectiveness of printed ads and then to complain that they couldn't run them seems a kind of microcosmic example of the Fieldings' propensity to swagger and then take offense when defied. But equally interesting for our purposes is Z.Z.'s reference to *The Daily Advertiser*'s lack of entertainment value, for in it perhaps lurks the seed of *The Covent-Garden Journal*.

Fielding's establishment of *The Covent-Garden Journal* seems to have been an attempt to do what the daily advertisers couldn't effectively do at this point in their history: use entertainment as a primary means of calling attention to the products and services they advertised.[31] *The Covent-Garden Journal* would provide such entertainment both in traditional forms (topical essays and letters) and in more innovative ones (regular reports from Fielding's court and, in the "Modern History" column, news with commentary). As Goldgar notes, Fielding's persona, Sir Alexander Drawcansir, despite its mock-heroic overtones, continued in the tradition of the *Champion* and *Jacobite's Journal* "the role of Censor on the Roman model, the overseer and judge of the nation's moral health, charged with examining into the lives and manners of its citizens," and predictably Fielding's first leader concentrated on issues of authorship and commercial publication, noting conventionally that there was too much of both, promising better material, and justifying its three-shilling price since it contained "almost twenty Times as much as is generally contained in the Daily Advertiser."[32] But more paradoxically, after renouncing "Slander and Scurrillity" and incursions into the "Land of DULLNESS," Fielding, in keeping with the "total war" concept advocated by his persona's prototype in *The Rehearsal,* declared a "PAPER WAR between the Forces under Sir ALEXANDER DRAWCANSIR, and the Army of GRUBSTREET"— thereby providing an open invitation to slander, scurrility, "Dullness," and the army of Grub Street to join in what he no doubt hoped would be a sales-raising melee.[33] In effect, Fielding seems to have replicated in the society of Grub Street journalism the stated commercial mission of the Universal Register Office: to provide "a Place of universal Resort, where all the Members of the Society may communicate all their mutual Wants and Talents to each other. So that no Person may want what another is capable of supplying him with, provided he is able and willing to pay the Price." Like the register office, *The Covent-Garden Journal* became a nexus of exchange: a focal point for writers to engage in mutually beneficial (or disciplinary) interaction. In a move that translated John Fielding's equation of "Dullwin" with "Dulness" (that is, the Public Register Office with Grub Street) back into the world of journalism, Henry Fielding melded the Public Register Office and dunces as targets of *The Covent-Garden Journal*—a publication sponsored by the Universal Register Office—in an attempt to contest simultaneously the realms of brokerage and authorship. As Fielding surely must have known, such a project, particularly when couched in the bombastic tongue-in-cheek that characterizes Drawcansir's early manner, would provoke an instantaneous and massive exchange of talents worthy of his fondest brokering dreams. What the participants supplied, however, were not goods or services, but opinions and entertainment.[34]

The progress of the resulting paper war, in which Fielding paid perhaps a greater "Price" than he had anticipated, has been well-documented, although most accounts again have tended to emphasize Fielding's innocence and good intentions and to attack the moral or verbal turpitude of his opponents.[35] The war became something of a publishing bonanza, provoking contributions and commentaries from John Hill, Smollett, Thornton, Macklin, Smart, Kenrick, and others. Some authors, like Hill and Smollett, seem to have been driven by real anger (though in Grub Street this is often hard to distinguish from the fictional variety), while others were clearly in it for the fun—and the money. William Kenrick's contribution, in fact, was called *Fun*—a Shakespearean send-up that laughs not only at Fielding, Hill ("Mountain"), and Thornton ("Roxana Termagant") but translates the commercially symbiotic relationship of these writers into sexual terms. Kenrick's "Roxana" exclaims:

> Raise all my Powers, the Powers of Grub-street raise,
> Drawcansir trembles at the Name of me,
> My ranks in King-street shine—but oh my Heart!
> I'm sick of Love, and for my mortal Foe;
> Drawcansir's Charms have pierc'd my tender Breast.[36]

The sexual analogy here alludes to Bonnell Thornton's close parodies of Fielding's style ("*Drawcansir's* Charms") in *Have At You All; or, The Drury-Lane Journal*, a publication originating from D'Halluin's Public Register Office in King Street, Covent Garden. As D'Halluin had imitated and contested the Fieldings' business methods, so his hired pen, Thornton, was imitating and contesting Henry Fielding's journalistic ones.

In *The Drury-Lane Journal* (which commenced publication on January 16, 1752), D'Halluin's somewhat cheeky, insubordinate attitude toward the motives and practices of the "gentlemen" over at the Universal Register Office finds fictional articulation in "Madam Roxana Termagant's" irreverent send-ups of Sir Alexander Drawcansir. Thornton's Roxana is a significant figure in the textual representation of register offices for several reasons. First, she is an aggressive female taking on Fielding's "tongue-doughty giant SIR ALEXANDER DRAWCANSIR."[37] Secondly, she is an implied former prostitute or bawd, full of experience and resentment, with a sharp eye for the "gentleman" Fielding's literary/moral tricks and evasions. In an autobiographical sketch, Roxana calls attention to her questionable past by protesting it rather too often: "I was born at a little town in the West of England; no matter where, no matter when.—'Tis an usual practice, I know, with the miserable creatures of the Courtezan order (of which if any one suspects me to be, I here assure him to the contrary) to incite the compassion of their casual gallants by pretending to be, what they call, Parson's daughters"—which is just what Roxana then pretends to be (31–32). Later Roxana tells how a young man was found by her bedside at her clergyman-father's school and caused her to be sent to a relative at Cambridge. There she fell in love with a student who tutored her in love and classics, and eventually recommended her to his mother as servant/companion for his sister. In service she continued her relationship with the brother: "Some unguarded indiscretions (I leave the reader to guess them) at last broke the union between us: the mother had observ'd us more intimately connected than we intended she should" (36–37). She was expelled, became an actress's dresser, a strolling player, and finally an author. Although Roxana, of course, does not explicitly state that at any time she was a prostitute, Thornton's innuendoes construct her as an ambitious country girl, turned servant, turned mistress, turned authoress, who reveals her past as she attempts to refute it.

In the sociology of Grub Street, Roxana is the rhetorical and symbolic sister of Christopher Smart's unruly Mary Midnight, who, as I have suggested elsewhere, embodies the irreverence and resentment of the underclass.[38] In fact, in the fantasy Grubean world constructed by the friends Thornton and Smart, the two actually meet: Midnight visits Termagant at her hack writer's chambers above a "rotting Chandler's shop" in Drury Lane, where a broken window is covered "with proof-sheets of the *Drury-Lane Journal* . . . and the bare walls were set off with five wooden pictures, half torn, of the *Harlot's Progress*" (60–61). Roxana epitomizes the "resentful upper servant's view of society" that Morris Golden describes as the defining characteristic of Smart's journalism.[39] Not surprisingly, she seems intent on exposing the material interest elided by Sir Alexander's gentlemanly professions of disinterested public good. Thus when Sir Alexander writes (with some irony on Fielding's part?) that money is "infinitely below my Consideration," Roxana answers by making material interest, in fact, *material*:

> The scribbling haberdashers of small wares, I agree, with you, are already so numerous, that a Witmonger now a days finds it an hard matter to live by the trade.—Yet give me leave to open my shop among the rest: and, as I intend never to impose on my customers any of your second-hand garbish, your ordinary patch-work, and common commodities, I don't despair, tho' a beginner, to please them full as well as Sir ALEXANDER, (who is an old dabbler in this sort of merchandize) or any other Retailer of Scraps and Literary Piece-Broker.—At least, I invite every body with the usual salutation, to see for love and buy for money.
>
> I do not pretend, with your Worship, to a spirit so disinterested, as to be entirely regardless of Profit in the business.—Every one has a right to as much as he can earn: and the genius, whose brains spin materials for the mind, ought equally to be rewarded with the mechanick, whose hands furnish out coarser stuff for the body (4).

Here Roxana anticipates James Ralph's argument in "The Case of Authors by Profession or Trade" (1758)—"the writer . . . has as good a Right to the Product in Money of his Abilities, as the Landholder to his Rent, or the Money-Jobber to his Interest"—by taking the radical duncean position that writing is a commodity pure and simple.[40]

More importantly, however, Roxana parodies the "Covent Garden" columns in a way that suggests she understands Fielding's moral evasiveness. In her "MOLL DRAGGLETAIL" passage (quoted above), she attacks Fielding as both "Sir Alexander Drawcansir" (whose "style and manner" are being parodied) and as "Justice Scribble" (before whom the streetwalker is dragged), accusing him of harboring a secret fascination for the corrosive language and sordid behavior of those "blundering servant girls" and whores over whom he exercises legal power and whose "misfortins" he turns to commercial literary use. Although it wears its protest lightly, Thornton's journal, like Smart's *Midwife*, seems to empower marginal women. Regardless of its humorous exaggeration, the ideological intonation of Thornton's text is clear: it mimics the resentful voice, sometimes rough, sometimes shading toward the genteel, of a working girl telling a puffed-up gentleman that she sees through his high-flown rhetoric to the morally compromised world with which he colludes.

II

To the reader who takes it whole, rather than as an edited set of leaders extracted from surrounding material, *The Covent-Garden Journal* seems less a vehicle of moral/literary commentary than an overview of interesting transactions in the world of vice.[41] Besides the numerous leaders that discuss sordid or bizarre goings-on in London—for example, essays on the Robinhood society (Nos. 8 & 9); the notorious parricide Moll Blandy (mentioned Nos. 11 & 12); the punishment of felons (No. 25); the power of the mob (Nos. 47 & 49); prostitution (Nos. 50 & 57); adultery (Nos. 66, 67, & 68), and so forth—*The Covent Garden Journal's* regular features, "Covent Garden" (Bow Street reports) and "Modern History" (news, mostly criminal), usually emphasize malfeasance and mayhem. The second feature in particular gave Fielding the freedom to search out the most interesting bits from other papers and to comment on them, often satirically and sometimes seriously, but always with a keen eye for sensation. "Modern History," March 3, 1752, from *The General Evening Post:*

> A Man and his Wife are committed to Malden Goal, for threatening to kill their Neighbours for upbraiding them with Cruelty. It seems, the Woman used frequently to stick Pins in a Child (to which she was Mother-in-law) and stir up the Fire with its Feet, so that its Toes rotted off; on which the Parish took it from her on the Neighbour's Complaint, and put it in the Workhouse, where it is since dead: But we don't hear that there are any Proceedings against her yet on this Score. Id.——
>
> *More Murders and horrid Barbarities have been committed within this last Twelve-month, than during many preceding Years. This, as we have before observed, is principally to be attributed to the Declension of Religion among the common People.* C.[42]

As in the Covent Garden columns, the sensational subjects and lurid details of such episodes seem scarcely justified by the protestations of indignation or outrage that succeed them. They seem intended to attract a readership more interested in the event than in the commentary. And like Fielding's descriptions of prostitutes, they suggest his own fascination with such material, possibly for its own sake and certainly for its ability to sell journals.

As we have seen, Fielding's "enemies" were not blind to this orientation—and were quick to extend it from Fielding's journalistic to his judicial practice. Accusations that Fielding was a "trading justice"—in cahoots with the very criminals he judged—occurred in productions ranging from Smollett's *Habbakuk Hilding* to the anonymous parody, *A Scheme for a New Public Advertiser.* Although, by eighteenth-century standards, Fielding seems in fact to have been a relatively honest and hardworking justice, a close scrutiny of the accusations leveled at him provides insights not only into the subtleties of Fielding's individual morality but, more importantly, into the social and ideological workings of the structures through which his judicial, entrepreneurial, and social roles were expressed. In *A Scheme for a New Public Advertiser,* for example, lists and advertisements are themselves cast as vehicles for promulgating vice. A hit at Fielding's promotion of *The Public Advertiser,* the parody calls Fielding "Justice Fail-Paper, in Arrow-street" and claims that his new advertiser will include "a true and perfect List of all Bawdy-Houses," ads for stolen goods inserted by criminals for the information of pawnbrokers, and so forth—thus inverting the intended ethical effect of Fieldings notices while remaining remarkably close to them in form. The parody also contains a list of subscribing whores, pimps, thieves, and other criminal elements.[43] Of course, it was an eighteenth-century commonplace that the criminal world of "business" mirrored and inverted the "legitimate" world of business, just as Grub Street "literature" mirrored and inverted "legitimate" literature. And Jonathan Wild himself had proved the criminal value of advertisement.[44] But the implication that specific contemporary commercial forms and institutions—which were materially connected both to literary production and criminal apprehension—might in fact serve to exacerbate the conditions they pretended to cure seems to me worth probing further.

This is not to imply that Fielding, as a justice or a businessman, was consciously engaged in promoting vice and illegal behavior. But it is to suggest that Fielding was an author and promoter capable of mystifying his own commercial relation to the darker side of human nature. If Fielding could write (in the guise of an admiring correspondent) that the *Covent-Garden Journal* should be considered "a *Universal Register Office* too, but of a different Kind; . . . you regulate the Minds of one Part of the World, whilst he employs the Bodies of the other," one is compelled to ask what effect the intense interest in vice and criminality shown by the "Minds of one Part of the World" might have had on the potential "employment" of the brokered "Bodies of the other"?[45]

Some answers are suggested by the complicated evidence of the June 3, 1751 letter to John Hill's "Inspector" column in *The London Daily Advertiser.* The correspondent, "Z.Z." (usually assumed to be John Fielding, but see below), reports on a visit to the Universal Register Office, where he found himself "a Spectator of one of the most agreeable Scenes I ever saw": specifically, a series of vignettes in which various customers of the register office fulfill their fondest desires. Z.Z.'s first "sensible Pleasure" arises from the questioning and cautioning of servants. Then the small drama of a clergyman registering for a curacy "awakened a Tenderness in my Mind, I always feel in seeing a Clergyman under Difficulties; but how great was my Joy, when I heard one of the Gentlemen tell him, that a Curacy, and being Usher to a School in the same Village was vacant. . . . The Surprize and Joy which sparkled in his Eyes were too visible to escape me, and his Thanks, and manner of taking his Leave, plainly discovered he had succeeded beyond his Expectation."[46] This kind of vicarious emotional satisfaction is repeated at a lower pitch as a husband and wife find more lodgings "in five Minutes . . . than a Man could see in a Month," and an artist thanks the proprietors for placing him with a nobleman. But the culminating moment, according to Z.Z., was "one Scene, which greatly affected me":

> This was the Person of a genteel young Woman, who came to acquaint the Gentlemen, that the Lady had hired her; indeed those were all the Words she was capable of expressing; for the Thanks which she was going to give, were suppressed by that Excess of Gratitude and Tenderness which burst into Tears, and she departed with a Look that struck my very Soul. Such an Object could not possibly escape my Enquiry; and I was informed, that the Parents of the young Creature had, by a false Pride, lived beyond their Circumstances, and, after bestowing Education upon her with a lavish Hand, died, and left her without the least Means of Support, and from the Office she had been recommended to a Lady of Quality as her own Maid; adding, that several young Creatures, in like Circumstances, had by the Office been provided for, and possibly rescued from the Misery of Prostitution.

In the story of the "young Creature" (and those that precede it), sentiment and efficiency combine in the advertiser's dream come true. The work of the register office is not only dramatized as remarkably successful, but the "Curious" are wooed by the promise of emotional catharsis: "prevail upon them to *see* the Office," Z.Z. enjoins the Inspector, "tell them their Understandings will be *charmed* with the Scheme" (my emphasis).[47] The language of physical expression dominates the scenes, making conversation secondary or useless: the joy that "sparkled" in the clergyman's eyes evokes an equal joy in the spectator; the young woman is struck dumb by emotion, but her "Look" strikes the spectator's "very Soul."

The strong emphasis on the visual in this letter suggests to me that Henry Fielding had a hand in it.[48] John Fielding was blind, and although this would not have precluded his imagining a scene predominantly in visual terms, it seems to me that Henry Fielding, schooled in the spectacle of the theater and the discursive authority it provided the spectator, would have been far more likely to conceive of the register office as a theatrical site and to provide at least the *ideas* for the clergyman's sparkling eyes and the young lady's evocative look.[49] Like the theater patron, the spectator at the register office does not have to participate in the performance, but can respond visually and emotionally to the evocative gestures and expressions of the clientele—responses unavailable to a blindman. For the sighted, genteel visitor (or prospective employer) the register office is verbally constructed as a site not only for business and employment but for stimulating and gratuitous entertainment as well: a place where, to use Z.Z.'s words, the "sensible Part of Mankind" might expect to be "charmed" by such spectacles as the "Person" (i.e., body) of the "young Creature" and the commodification of her history as an "Object" to be savored for sentimental frisson.

But the most striking element of this vignette is its similarity to Henry Fielding's descriptions of the beautiful young prostitutes at the Bow Street Magistrate's Office. In both cases we find reportage from institutions in the business of saving young women (especially good-looking ones), an intimate probing into the history and circumstances of the "Object," and a rescue from prostitution. We also find short, evocative narratives posing as factual reports, and the publication of these reports for their advertisement and entertainment value. Just as the history of the St. Clement's prostitute allures the reader to reconstruct "all the Secrets of her late Prison House, Acts of Prostitution, not . . . proper to be made public," so the genteel young woman's story invites the reader to thrill to the emotional surrender and willingness to please suggested by her "Excess of Gratitude and Tenderness that burst into Tears." Both women are examples of what Fielding described as "young, thoughtless, helpless, poor Girls"—beautiful, gullible, in need of protection. And it is the job of the magistrate's office and the register office to protect them. But what the Fieldings don't seem to recognize is the provocative nature of their advertisements. And what they do not ask (or even seem to understand as a potential question) is whether these "young, thoughtless, helpless, poor Girls" could have been, or could become, the unintended victims of the "enlightened" institutions ostensibly intended to aid and protect them. For as the parallel passages above suggest, in Fielding's court and in the register office, women were deterred from selling their bodies in one venue only to have their bodies textually merchandised in another. Given this structural relationship, we must, I think, be prepared to ask if there is perhaps a more insidious connection between the world of prostitution and the register offices, between the cataloguing of goods and servants and the cataloguing of criminal prosecutions, between the prostituted muse of Grub Street and the human prostitutes on every other street?

Evidence toward an answer accrues in the dynamics of the most visible activity of the register offices: the assessment and placement of servants, especially country people coming to seek domestic service in

London. As we have seen, the Universal Register Office was particularly assiduous in discovering and listing the background and qualification of its servants: "Age, married or single, whether had the Small Pox, what Place lived last, and how long; with every Particular of their Characters."[50] The competing Public Register Office, for its part, went as far as to emphasize that it specialized in a particular kind of servant: those "in any upper station . . . Housekeeper, Waiting-woman, Chamber-maids."[51] This specific clientele—young, ambitious, and sometimes pretty women in search of places in an "upper station"—formed a ubiquitous population in the register offices because places in an "upper station" were in short supply. In 1758 John Fielding wrote of the "amazing number" of female servants out of place:

> The body of servants . . . that are chiefly unemployed and out of place, are those of a higher nature such as chambermaids, &c., whose numbers far exceed the places they stand candidates for; and as the chief of these come from the country, and are far distant from their friends, they are obliged, when out of place, to go into lodgings, and there subsist on their little savings till they get places agreeable to their inclinations; but as this frequently does not happen till their all is spent, they, from pinching necessity, become prey to their own passions, the pimp, and the debauchee; and this is one of the grand sources which furnish this town with prostitutes.[52]

Here the manager of the Universal Register Office suggests the mystified connection between the newest commercial institution and the oldest profession. The Fieldings, of course, felt that the Universal Register Office—like the Bow Street Magistrate's Office—helped young girls to avoid or escape the prostitute's fate. But as Pamela and Moll Flanders and thousands of other pretty, young girls would remind us, being placed as a chambermaid or maid in an upper station did not necessarily save one from the misery of prostitution. More often than not, in fact, it put the commodified victim directly in harm's way.[53] Moreover, the register offices acted as something of a mart for this kind of transaction, for potential employers seem to have been able to examine *personally* (I intend the term to carry its full eighteenth-century allusive freight) large numbers of servants in advance. At least this is the message of Thomas Rowlandson's engraving of 1803, *The Registry Office* (plate 2.1). Here we see a "show day" in which prospective employers survey the market. Servants stand about like so many disposable goods; old men inspect—close up—young women they may hire as "chambermaids." Robert Wark says of the print that it "must be admitted that there is nothing inherently funny about the situation Rowlandson depicts; it could be regarded as sordid and nasty," but goes on to make the case that its "humor is due to a complex intermingling of various factors: caricature, action, pictorial arrangement, verbal labels, and, ultimately, the actual medium in which the drawing is executed."[54] I disagree. It seems to me that the humor resides almost wholly in the reversal of gender roles that occurs on the left side of the print where a grotesquely large and aggressive woman (replete with a muff and umbrella resembling male genitalia) eyeballs a disconcerted young male servant. If this passage is edited from the print there is nothing funny left: it is simply a graphic record of the sexual jobbing of female servants in a register office.[55]

In fact, the perception of the register office as a kind of quasi-brothel seems to have developed in relation to "intelligence offices" even before the founding of the Fieldings' more grandiose establishment.[56] And by 1761 Joseph Reed would go so far as to write that register offices were places where "the good old Trade of Pimping is carried on with great Success and Decency. I believe as many Proselites have been made to the Flesh, by the Knavery of this Rascal [the proprietor], as by the most successful Bawd in Town."[57] In his play, *The Register Office: A Farce,* Reed explicitly portrayed the sexual marketing of a servant girl in the story of Maria, a pretty housekeeper from the country, who is recommended to Lord Brilliant by the proprietor: "I have one of the finest Women in the World to provide for—I expect her here every minute—Will your Lordship be pleased to step into that Room—You may see her thro' the Lattice—You will find *Rochester's* Poems, and the *Memoirs of a Woman of Pleasure* to entertain you."[58] The mention of William Cleland's *Memoirs of a Woman of Pleasure* (1748–49) alludes not only to Lord Brilliant's sexual interests, but perhaps to the earliest portrayal of the fate of a young country girl in a register (or intelligence) office. The novel, published in two parts a year before the Fieldings opened the Universal Register Office, describes Fanny Hill traveling to London from "a small village near *Liverpool*" to look for a "place." She is advised that there are "more places than parish-churches" and that she can secure information about them at "an intelligence-office." There Fanny finds "an elderly woman, who sat at the receipt of custom, with a book before her, in great form and order, and several scrolls, ready made out, of directions for places":

> Madam having heard me out, with all the gravity and brow of a petty-minister of state, and seeing, at one glance over my figure, what I was, made me no answer, but to ask me the preliminary shilling, on receipt of which she told me, places for women were exceeding scarce, especially as I seemed too slight-built for hard work; but that she would look over her book, and see what was to be done for me, desiring me to stay a little till she had dispatched some other customers.[59]

Plate 2.1 The Registry Office, by Thomas Rowlandson 1803. Courtesy of the Huntington Library.

Thus is Fanny set up to be hired by a bawd who sat "in the corner of the room" and "look'd as if she would devour me with her eyes, staring at me from head to foot, without the least regard to the confusion and blushes her eyeing me so fixedly put me to" (7). The scenario of oppressive spectation described by "Z.Z." and eventually illustrated by Rowlandson combines with John Fielding's observations about the difficulty of securing a place in an upper station (as opposed to the available "hard work") to historically corroborate this fiction. What Cleland adds is the potential servant's feelings: "confusion" and "blushes" at being the object of intense visual examination.

Country girls are also singled out as the most unfortunate victims of the register offices in *An Appeal to the Public Against the Growing Evil of Universal Register-Offices* (1757) by "Philanthropos" who laments the "many poor Girls . . . ignorantly sent out of the Country, by their Town Acquaintance, and taken from a Life of Innocence and Industry, under the false Pretence of *bettering* themselves, . . . and then turned over to these *Offices* for a Place."[60] But Philanthropos also registers a contrasting point of view when he protests that only the worst of experienced servants (those discharged for "Lewdness, Sauciness, Laziness, or Dishonesty") use the register offices, while only the worst masters ("*Publicans, Vintners, Bawds, Bailiffs*") hire them.[61] Thus it seems that register offices might simultaneously function as a false refuge for country innocents and a convenient mart for servants with "lewd" experience. Paradoxically, the very procedures developed to protect against servants with questionable pasts may have worked against virtuous servants. For in order to prevent the register office from becoming a clearing house for whores and thieves, inspection and interrogation were necessary; yet such practices—especially at the hands of prospective employers—opened the door for the exploitation. In the register office, the proprietors played a role akin to procurers, providing a structure that facilitated close inspection on the premises. Not only were young servant girls (and, if we believe Rowlandson, men) reduced to the status of listed commodities, but the register offices allowed and in certain ways encouraged "hands-on" evaluation. This "personal touch" was allowed not only to prospective employers but even to voyeurs. To view, to inspect, to enjoy emotional responses—these were the invitations implicit in Z.Z.'s newspaper description of the Universal Register Office. Though Cleland, Reed, and Rowlandson may exaggerate the overt sexual climate of the register offices, it seems likely that at the very least such places were steeped in an atmosphere of sexual harassment—a crime that remained sociologically and legally unnamed until the second half of the twentieth century.[62]

Domestic service was clearly recognized by eighteenth-century society as the premier site of institutionalized sexual harassment (and textualized as such in, for example, *Moll Flanders* and *Pamela*).[63] As a clearing house for domestic servants, the register office must have seemed a kind of showcase for it. Yet so many kinds of male-female relations in the eighteenth century (romance, courtship, not to mention the kind of competitive debauchery associated with being a "rake") seem pervaded by what today would be called sexual harassment that perhaps the concept is too anachronistic to aid understanding. Perhaps Fielding was simply wise enough to know that all worldly relations involve usage, and canny enough to rationalize that the potential sexual usage of domestic service was generally better than the assured sexual usage of prostitution.

A more insidious usage, however, may have occurred outside the offices in the texts that advertised them. For in *The Covent-Garden Journal, The Drury-Lane Journal,* and newspaper advertisements, the Fieldings, D'Halluin, and Thornton, while recognizing and repudiating overt prostitution, seem simultaneously to mystify and promote the connection between prostitution and employment services. The Covent Garden columns record the interrogation of prostitutes in a journal sponsored by the Universal Register Office, and the Fieldings, while stressing that their brokerage actually rescued women from prostitution, repeatedly remind the reader (or prospective employer) of the connection between register offices and available "young, thoughtless, helpless, poor" girls. D'Halluin's Public Register Office, for all of its egalitarian rhetoric (or perhaps because of it), pointedly advertised itself as specializing in a particular kind of servant: those "in any upper station . . . Housekeeper, Waiting-woman, Chamber-maids"— just those female servants most vulnerable to the blandishments of domestic prostitution. For his part, Thornton, in creating the persona of Madam Roxana Termagent, a former prostitute, seems to propose simultaneously that underclass women have a voice to raise against the patriarchy (as Roxana does against Sir Alexander), but that they remain sexually open and available. The fact that Roxana is a prostitute pretending to be something else and that her history includes her lover's recommending her as a servant calls attention to precisely the sexual/service dynamic at play in the register offices.[64] This crucial connection is startlingly highlighted by Thornton when, with tongue presumably in cheek (and yet possibly stating the whole truth), he has Roxana's printer suggest that "instead of the Drury-Lane Journal, suppose you was to call yours *The Bawd's,* or *The Kept Mistress's* MAGAZINE?" (49). Could Thornton be "humorously" encoding a message he is eager to have deciphered? Was the Public Register Office meant to be understood as a storehouse of potential kept mistresses?

Such mystified connections (encompassing the listing of servants in the register offices, the listing of crimes in *The Covent-Garden Journal,* and the satirical suggestion in the *Scheme for a New Public Advertiser* that the Fielding's judicial notices and advertisements include "a true and perfect list of all Bawdy-Houses") are strikingly contextualized by what, it could be argued, amounted to another kind of "register office"—one that carried on its business next to the entrance to the Covent Garden Theatre, a scant one block east of the Public Register Office and one block west of Fielding's court in Bow Street. This was the bar of the Shakespeare's Head Tavern, renowned resort of literary men, where since the 1740s the chief waiter, Jack Harris, had kept an unpublished list of the best prostitutes in town. H. W. Bleackley writes that Harris would "arrange the *petites affaires* of all the women of the town, and it was an honour to figure in his list."[65] The tradition of the Shakespeare's Head being simultaneously a literary resort and a register office for prostitutes seems to have been well-known both in print and in fact. In a scene with remarkable structural parallels to the procedures of the register offices, Boswell picked up "two very pretty little girls" on May 19, 1763 and took them to the Shakespeare's Head:

> So back to the Shakespeare I went. "Waiter," said I, "I have got here a couple of human beings; I don't know how they'll do." "I'll look, your Honour," cried he, and with inimitable effrontery stared them in the face and then cried, "They'll do very well." "What," said I, "are they good fellow-creatures? Bring them up, then." We were shown into a good room and had a bottle of sherry before us in a minute. I surveyed my seraglio and found them both good subjects for amorous play. I toyed with them and drank about and sung *Youth's the Season* and thought myself Captain Macheath; and then I solaced my existence with them, one after the other, according to their seniority. I was quite *raised*, as the phrase is: thought I was in a London tavern, the Shakespeare's Head, enjoying high debauchery after my sober winter.[66]

The waiter's parody of the register offices' "examination" of servants—in this case "two pretty little girls"—stands as a revealing inversion (or perhaps more overt inactment) of register office practice.

Fielding, of course, had frequented the Shakespeare's Head, as had Thornton and most of the other "wits" of London. They clearly knew Jack Harris and certainly knew exactly what went on upstairs. Why Fielding should trouble himself with saving pretty, young prostitutes in court while suffering a tavern a block away that registered, retailed, and provided "good rooms" for them is an interesting question. Laws against disorderly houses were traditionally difficult to enforce, but those who wish to cast Fielding as an exemplary justice may not take much comfort in this fact. We must at least admit the possibility that Fielding's was a genuinely bifurcated ethical consciousness that somehow assigned certain "moral" responses to "official" or "public" venues and other less conventional ones to the private sphere.[67] In print, however, the two often bled textually and tonally into one another, introducing precisely the kinds of ambiguous coded messages and advertisements found in Fielding's and Thornton's journals.[68]

In this light, it is particularly interesting to recognize the similarity between the titles of both Fielding's and Thornton's register office publications and the later published version of Harris's prostitute register: *Harris's List of Covent-Garden Ladies* ("Containing, an exact description of the persons, tempers, and accomplishments of the several ladies of pleasure who frequent . . . this metropolis").[69] A typical entry from *Harris's List* focuses, as the title page indicates, on the "persons, tempers, and accomplishments" of the ladies, much as Z.Z. in his description of the "genteel young Woman" had touted her "Excess of Gratitude and Tenderness," the "Education [bestowed] upon her with a lavish Hand," and her "Look that struck my very Soul." In *Harris's List* for 1764, for example, a "*Miss* B-wen, *Castle Street. Mews*," is described as "tall, genteel, and elegantly shaped. . . . Her complexion is fair, and she has good hazel eyes. . . . She has a remarkable fine hand and arm, and has, perhaps, made as many conquests by them as by her eyes. . . . Her education is much superior to the generality of women of pleasure, and her conversation is very entertaining."[70] Given these textual examples, one can only wonder how closely the actual marketing of attractive, genteel servants in the register office conformed to the marketing of attractive, genteel prostitutes elsewhere.

At the very least, the procedures of the register offices may have lent themselves to a potentially exploitative process. The extent of Fielding's recognition of his conflicted position is, of course, impossible to ascertain. In addressing one local, contradictory element of the register offices' activities, I do not intend to detract from the positive contributions of such institutions, including the placing of servants in good jobs and perhaps the saving of some from the miseries of prostitution. But Fielding's intentions, however benevolent, do not completely efface his evident interest in the more seamy or sensational side of the register offices or the court—nor indeed his lifelong fascination with transgressive or exploitative master-servant relations.[71] This seems to be the sense of the ubiquitous Grubean accusations that Fielding's was a hypocritical muse—"Here the Debauched, the Diseased, the Rotting and the Rotten, may be instructed and amused, if not cured and reformed: Here will be seen the quaint Device, the Old *Badger* preaching Continence (in the *Aesopian* Stile) to the young *Wolf*,—The Type of Impotence correcting Vice!"[72] After all, Fielding himself gave his enemies the most exquisite example of the vexed relationship between the register office and its advertising vehicles when in composing the original edition of *Amelia* ("sincerely designed to promote the cause of virtue")[73] he thought it prudent to include a series of puffs for the Universal Register Office, headlined by the ill-advised comment that, in exposing Miss Mathews (an attractive, genteel prostitute), "Many other Materials of a private Nature were communicated by one of the Clerks of the Universal Register Office; who, by having a general Acquaintance with Servants, is Master of all the Secrets of every Family in the Kingdom."[74] A more sensational and counterproductive admission, especially couched as a boast, can scarcely be imagined; an impression reinforced by his rival D'Halluin's assurance, two weeks before the publication of *Amelia,* that at his register office, for "the better Conveniency of Ladies and Gentlemen, distinct Offices are provided for treating with them, or for taking their Directions or Commands; so that when any Lady or Gentleman has Business to do, there will be no Necessity of discovering the Particulars of their Business to a Number of Servants and other Persons who may be in a Public Room; but here they will be quite free, and not incommoded in any Sense whatever."[75]

In a reversal of all the moral packaging, the register offices, by finding service jobs for women, may have actually promoted rather than prevented prostitution; and by ferreting out servants' histories they may have created a mart for masters' secrets. The binary separation of servant and prostitute collapses, as do conventional power relations between servants and masters. Servants are no longer passive objects whose personal secrets must be found out; they are the possessors and manipulators of family secrets that masters seek to conceal. Servants with secrets, masters with secrets, prostitutes with secrets, innocents who may be prostitutes, prostitutes who may be innocents—such was the world that Fielding advertised in the Covent Garden columns, in ads for the Universal Register Office, and in *Amelia.* And it is to *Amelia,* as a distillation of Fielding's experiences in his last offices, that we now must turn.

Chapter 3

Interest in *Amelia*

I

Interrogation, confession, desire, sexual exploitation (real and potential), un/employment, prostitution, and, above all, the advertisement of these activities are the themes that emerge from an examination of Fielding's work in his last offices. They are, not surprisingly, themes also central to his last novel, *Amelia*. While the importance of the court and the prison to the novel has long been appreciated, Fielding's representation of motives and behavior in the magistrate's office and Universal Register Office provides an enriched environment for reviewing not only scenes of commitment, incarceration, and sexuality as they are structured by Fielding's experience on the bench, but the crucial issues of employment, insecurity, and interest that, I will argue, constitute the very heart of the novel and derive from Fielding's lifelong experience in the capricious world of clientage, connection, and chance that his register office scheme sought (ostensibly) to remedy.

It has often been noted that the opening scene of *Amelia* is structured primarily by interrogation, and that the subsequent overview of the prison seems to derive from Fielding's direct experience: the vignette at Justice Thrasher's and the following description of Newgate and its inmates have been fully contextualized in relation to Fielding's judicial activity.[1] But much less attention has been paid to the most obtrusive yet perplexing narrative element of the novel, one that brings together at length the dynamics of interrogation and imprisonment: Fielding's decision to devote the entire first volume to the tales of Miss Mathews and Booth.

Miss Mathews and Booth interrogate each other—or listen to each other's depositions—for hours and hours. During these sessions, much information (of varying truth value) is revealed at secondhand, and it seems to me that the indirection of the narrative here has always constituted a

major flaw of the novel.[2] The dialogue blocks Fielding's authorial voice for
the most part while at the same time not achieving enough idiosyncrasy
of style to tell us much about the speakers' inner lives.[3] It drones on and
on, perhaps as Fielding's cases did. But its liveliest and most revealing moments, and those perhaps best illuminated by (and illuminating) Fielding's
practice at court, are the moments when the tale-telling stops, and Booth
and Miss Mathews exchange witty or passionate observations or revelations. Here Fielding subtly charts their evolving relationship with each
other, their secret desires, and their subterfuges—the deep emotional and
sexual drives that propel the interminable talk. Like Fielding's reports from
the bench, the talk is personal history punctuated by ethical rhapsodies dis-
guising real negotiations of sex and power.

The younger Fielding has long been identified with the shiftless
William Booth, but here I would like tentatively to identify the older
Fielding with Miss Mathews.[4] For Miss Mathews listens and questions—
and in so doing accrues power. She, like Justice Fielding, extols virtue
while mining for dirt. When Booth mentions a complimentary description of himself "which my Modesty forbids me to repeat," Miss Mathews's encouragement is simultaneously admiring and suggestive: "'I insist
on your Conquest of that Modesty for once.—We Women do not love to
hear one another's Praises, and I will be made amends by hearing the
Praises of a Man, and of a Man, whom perhaps,' added she with a Leer, 'I
shall not think much better of upon that Account'" (90). What can she
mean by the final phrase? That no matter how good the description is, it
couldn't match Booth's virtuous reality? Or that no matter how virtuous
the description is, it won't change Mathews's sense of his moral weakness
and sexual availability?

The tension between the two readings summarizes the complex
problem of Mathews's character. For in the opening dialogue Mathews is
a smart, witty, emotionally hopeful, and rationally cynical woman, fully
capable—given a different impulse in her creator—of becoming the
"Mrs. Waters" of *Amelia*. Compared to her, Booth is a tiresome, vice-ridden innocent, fully predictable and not very intelligent. In manipulating
Booth, Miss Mathews strikes an ethically dissonant chord that resonates
with the older Fielding's performance on the bench and the tension between his official aspirations and personal desires. In ways strikingly similar to Fielding's praise (Covent-Garden, January 10) for the "less
abandoned" young prostitute who is "fixed on as the Proper Person" to
reveal all the juicy "Secrets of her late Prison-House, Acts of Prostitution,
not . . . proper to be made Public," Mathews's ambiguous insistence on
Booth's "Conquest of that Modesty for once" seems to point toward her
hope that more sordid and interesting revelations will follow. If he can

be made to forget modesty awhile in singing his own praises, he may be amenable to exposing much more. While I am not suggesting that such personal identification was intended by Fielding (indeed he would have probably vehemently denied it), many of the techniques and characteristics of his conflicted official style seem transposed into the seductive verbal manner of an intelligent, incarcerated prostitute. As bizarre as it may sound, there may be a sense in which Miss Mathews's treatment of Booth represents the older Fielding deposing (in both senses of the word) the younger one.

The phrase "Secrets of her late Prison-House," from the interrogation of the young prostitute, echoes suggestively the title of Book I, Chapter IV of *Amelia*, "Disclosing further Secrets of the Prison-House." This chapter, it will be remembered, contains the familiar vignette (in terms of the Covent Garden columns) of the "very pretty Girl" who turns out to be a "common Street-walker" capable of discharging "a Volley of Words, every one of which was too indecent to be repeated" (33), a scene that simultaneously recalls the actual prostitute's sexual secrets "not proper to be made public" and Thornton's ironic voicing of prostitute's oaths in the Justice Scribble squib.[5] It is followed by horrifically ugly Blear-Eyed Moll's roughing up a man "for certain odious unmanlike Practices, not fit to be named" (33)—again emphasizing in a way seemingly typical of Fielding at this period that there are all sorts of phrases and practices in the world of vice that while too indecent to be repeated, or not proper to be made public, or not fit to be named, are in fact quite fit enough to be suggestively alluded to, winked at, and retailed in commercial journalism and fiction.[6] It is particularly this inconsistency of response, this dialectic of morality and desire, this reluctance to name or reveal while alluding to all that might be named or revealed, that characterizes the discourse and performance not only of Fielding (in court and print) but of Miss Mathews (in jail). And it is she who appropriately makes her entrance at the end of the chapter.

Miss Mathews's stock-in-trade is secrets. Strategically keeping or revealing them, she barters (or attempts to barter) her way to power. As she opens her tale, she specifically laments her current secret deficit: "Alas! I could keep a Secret then: now I have no Secrets; the World knows all; and it is not worth my while to conceal any thing" (47). While intended to refer to the secrets of Mathews's own life, this confession takes on a wider applicability in the context of the dialogue that follows, first because Mathews indeed does have a secret, one which she reveals a few pages later. "'It was now,' she tells Booth confidentially, 'that I began to survey the handsome Person of *Hebbers* with Pleasure. And here, Mr. *Booth*, I will betray to you the grand Secret of our Sex.—Many Women, I believe, do with great Innocence, and even with great Indifference, converse with Men of the

finest Persons; but this I am confident may be affirmed with Truth, that
when once a Woman comes to ask this Question of herself; Is the Man
whom I like for some other Reason, handsome? Her Fate and his too very
strongly depend on her answering in the Affirmative'" (51). Whether this
practice is indeed true of all women is open to question; but, as we have
seen, it was (with gender transposition) remarkably true of Fielding's judicial practice in the case of prostitution. Secondly, Mathews adumbrates
here precisely the dynamic that compels her to seduce Booth despite her
seeming admiration for Amelia and domestic virtue, and which causes
Booth, after interminable pages of sentimental admiration for his wife, to
hop straight into bed with Mathews. And finally it introduces the larger
theme of secrets-as-power, one that derives its particular force in *Amelia,* I
think, from Fielding's experiences in the register office and the court. Early
on, the theme is dramatically exemplified in Booth's story of the mutual
blackmail practiced by him and Mrs. Harris's servants (82), and it eventually pervades the social relations of practically every character in the novel.
This is not to suggest it is a new theme for Fielding; there are powerful secrets aplenty in *Joseph Andrews* and *Tom Jones.* But they are not, I think, as
central nor as defining as in *Amelia.*

   In any case, Miss Mathews's biggest secret is that she wants to sleep
with Booth even though she seems truly to admire his domestic virtue
and loyalty to Amelia. This second element is important. Too many critics, if they address her character at all, have been quick to dismiss Miss
Mathews as, to adapt Boswell's phrase, a "consummate dissembling
whore."[7] Claude Rawson, for example, tells us that "Fielding means us to
dislike Miss Mathews' shallowness (her vulgarly sentimental voyeurism is
noted more than once), but there is an odd nastiness which Fielding does
not have entirely under control in the fact that she is an ex-mistress
preparing to enjoy the account of a loving and painful scene between her
former lover and his wife" (87). Why, in fact, an "ex-mistress" (which in
this case simply means a woman with whom one has had a sexual relationship) enjoying a scene of tenderness between her former lover and his
wife should be found so signally offensive is not explained. As to Miss
Mathews's alleged "shallowness," one can only reply that she seems far less
shallow in every respect than Booth, who after all is telling the story.[8]
Morris Golden, on the other hand, finds that "Miss Matthews, though a
whore, yet has occasional decent sentiments, is capable of considerable
generosity, and gladly acts for the right in the rare situations when her
passions are not involved against it."[9] This is closer to the mark, though
one has to wonder who is more the whore in the prison scenes, Mathews
(who dispenses money) or Booth (who takes it). Andrew Wright remarks
(inaccurately I think) that Mathews "is an extraordinarily strange exam-

ple of womanhood," but senses the oddity of Fielding's technique, given his professed purpose: "the structural principle of the . . . first quarter of the novel . . . is founded upon the seduction intended, planned, and executed by Miss Matthews. . . . In this light, the cautionary flavour of Miss Matthews's tale assumes a curiously ironical aspect, for as she tells it in the first book, she reveals that she is not a reformed sinner preaching virtue but a temptress spreading her net" (110). Although Wright gets the cart a little before the horse here (since the "ironical aspect" of Mathews's tale cannot appear "in this light" until the "light" generated by the "first quarter of the novel" is cast back upon her tale; that is, it cannot be discerned "as she tells it"), his emphasis on the importance of Mathews and her complicating role is significant. But the best and most sympathetic reading of Miss Mathews' complex character is Robert Alter's: "In the splendid figure of Miss Matthews, who lamentably is reduced later in the novel for didactic reasons to a venomous Rejected Mistress, Fielding hints at an ironic doubleness of attitude toward the very pursuit of sentiment which is undertaken elsewhere in the novel with distressing single-mindedness. Miss Matthews is presented to us as a reader, or rather listener, of sensibility par excellence."[10] Where Rawson had found this "sentimental voyeurism" superficial and nasty, Alter finds it sincere. But it is Alter who poses the crucial question: "Does Miss Matthews have a sensible heart, or merely the superficial empathy of an envious one, the keen imagination of unsated desire?"[11]

If we substitute "Justice Fielding" for "Miss Mathews" in this formulation, the significance of the magistracy to the first quarter of *Amelia* suddenly snaps into place. For the conflict between a "sensible heart" and "the keen imagination of unsated desire" constitutes the ethical dialectic of Fielding's performance in Bow Street. It is a dialectic central also to the character of Miss Mathews: "We have already been given enough hints to guess that Miss Matthews throughout has been preparing the way for the seduction of Booth, but, at least in this first part of the novel, she shows a warm sympathy and generosity which probably cannot be wholly explained away as stratagems of seduction."[12] This could not have been better said—unless Alter had noted that "warm sympathy and generosity" are not necessarily antithetical to the "stratagems of seduction." In fact, they often heighten and soften the purely predatory sexual impulses "seduction" implies. Throughout the first quarter of the novel, Miss Mathews seems genuinely overcome with empathy and admiration for Booth and Amelia, but this response often acts as something like an emotional prelude and simulacrum to the sexual impulse that follows. Thus, for example, when Booth rhapsodizes on "'that delicious Dream of Bliss in which the Possession of *Amelia* had lulled me,'" Miss Mathews "sighed, and cast the tenderest Looks on *Booth*" (91). Soon thereafter Miss Mathews admires the marital state of "'the happy *Amelia*'" and laments her own fate, only to have Booth tell her to "'banish such gloomy Thoughts. Fate hath, I hope, many happy Days in Store for you.'—'Do you believe it, Mr. *Booth,*' replied she, 'indeed you know the contrary—You must know—For you can't have forgot. No *Amelia* in the World could have quite obliterated—Forgetfulness is not in our own Power. If it was, indeed, I have Reason to think—But I know not what I am saying.—Pray, do proceed in that Story'" (98–99). Here Miss Mathews's emotional admiration of Amelia's state seems to convert almost instantly to sexual frisson at Booth's mention of "'happy Days'"—a phrase that for Booth presumably refers to Mathews's hypothetical future marriage to someone else and that for Mathews (based on past experience) conjures images of future sex with Booth. The latter more selfish response does not at all cancel the earlier generous one, but in fact grows emotionally from it. In other words, the answer to Alter's initial question (a "sensible heart" or "the keen imagination of unsated desire"?) seems to be—for Mathews in jail and Fielding on the bench—both.

One of the unremarked virtues of *Amelia*'s flawed first book may be that Miss Mathews's responses to Booth provide a lens through which Fielding's generous sympathy for "young, helpless, thoughtless, poor girls" and his simultaneous desire to use them as sex objects (physically in theory; textually in fact) becomes more explicable. As a potential repository of the unwitting Fielding's most deeply guarded secrets, her complicated responses to the attractive, vice-ridden, innocent Booth (a young, helpless, thoughtless, poor boy) may enact precisely the contradictory skein of emotions a long and intimate revelation by a desirable young prostitute might have provoked in Fielding. But we must also remember that Miss Mathews is a young, attractive, genteel prostitute herself, and that her own vacillating emotions faced with the attractive ideal of domestic virtue and the thrill and freedom of illicit sex may also function as Fielding's reading of the girls he wishes to rescue.[13] In Miss Mathews's case, however, no such rescue occurs.

It is, in fact, precisely at the moment Miss Mathews performs physically the sexual liaison that Fielding can only dream about that he parts empathetic company with her forever. Booth, as the young Fielding, may transgress and be forgiven; but Mathews, as the repressed older one, forfeits sympathy by abandoning repression. Booth, we are told, speaks to her "with great Tenderness: For he was a Man of consummate Good-nature" (150)—about the closest Fielding ever comes to saying "consummate sex drive." Miss Mathews responds in kind, and Fielding's farewell to her is both heartfelt and sad:

Miss *Mathews* did not in the least fall short of Mr. *Booth* in Expressions of
Tenderness. Her Eyes, the most eloquent of Orators on such Occasions, ex-
erted their utmost Force. . . . In real fact, this Mr. *Booth* had been her first
Love, and had made those Impressions on her young Heart, which the
Learned in this Branch of Philosophy affirm, and perhaps truly, are never to
be eradicated. (151)

Good-byes said, Miss Mathews becomes predatory, possessive, and increasingly stereotyped. Her physical seduction of Booth is not at all a "very
Mysterious Matter" (as the chapter title ironically calls it) but straightforward and remarkably efficient. She recounts her first meeting with Booth
in detail, dismisses any lingering vision of Amelia ("the happy *Amelia* in
those days was unknown"), orders punch, makes Booth an offer he can't
refuse ("'suppose,'" she says, "'the Captain and I should have a mind to sit
up all Night'"), blushes when the Governor in naming his price calls the
proposition what it is ("'It is but the Price of the Bagnio'"), and has her
way. Fielding immediately sides with the gentleman ("we are much more
concerned for the Behaviour of the Gentleman, than of the Lady") and
seems for just a moment to understand the unstated judicial performance
implicit in Miss Mathews's former role as listener, sympathizer, and exploiter. For as the unstated judicial metaphor dissolves, Fielding, as it were,
switches sides and in an overt litigation metaphor becomes the defense at-
torney for Booth-as-young-Fielding. And Miss Mathews, deprived of the
complex ethical dimension of the older Fielding, dwindles to a simulacrum of the genteel young prostitutes in Fielding's court, titillating one
final time his audience and his past and present selves:

We desire . . . the good-natured and candid Reader will be pleased to weigh
attentively the several unlucky Circumstances which concurred so critically,
that Fortune seemed to have used her utmost Endeavours to ensnare poor
Booth's Constancy. Let the Reader set before his Eyes, a fine young Woman,
in a manner of first Love, conferring Obligations, and using every Art to
soften, to allure, to win, and to enflame; let him consider the Time and Place;
let him remember that Mr. *Booth* was a young Fellow, in the highest Vigour
of Life; and lastly, let him add one single Circumstance, that the Parties were
alone together; and then if he will not acquit the Defendant, he must be
convicted; for I have nothing more to say in his Defence. (154)

Like the description of beautiful prostitutes in the Covent Garden
columns, this quasi-legal summation manages to enjoy the fine young
Woman's ability to "soften, to allure, to win, and to enflame," while simultaneously presenting such attractive talents as a defense for having suc-
cumbed to them.

II

Amelia not only refigures the dynamics of seduction implicit in judicial interrogation, it fictionally examines many of Fielding's other concerns during the period, particularly concerns arising from the theory and practice of the Universal Register Office. Booth, for example, is not only sexually lax, but unemployed—as are most of the major characters in the novel. Moreover, when unemployed, Booth and his officer friends, Bath and James, inevitably get into trouble, and in so doing seem to represent in microcosm a population that during this period caused Fielding great difficulty in his role as magistrate: demobilized military men. As a magistrate, Fielding would have had professional reasons for deploring the irresponsibility of unemployed military men; and as a proprietor of the Universal Register Office he may have had material motives for delineating the evils of unemployment in general. But even more personal motives may have played a part in his portrayal of the chaotic consequences of martial energy uncontrolled by employment. For in October 1748 (the same month that Fielding took the oaths for the Westminster magistracy) the signing of the Treaty of Aix-la-Chapelle brought an end to the War of the Austrian Succession and loosed on the London streets thousands of discharged sailors and soldiers.[14] As always, a redundancy of military men gave rise to an immediate increase in prostitution, drinking, gaming, and rioting—activities that at a somewhat more exalted level (prostitution transformed into seduction and rioting into dueling) constitute the primary activities of the "broken" and unemployed officers of *Amelia*. In July 1749 a particularly nasty riot occurred, the consequences of which eventually dragged Fielding's judicial reputation to its nadir. It involved sailors attacking bawdy houses, and it led to the hanging of Bosavern Penlez.

On July 1, 1749, a mob of disgruntled sailors demolished a brothel and burned its contents in the street. Over the next two days, the riot grew into a general mob action against bawdy houses in which thousands of unemployed sailors were involved. Rioting and destruction turned to looting, and by the time peace was restored, primarily through the actions of Saunders Welch and Fielding himself, several men had been arrested, including Bosavern Penlez, a peruke-maker, who had been caught drunk and in possession of "ten lace caps, four lace handkerchiefs, three pairs of lace ruffles, two lace clouts, five plain handkerchiefs, five plain and once laced apron" taken from a brothel known as the Star.[15] Fielding was immediately caught up in the controversy that developed over the quelling of the riots and the prosecution of Penlez. His enemies accused him, first, of defending bawdy houses because they paid him protection money and, second, of unjustly advocating the hanging of Penlez despite strong public sentiment for mercy. Given Fielding's reputation as a former rake and man-about-town, accusations of collusion with bawdy houses must have been especially galling. More importantly, in abetting Penlez's martyrdom Fielding offended public sentiment and made himself more widely known and disliked than at any other time during his career as a magistrate. Both circumstances haunted him and his political allies during the elections that followed Penlez's hanging on October 18, 1749, and caused Fielding to publish, on November 18, 1749, *A True State of the Case of Bosavern Penlez,* a pamphlet in defense of the ministry and himself.

The Penlez incident developed just at the moment Fielding was preparing to write *Amelia,* and two features of Fielding's experience in the Penlez incident seem significant to the novel.[16] First, facing from an unfamiliar position of power the destructive misconduct of idle military men, Fielding would have had reason to recognize, to perhaps a greater degree than ever before in his life, the deep social risk inherent in groups of what in earlier times might have been called "masterless men."[17] In *Amelia,* this insight would manifest itself in the self-indulgent and chaotic behavior of officers without purpose, whose unemployed energies turn to drink, seduction, prostitution, and violence.[18] But more intriguing, especially in light of the evasive marketing of sex we have seen at work in the register and magistrate's offices, is Fielding's response to the subsequent charge that he protected brothels. Battestin adamantly denies the charge, and even Linebaugh grudgingly admits that there is "no reason to believe that Fielding added to his income" by accepting bribes.[19] Certainly Fielding's contention that he had to protect life and property, even if the life was a prostitute's and property a brothel, cannot be refuted. But, as Linebaugh notes, while Fielding had railed against bawdy houses in his *Charge delivered to the Grand Jury* a few days before the riots, he had also admitted that "to eradicate this Vice out of Society . . . is, perhaps, an impossible Attempt."[20] Moreover, Linebaugh points out that Fielding subsequently does not mention "prostitution or brothel-house-keeping as a cause of crime" in *An Enquiry into the Causes of the Late Increase of Robbers* (1751). I would add that in his "Bill to reform the Police" (1749), discovered by Battestin and published in 1989, Fielding takes great pains to delineate the various forms of streetwalking that should be liable to legal action—"all Women who shall stand in the streets or in Corners & Byeplaces to pick up Men for lewd purposes & who shall walk the street for such purpose & by their indecent behaviour manifest their said Intentions"[21]—but makes no mention of brothels whatsoever.

As with his tendency to overlook Harris's pimping operation at the Shakespeare's Head or the potential fate of servant girls placed by the Universal Register Office, Fielding may have adopted the motto "out of sight, out of mind" when it came to most brothels. The overt, public, or outdoors sale of sex provoked his official wrath, but what might be called privatized or surreptitious sexual brokering (mitigated perhaps by its connections to property and employment?) may have seemed a more problematic issue. Certainly, the prosecution of bawdy house keepers was both notoriously difficult and easy to evade. Even after the passage of the new anti-prostitution Act of 1752, justices were required to prosecute persons accused of keeping bawdy houses only when "information was provided by two inhabitants of the parish paying scot and lot and willing to enter into a recognizance of 20 pounds each to produce evidence against the accused."[22] But Fielding in his role as a social essayist never singles out or attacks by name any of the numerous bawdy house keepers within easy walking distance of the Bow Street Magistrate's Office—and presumably there was nothing to keep him from doing so. His enemies at least were happy enough to accuse him of collusion; a writer in *Old England,* for example, claimed Fielding was "imbitter[ed]" by efforts to "abridge the Perquisites of the good *old Shop,* and lessen the *Trade thereof.*"[23]

In *Amelia,* Fielding's response seems to have been to expand the definition of prostitution in a fiction about the interrelations of sex, interest, employment, and marriage, with the chief exhibit being the prostitution of wives. Set in a society where insecurity and unemployment are rampant, where the cultivation of personal favors and interest is the only way to thrive, where intense gratitude seems at times an almost sexual event, *Amelia* presents prostitution (in various guises) as a bad but perhaps understandable antidote to neglect, unemployment, poverty, and starvation.

Indeed, if the central emotion pervading *Amelia* had to be summed up in a word, that word would have to be "insecurity." Nowhere in eighteenth-century literature do we more tangibly feel the lack of a "social safety net," the promiscuity and changeability of friendship, the impossibility of rational reliance on anything. Deprived of employment and income, the Booths worry incessantly about money, debt, and arrest, and incessantly attempt to gauge the sincerity of their volatile friends' purported benevolence. They spend their lives guessing at the meaning of events and the shape of their future. Over and over it seems Booth is "greatly puzzled and perplexed" at James's behavior, "so indifferent from what it had been formerly" (185); or "not more hurt than surprized at [Bath's] Behaviour, and resolved to know the Reason of it" (209).[24] Likewise, Mrs. James receives Mrs. Booth "with a Degree of Civility that amazed *Amelia,* no less than her Coldness had done before. She resolved to come to an Eclaircissement" (207).[25] Indeed, John Coolidge's description of the experience of reading *Amelia* seems perhaps even more applicable to the Booths' perception of characters within the world of the novel:

"People come into the story in the same way that people come into our lives . . . Our knowledge of a person's character is always provisory, pending further discovery. A new word or act may bring a new revelation, causing a shift in interpretation and evaluation."[26] Booth not only has to worry about the shifting economic prospects represented by James's and the Noble Lord's shifting moods and desires; he has to watch every word he speaks for fear that some perceived innuendo against honor will set his friend Colonel Bath off on a bloody rampage. It comes as something of a relief, I think, when Booth finally does run Bath through. At least he's done something besides worry, drink, and gamble.

It is notable that while Booth's narrative to Miss Mathews contains its share of tribulations, they are essentially the predictable ones of young romance and military service. Only at the moment when that romantic story ends does the second story of truly radical insecurity begin: driven off the farm, the unemployed Booth arrives in London, wanders the streets, gets into a fight, is arrested and tossed into prison, and meets Miss Mathews. The events immediately preceding and following this moment are crucial, because they introduce in miniature the engine that will drive the rest of the novel: the power of interest in a radically insecure world. Miss Mathews, we soon discover, has been an "interested" listener, not only in the modern sense of "curious" but in the primary eighteenth-century sense: "influenced by considerations of personal advantage."[27] She is clearly fascinated by Booth and his story, but she is also operating in the full knowledge that Booth's unemployment and imprisonment make him susceptible not only to social but to criminal conversation. Her genuine joy at looking at and listening to him is infused with an equally genuine desire to have him under her sexual control.

Miss Mathews succeeds in converting fascination into possession, and in so doing enacts an exemplary paradigm for the rest of the novel. For her, possessing Booth is facilitated early on by a gift of money (60) and later by the influence of her interest and money on the jailkeeper (153). Having succeeded in possessing Booth, Miss Mathews "to whom Money was as Dirt, (indeed she may be thought to have not known the Value of it)" (158) then attempts to sustain the client relationship by doing Booth more favors with the money supplied unwittingly by Colonel James. She buys his discharge, dramatically presents it to him, and orders "a Hackney Coach, without having yet determined whither she would go, but fully determined . . . wherever she went, to take Mr. *Booth* with her" (159). Her scheme, however, is dashed by Amelia's sudden entrance.

For the generous, luxurious, and impecunious Fielding (as Battestin writes, "his ability to run through money at speed is extraordinary—almost a talent"),[28] this moment must have possessed some resonance, for similar transactions are repeated (either abortively or with complete delivery) again and again throughout the novel. Such transactions involve the promise or dissemination of money or material interest in the service of satisfying ocular and emotional interest in another person, with the "interested" end in view of securing sexual possession of that person's "person." This is the Noble Lord's modus operandi in his relations with both the Booths and the Bennets. It is an application of power named early and explicitly by Fielding, when he has the Noble Lord respond to Mrs. Ellison's request that he help Booth. "'Cousin *Ellison*,'" replies the Lord with some double entendre, "'you know you may command my Interest; nay, I shall have a Pleasure in serving one of Mr. *Booth's* Character'" (193). As we shall later discover, the Noble Lord's anticipated "Pleasure" has more to do with his prospective relations with Amelia (about whom he has been told by Ellison) than any benevolence toward Booth (though this, I would suggest, should not be totally disregarded). Fielding, however, assumes we are taken in and drops a hint that summarizes the recurring trajectory of interpersonal relations in the novel:

> The Reader, when he knows the Character of this Nobleman, may perhaps conclude that his seeing *Booth* alone was a lucky Circumstance; for he was so passionate an Admirer of Women, that he could scarce have escaped the Attraction of *Amelia's* Beauty. And few Men, as I have observed, have such disinterested Generosity as to serve a Husband the better, because they are in Love with his Wife, unless she will condescend to pay a Price beyond the Reach of a virtuous Woman. (193)

At this intersection of sexual interest and material interest, we confront the central source of ethical and epistemological confusion in *Amelia*—a confusion engendered not so much by misapprehensions of class and gender roles, as Jill Campbell implies, or by Fielding's ambivalence concerning the relationship of "the new psychology" and the tradition of Christian humanism, as Battestin suggests, but by Fielding's acute experience of the mid-eighteenth-century world of clientage and connection, where sexual desire could determine generosity and material desire condone lubricity.[29]

The emotional complexity of the relationship between visual interest, sexual interest, and material interest is brilliantly played out as the Noble Lord mounts his campaign, first assuring Booth of his "Pleasure in doing any thing in my Power to serve you" (197), then visiting the Booths to announce "no doubt of my Success" (202), then visiting them again to reiterate his "further Hopes . . . of Success" (216).[30] The sly allusion to the trajectory of seduction implicit in the triad of "pleasure," "hopes," and "success" charges those terms with a fine irony that delicately redirects them away from Booth and toward Amelia. It is a relocation the Noble Lord himself dramatizes during a conversation at Mrs. Ellison's apartment when, although "he applied his Conversation more to her than to *Amelia*," his "Eyes indeed were now and then guilty of the contrary Distinction, but this was only by Stealth; for they constantly withdrew the Moment they were discovered" (216). The Noble Lord's visual interest is fully recognized by Amelia—who must be the one doing the "discovering"—but by some form of sublimation it is converted (by her or the narrator) into his treating her "with the greatest Distance, and . . . the most profound and awful Respect." Having rationalized the Noble Lord's stealthy ogling, she does not shrink from his gaze but on the contrary praises his "conversational" skills, conflates his evident interest in her person with his material interest in advancing Booth, and responds to both with a burst of almost illicit pleasure: "his conversation was so general, so lively, and so obliging, that *Amelia*, when she added to his Agreeableness the Obligations she had to him for his Friendship to *Booth*, was certainly as much pleased with his Lordship, as any virtuous Woman can possibly be with any Man, besides her own Husband" (216–17). In this highly receptive state, Amelia is suddenly informed that Colonel Bath will live (thus saving Booth from criminal charges) and rises in a new burst of "satisfaction" to a kind of orgasmic glow: "This made her Satisfaction complete, threw her into such Spirits, and gave such a Lustre to her Eyes, that her Face, as Horace says, was too dazzling to be looked at" (217). Indeed, once the Noble Lord leaves, Amelia's "Raptures" seem to know no bounds: "*Amelia*, without making any Exception, declared he was the finest gentleman, and the most agreeable Man she had ever seen in her Life; adding, it was a great pity he should remain single" (217).

Such a reading suggests a modification early in the novel to the dominant critical assumption that Amelia is a paragon of "female strength and virtue" or, in Jill Campbell's words, that the "post of domestic 'angel,' which we often think of as really materializing in the Victorian era . . . is apparently already available to Amelia as an active and coherent role."[31] Indeed, even those critics who acknowledge Amelia's potential for subversive sexual agency universally locate its manifestations far later in the novel. Terry Castle suggests that Fielding's "moral certainty" about Amelia is compromised at the masquerade by "a tropology of ambiguity and complexity" and that the narrator's later admission that Amelia felt a "momentary Tenderness" toward Atkinson is "shocking" in its "morally subversive implications."[32] Likewise, Alison Conway argues that Amelia's "potential for desire" and "first move away from the path of righteousness" become evident only in her emotional response to Lt. Atkinson's confession and her subsequent pawning of her own portrait miniature—an act that "links sentimentalism to materialist eroticism."[33] But sentimentalism, materialist eroticism, and moral subversion have been linked far earlier, when Amelia displays herself for the Noble Lord's erotic enjoyment and cloaks her resulting *frisson* in the language of sentimental gratitude.

There is an adulterous quality to this episode, recording as it does Amelia's openness to the Noble Lord's ogling, her suffering the Noble Lord to view her body until "discovered" (then suffering him again and again), her subsequent orgasmic glow, the gradual elision of Booth from her effusions (at first she is "as much pleased" as a woman can be with any man "besides her own Husband," but later she declares "without making any Exception" that the Noble Lord was "the most agreeable Man she had ever seen in her Life"), and her rather yearning reference to his marital status ("a great pity he should remain single") that suggests that Amelia is willing to trade sexual "views" for material ones. Amelia knows she is alluring, allows certain ocular freedoms to the Noble Lord, and consummates an emotional relationship with him that replicates the trajectory of sexual conversation. Amelia's raptures of gratitude betray not only a "potential for desire" but a realization of it that is manifested as verbal and physical excitement.[34]

Of course, the "interested" proffering of orgasmic compliments and thanksgiving was a basic skill in the world of clientage and connection—and Fielding himself was an adept. During exactly the period *Amelia* was being composed, he wrote to the Duke of Bedford (May 29, 1750) expressing his gratitude for a position he eventually would not receive:

> I sit down in a Rapture of Gratitude to thank your Grace for the immediate Notice you was pleased to take of my Application, in the midst of Engagements with which if I had been acquainted I should not have presumed to have written on any Affair of mine. Success in this Matter, I most solemnly declare will be trifling compared to the Joy I taste in reflecting on so much Goodness, and on the Honour done me by the Duke of Bedfords Patronage and Protection. The great Business of my Life shall be, my Lord, to deserve these, at least to the utmost of my Power: and I heartily pray for some Opportunity to convince your Grace with what Zeal and Devotion I am,

My Lord,
Yr Graces most obliged
most obedient, and dutiful
humble Servant
Henry Fielding[35]

"Rapture . . . Success . . . Joy . . . Zeal . . . Devotion"—were Fielding a woman, one must tremble for his fate. Fielding is teased by imagined material success into a posture of exaggerated verbal submission, just as Amelia is teased by the imaginative projection of her husband's success into similar verbal and physical posturing for the Noble Lord. Euphemizing her ulterior display, she allows herself to tantalize and partially to submit to a person whose interest she seems to desire above all else.

That the demure Amelia at some level both knows and relishes the power generated by her beauty seems to contradict Fielding's predominant implication that she is a paragon of modesty and virtue. Yet Amelia's agency in both recognizing and making use of her power is explicitly stated twice in the novel. First, responding to Mrs. Bennet's observation that "'the first wish of our whole Sex is to be handsome,'" she and Amelia assess their mutual qualifications: "Here both the Ladies fixed their Eyes on the Glass, and both smiled" (276). And later when Dr. Harrison teasingly tries to downplay Amelia's compliments—"'If I could but persuade you . . . that I thought you not handsome, away would vanish all Ideas of Goodness in an Instant. Confess honestly, would they not?'"—Amelia in a remarkably frank self-assessment replies, "'Perhaps I might blame the Goodness of your Eyes . . . and that is perhaps an honester Confession than you expected'" (376). To the reader who has been lulled by Amelia's usual abnegation, this statement comes as a bit of a shock: it is the confession of a woman who has spent some time thinking about the social implications of her own beauty.[36]

Moreover, Amelia seems to recognize that signs of her physical charm may be diversified, as when she constructs her children as extensions of her person and thus visual treats for the Noble Lord: "I am resolved to shew him my little Things . . . I may say without Vanity, he will not see many such" (217). Amelia's "little Things" are not only her children, but her children as products of her sexuality and as replications of her beauty. Indeed she so aggressively makes herself and her children available to the Noble Lord that even the obtuse Booth is forced to call it what it is: "this Behaviour of ours puts me in mind of the common Conduct of Beggars; who, whenever they receive a Favour, are sure to send other Objects to the same Fountain of Charity. Don't we, my Dear, repay our Obligations to my Lord in the same manner, by sending our Children a begging to him?" (218). But Booth is ignored, and Amelia's efforts do in fact reap immediate benefits when the Noble Lord sends expensive toys to the children (231).

Amelia (and, by extension, Fielding) is on very complicated ethical ground here, for in marketing a glimpse of her charms she risks becoming a sexual commodity along the lines of the now-dwindled Miss Mathews. The rights to Miss Mathews, it will be remembered, had seemingly been sold by Booth (after his release from prison) to James for a gift of 50 pounds and an offer of employment (169–73). Now, in the wake of the

Noble Lord's generosity, James and Booth discuss their respective sexual and financial desires. James's desire is to possess Miss Mathews—"'curse me, if I don't think her the finest Creature in the Universe. I would give half my Estate, *Booth,* she loved me as well as she doth you'" (226). Booth's desire is to possess the Noble Lord's influence, and James assures him "if you have his Interest you will need no other" (227). During the course of this conversation, however, their material and sexual desires become confused, with Amelia suggestively blended into the mix, as James reveals the Noble Lord's fascination with women and advises Booth to "carry your Goods to Market." Understandably—given James's recently expressed desire for Miss Mathews—Booth assumes that by "Goods" he means Amelia and translates the market metaphor into a raw statement of fact: "'What to prostitute my Wife!'" (228). Although James quickly backpedals by explaining that "'the Goods I meant, were no other than the charming Person of Miss *Mathews;* for whom I am convinced my Lord would bid a swinging Price against me'" (228), the indeterminacy of the earlier reference remains troubling both to Booth and to the reader. James, actually or mistakenly, has suggested the equation of Miss Mathews and Amelia, and we are forced to acknowledge how close to realizing this equation Booth and Amelia have come. The cumulative effect of the episode is to expose Amelia's euphemized solicitations and domestic posing by eliciting from her husband the raw expression of the transaction with which she so insistently flirts; at the same time, Booth's "Smile" at being described as the man who can dispose of the "'charming Person of Miss *Mathews*'" reveals how close to the art of pimping his interested relations with all women have become.

Meanwhile, Amelia has become involved as a go-between in the unpredictable and interest-driven friendship between Booth and James. As she pursues her task of reconciliation, her beauty again does its seductive work: "such were the Charms now displayed by *Amelia* . . . that perhaps no other Beauty could have secured [James] from their Influence; and here to confess a Truth in his Favour . . . I am firmly persuaded that to withdraw Admiration from exquisite Beauty, or to feel no Delight in gazing at it, is as impossible as to feel no Warmth from the most scorching Rays of the Sun" (232). With this effusion Fielding not only launches James on his quest to seduce Amelia, but launches himself into an extended digression on the corruptive power of beauty:

> The Admiration of a beautiful Woman, though the Wife of our dearest Friend, may at first perhaps be innocent, but let us not flatter ourselves it will always remain so; Desire is sure to succeed; and the Wishes, Hopes, Designs, with a long Train of Mischief, tread close at our Heels. . . . In short . . .

not only Tenderness and Good-nature, but Bravery, Generosity, and every Virtue are often made the Instruments of effecting the most atrocious Purposes of this all-subduing Tyrant. (232–33)

Fielding's stark recognition that various virtues—tenderness, good nature, bravery, generosity—are not antithetical to desire but become "Instruments" of it may be the central insight of *Amelia,* and the one that most revealingly links the novel to his experience in court and in business. From Fielding's own delight in gazing at and textual exploiting of beautiful young prostitutes for whom he also felt genuine concern (and genuinely tried to help), to the register offices' (mystified) sexual marketing of maidservants in order to save them from becoming prostitutes, to the remarkably mixed motivations of almost all the characters in *Amelia,* the conflation of benevolence and desire central to the transactions of interest provides a crucial heuristic for understanding the contradictions of Fielding's later career. In his final novel, this structure of feeling is linked to a relentlessly repetitive plot of hope, betrayal, disaster, and renewed hope. In this world there are no unadulterated villains, many people who do good deeds, and primarily people who do good deeds based on self-interest and who are quick to betray their friends. While numerous critics have cited the jaded Nobleman's conversation with Dr. Harrison on the necessity of political corruption as Fielding's definitive statement on the way of the world (see below), this episode seems crudely simplistic compared to the incremental development of "interest" as it recurs in scene after scene throughout the novel.

Fielding's exploration of the complexities of "interest" is enabled, and probably inspired, by a semiotic expansion that would transform the meaning of the word by the end of the eighteenth century. Already by the mid–eighteenth century, the normative definition of "interest" as "an objective or legal share in something" had been expanded to include "the sense of general concern or having the power to attract concern" and, because of its association with relations of power, the more pejorative connotation of "influence" exerted or solicited with "considerations of personal advantage."[37] Simultaneously, however, the word was developing a less materialist definition that would eventually make it "a common name for a general and natural concern" and eventually for "something which first 'naturally' and then just 'actually' attracts our attention."[38] Interest, in effect, could mean a material share, material influence, personal attraction, and something like "curiosity." The interpretational problem, Raymond Williams writes, "is that the sense of objective concern and involvement, derived from the formal and legal uses, is not always easy to distinguish from these later more subjective and voluntary senses." This

overlapping of formal and emotional meanings—excluding for a moment
the strictly financial definition of "money generating money"—recalls the
volatile mixture of objective and subjective motivations that generates the
ethical fog investing the real world of Fielding's offices and the fictional
world of *Amelia*. In situation after situation, in the court, the register office, and the novel, it is the "natural" interest in other human beings (en-
acting, though not deploying, the emergent definition of "interest" as
"attraction") that tends both to provoke and corrupt the more objective
and legal sense of "interest" as material or ethical investment, thus produc-
ing the intermediate (and ethically complex) relationship that is the primary meaning of "interest" in Fielding's world: a world in which influence
is most often promised or exerted "for considerations of personal advantage." "Interest as attraction" stimulates the concern of those who hold a
material "interest" in commercial, political, legal, or financial institutions,
and this conjunction of desire and power generates the exertion "interest
as influence" to help, but also to control or exploit, the object of original
(often emotional or sexual) interest.

Fielding's critics have tended almost universally to deplore such manipulation of interest on traditional moral grounds—an interpretive stance
that has led to the pervasive idea that the novel portrays, as Alter puts it,
"the insidious mesh of a pervasively venal social order."[39] But it is important to remember that Fielding seems very willing to forgive or excuse
those who engage in such behavior (not the least of whom is Booth himself); indeed it could be argued that there is no truly villainous major character in the work at all. Colonel James, for example, despite being a
"perfect libertine with regard to Women" and a relentless pursuer of
Amelia, "otherwise . . . deserved Commendation for Good-nature, Generosity, and Friendship" (174); Colonel Bath is "a perfectly good Christian,
except in the Articles of Fighting and swearing" (507); and even the Noble
Lord is shown consistently to deliver the goods he has promised in the self-
interested transactions in which he engages. Indeed, as Alter presciently
says of Col. James, "As with Miss Mathews, Mrs. Atkinson, Mrs. Ellison,
even Mrs. James, the characterization of the colonel would appear to point
toward complexities and ambiguities which Fielding himself was not ready
to confront or follow out."[40]

III

But if the ambiguities of characters created by a system of personal favors
and clientage remained ineffable to Fielding (as well he might wish, given
his own background and practice), the twisted functioning of the system—perhaps because it was something he thought might be corrected—

seems to have engaged his documentary and tinkering impulses in less problematic ways. As he portrays it, the system almost always works, but often capriciously, inefficiently, and unfairly—a problem addressed with unusual clarity at the exact midpoint of the novel, as Mrs. Bennet tells Amelia her story.

From the beginning, the Bennets' haplessness in a world of economic interest seems intended to remind the reader of the Booths' similar problems. We find that as a young girl Mrs. Bennet was sent to live with an Aunt when her father was seduced by an opportunistic widow, and that the Aunt abused Mrs. Bennet because of her poverty. We also discover that Mrs. Bennet's husband-to-be endured similar disappointmentss and betrayals in his quest for ordination and preferment. Although at first Mr. Bennet was supported by an uncle, who sent him to Oxford and purchased for him a prospective "Presentation of a Living," the uncle prematurely died, leaving the young man friendless. Exploitation quickly filled the void: his cousins ignored their father's dying request that they aid Bennet at Oxford, forcing him to borrow money on steep terms from another "Friend" in order to finish his degree; he was then refused a "Title to Ordination" by a Clergyman who held the living intended for him, and he was finally forced to become a curate to a rector whose whims he could not satisfy and yet whom he could not leave. In other words, devoid of interest after his benefactor's death, Mr. Bennet was exploited and betrayed by other interested parties.

After a series of such setbacks and "many fruitless Enquiries" about other curacies, Mr. Bennet (like Booth after him) "thought best to remove to *London, the great Mart of all Affairs* ecclesiastical and civil" (286). Here, something almost inexplicable occurs. After spending the first night in an inn (as Mrs. Bennet tells it): "the next Morning my Husband went out early on his Business and returned with the good News of having heard of a Curacy and equipped himself with a Lodging in the Neighborhood of a worthy Peer" who was his "Fellow Collegiate" (286). In *Amelia* such unexpected "good News" almost always precedes disappointment, but in fact Mr. Bennet is soon "settled in a Curacy in Town, greatly to his Satisfaction" (287). How he heard of the curacy we are not told; from whom he has it we do not know. It may be the only time in the novel someone secures employment without suffering the ulterior motives of an intermediary: there are no hypocritical promises, no wife-oglings, no pretended friendships. There seems, in fact, to be no intermediary at all. It is an almost magical episode of good fortune.

At least in the second edition. But here is the same episode as Fielding originally wrote it:

"After many fruitless Enquiries, Mr. *Bennet* was at last informed of an Office lately erected, opposite *Cecil-street* in the *Strand,* called the *Universal Register Office,* where he was assured he might probably have his Choice of above a hundred Curacies, in different Parts of the Kingdom. . . . To London we came, and took up our Lodgings the first night at the Inn where the Stage Coach set us down; the next Morning my Husband went out early to the Office, from whence he returned in a Kind of Rapture, saying, he had been at a Place where all the Necessities of Life were provided for. I have not only heard, said he, of a Variety of Curacies; but I have equipped myself with a lodging." (286, 552)[41]

Clearly Mr. Bennet has found (in the first edition) what so many characters in the second edition conspicuously lack: a place where his talents will be recognized, where he can find a job, where "all the Necessities of Life" are provided for. His "Rapture" at the Universal Register Office presumably resembled the clergyman's in Z.Z.'s letter: "The Surprize and Joy which sparkled in his Eyes were too visible to escape me, and his Thanks, and manner of taking his Leave, plainly discovered he had succeeded beyond his Expectation."[42]

Ironically, this episode has been generally dismissed by critics as nothing more than an embarrassing commercial puff. Contemporary wits ridiculed Fielding's blatant self-promotion, and Battestin remarks that we should be "glad . . . Fielding's desire to improve the coherence and integrity of his novel as a work of art prevailed over his wish to promote his commercial interests."[43] But I am not convinced that his revisions were prompted so much by artistic or thematic concerns as by a simple desire to avoid further ridicule.[44] On the contrary, I would suggest that despite Fielding's decision to remove all mention of his business from the second edition of *Amelia,* the story of Mr. Bennet's happy experience at the Universal Register Office originally transcended purely commercial considerations and was intended to suggest a kind of utopian vision of all the things the Bennets and the Booths (and by extension the young Fieldings and many middle-class couples) could *not* rely on in the then current state of eighteenth-century English society. The episode of the register office, rather than a commercial aberration, seems thematically central to the novel; so much so that if we turn to Fielding's *Plan of the Universal Register-Office*—written, we must remember, while *Amelia* was being composed—we find a phrase that might stand as a motto for those utopian social services whose opposites summarize the Booths' and Bennets' economic predicament: "no useful Talent in the Society will be idle, nor will any Man long want a Seller and Purchaser of what he is desirous either to purchase or dispose of; whereas at present many a Man is Starving, while in the Possession of Talents, which would be highly serviceable to others, who could and would well reward him." Idleness and starvation while in the possession of marketable talents are, of course, the central problems faced by the Booths and Bennets, problems that leave them vulnerable to (or, perhaps, in collusion with) an exploitative system of personal clientage and influence. In part *Amelia* may be an attempt to construct a detailed fictional survey of precisely the kind of malfunctioning social relations that the register office's enhanced communications and objective application of interest would remedy. The self-interested practice of *Amelia* may represent the dramatized antithesis of the theory of the Universal Register Office.

This is not to propose that *Amelia* is a merely book-length puff for the Universal Register Office, but that Fielding's thinking about the office may have had a larger influence on the development of the novel than is usually recognized. I would emphasize the word "thinking," for I would not suggest that the actual practice of the Universal Register Office much resembled its utopian portrayal in Mrs. Bennet's story. As we have seen, sexual and emotional interest had already infiltrated its various services. Indeed, we must remember that the language of the Fieldings' newspaper advertisements and puffs from this period specifically link the transactions of business and employment with more emotional transactions of curiosity and economic relief in a way that recalls the overlapping "interests" in *Amelia*: "here the Ingenious meet with Rewards, the Curious with every Gratification which Art or Nature can produce in this Kingdom, the Industrious with Employment, the Man of Business with every Convenience, and the Distressed with Comfort and Support."[45] Here, too, prospective servant girls could be ogled by potential future employers with all the intensity the Noble Lord reserves for his "clients," and the servants themselves could trade in the currency of secrets, such as those supplied in the novel "by one of the Clerks of the Universal Register Office; who, by having a general Acquaintance with Servants, is Master of all the Secrets of every Family in the Kingdom."[46] The innuendoes of the register office's advertising are dramatized in the defining thematic paradox of *Amelia*: that the "gratification" of the "curious" may be directly connected to the comfort and support of the distressed; as when Z.Z. thrills to the tears of the beautiful young lady saved from the miseries of prostitution; or, in *Amelia*, when the Noble Lord and Colonel James both attempt to gratify their sexual curiosity by ostensibly (and, despite their motivations, *actually*) comforting and supporting the Booths.

Nevertheless, the Universal Register Office in its theoretical form seems the absent (or deleted) presence at the center of the novel; a still point of objectified clientage that anchors a relentless fictional enactment of two more traditional and excruciatingly subjective forms of interest: influence-trading and the marketing of flesh. The register office in the novel, like the register office in Fielding's *Plan,* is an idealized paradigm against which the exploitative system of personal interest and connection must be measured. This, at least, seems to be the point Fielding intends to make when, immediately following Mr. Bennet's success at the office, he illustrates through the clergyman one of the most brutal instances of capricious "old interest" in the novel.

As Mrs. Bennet tells it: "Mr. *Bennet* was now settled in a Curacy in Town, greatly to his Satisfaction; and our Affairs seemed to have a prosperous Aspect, when he came home to me one Morning in much apparent Disorder, looking as pale as Death" (287). Extreme physical response to a social and emotional distress is not unusual in *Amelia,* where so much depends on the goodwill of others, but Mr. Bennet's suffering is particularly intense and derives from a snub suffered while attempting to revive a potentially rewarding connection. Having waited "'till he could put himself in decent Rigging,'" Mr. Bennet "'purchased a new Cassock, Hat and Wig, and went pay his Respects'" to a neighbouring Lord—an "'Old Acquaintance, who had received from him many Civilities and Assistances in his Learning at the University, and had promised to return them fourfold hereafter'" (287). The outcome of such high hopes is predictable: the Lord pretends not to know him, then coldly acknowledges the acquaintance and leaves—a reception that literally makes Mr. Bennet sick. Mrs. Bennet elaborates on the episode in a way that seems to reveal Fielding's personal investment in it: "'Tho' this Incident produced no material Consequence, I could not pass over it in Silence, as of all the Misfortunes which ever befell him, it affected my Husband the most. I need not, however, to a Woman of your Delicacy, make Comments on a Behaviour, which, tho' I believe it is very common, is nevertheless cruel and base beyond Description, and is diametrically opposite of true Honour, as well as to Goodness'" (288).

Yet, however "cruel and base" the peer's behavior may be, it is important to recognize that Mr. Bennet's motivation was not in fact "real Friendship" but the Lord's promise to return Mr. Bennet's "Civilities and Assistances in his Learning . . . fourfold hereafter" (287). Since presumably Mr. Bennet didn't need the Lord to help him with his homework, his expectation of fourfold return could only mean an offer of money and/or interest.[47] Indeed, Mr. Bennet's dressing up to impress a noble "friend" has a calculated element to it (does one need to dress up to visit a real friend?) that Fielding accepts implicitly. It is, for him, the way of the world, and in fact his own way: Battestin records in detail Fielding's currying of Dodington's and Bedford's favor while writing *Amelia,* and in so doing incisively recreates the volatile world of interest in which Fielding calculated his moves. Battestin suggests that the diatribes against ministerial politicians put into the mouth of Dr. Harrison were intended to flatter both Dodington (who had been in Opposition since 1749) and the "more powerful and munificent" Bedford (who resigned his place as Secretary of State for the Southern Department six months before *Amelia*'s publication): "Bedford," Battestin writes, "would have relished Dr. Harrison's righteous indignation against ministerial politicians, and on Bedford, Fielding entirely depended. It was Dodington, however, whom he chiefly meant to please." Unfortunately, he could not please them both, for by October 1751 Dodington, "thoroughly disillusioned" with the prospects of Opposition, "was trying once again to ingratiate himself with Pelham." Fielding conveniently "abandoned this Opposition line at the same time that his friend [Dodington] changed his political tune," but "Bedford . . . continued to oppose the government."[48] One only can imagine Fielding's consternation when his two powerful patrons capriciously shifted their political allegiances and thus their relationship both to each other and to himself. His predicament poignantly recalls the Booth's and the Bennet's problems when faced with the capricious favors and disfavors, brotherhood and enmity, aid and exploitation offered by feuding grandees and sometime friends upon whom they entirely depend. Battestin is surely correct when he writes that "*Amelia,* to a greater degree than any other of Fielding's novels, is a story rooted in the history of its time and in its author's personal experience," but he seems to limit his reference to the novel's inclusion of scenes from the jail and the sponging house and its reiteration of particular political positions and specific social problems that concerned Fielding at the time.[49] What seems to me more central to Fielding's experience of his times (and our experience of the novel) is the way that the emotional and ethical tensions that characterized his performance on the bench, in the register office, toward his clientele, and toward his patrons—the sometimes crude, sometimes delicate, often hypocritical, and almost always volatile and confused workings of interest and clientage—are dramatized again and again in the pages of *Amelia*.

Although Mrs. Bennet says that the episode with the Lord had "no material Consequence," I believe structurally it sets the stage for a succeeding episode of very material consequence, in which Mrs. Bennet sacrifices herself both to Interest and the Noble Lord in a high-stakes relationship meant to serve as a parallel and warning to Amelia. Down on their luck and out of money, the Bennets at first do "not perceive any possible Views of Interest" (290) in Mrs. Ellison's advances and are dazzled by their introduction to the Noble Lord—a Lord whose behavior seems so opposite that of Mr. Bennet's old schoolfellow. And when they are informed that the Noble Lord has paid Mr. Bennet's Oxford debt, their gratitude knows no bounds. As Mrs. Bennet tells it, "Tears burst from my poor Husband's Eyes; and in an Ecstasy of Gratitude, he cried out, 'Your Lordship overcomes me with Generosity'" (292)—probably just the emotional response he had previously hoped to indulge during his meeting with the collegiate friend, before being rejected and having to settle for heartsickness.

Bennet's simultaneously strategic and intensely emotional gratitude to the Noble Lord (and Amelia's raptures earlier, and for that matter Fielding's smarmy, selfinterested letter to Bedford) marks one of the most startling measures of the distance between expected behavior in Fielding's times and our own. Compared to modern gratitude, such effusions strike the modern reader as at once crudely calculated and bizarrely overdramatized.[50] They have a curiously ritualized quality—although their conventions and limitations are well-known, they seem to open up space for deeper and more dangerous games at the boundaries where interest and gratitude lapse into prostitution and personal degradation. These are boundaries Amelia is fast approaching (and which Fielding himself seems to have crossed and recrossed many times)—boundaries Mrs. Bennet seeks to warn Amelia against in a raw narration of her suceeding transgression with the Noble Lord. It is an episode central to Fielding's exploration of sex and interest, one in which Mrs. Bennet represents Amelia's hapless double as she attempts to parlay her sexual desirability into material advancement for herself and her husband:

> "I will disguise Nothing from you: I now began to discover, that he had some Affection for me; but he had already too firm a Footing in my Esteem, to make the Discovery shocking. I will—I will own the Truth; I was delighted with perceiving a Passion in him, which I was not unwilling to think he had had from the Beginning, and to derive his having concealed it so long, from his Awe of my Virtue, and his respect to my Understanding. I assure you, Madam, at the same Time, my Intentions were never to exceed the Bounds of Innocence. I was charmed with the Delicacy of his Passion; and in the foolish, thoughtless Turn of Mind, in which I then was, I fancied I might give some very Distant Encouragement to such a Passion in such a Man, with the utmost Safety; that I might indulge my Vanity and Interest at once, without being guilty of the least Injury." (295)

Mrs. Bennet's professions of innocence are perhaps descriptive of her sexual intentions, but certainly not of her economic ones. There is nothing "thoughtless" at all in the way she calculates the indulgence of her "Vanity and Interest." She plans to give the Noble Lord a little thrill, feed her self-esteem, and realize some sort of material gain. Unfortunately for her, she's drugged and raped by someone who knows the interest game better than she does.

Mrs. Bennet's fall clearly serves as an enactment by surrogate of Amelia's never-realized transgressions and, curiously, seems to provoke in Fielding a kind of sadomasochistic fury. Whatever his motivations (the violation by proxy of his "favorite child"? a reflexive loathing of his own sometimes exploitative behavior?), Fielding, in a scene of uncharacteristically graphic violence, has the despoiled and willing Mrs. Bennet enjoy a cathartic beating at the hands of her husband:

> "He snatched off a large Book from the Table, and with the Malice of a Madman, threw it at my Head, and knocked me down backwards. He then caught me up in his Arms, and kissed me with most extravagant Tenderness; then looking me stedfast in the Face for several Moments, the Tears gushed in a Torrent from his Eyes, and with his utmost Violence he threw me again on the Floor—Kicked me, stamped upon me. I believe, indeed, his Intent was to kill me, and I believe he thought he had accomplished it.
>
> I lay on the Ground for some Minutes I believe, deprived of my Senses. When I recovered myself, I found my Husband lying by my Side on his Face, and the Blood running from him. It seems when he thought he had dispatched me, he ran his Head with all his Force against a Chest of Drawers which stood in the Room, and gave himself a dreadful Wound in his Head.
>
> I can truly say, I felt not the least resentment for the Usage I had received; I thought I deserved it all." (299)

In this scene, Mrs. Bennet is judged and punished twice: first, her husband literally "throws the book at her" and stomps her into insensibility; second, she convicts herself and accepts both the guilt and the beating as her due. In its circumstantiality, Mrs. Bennet's testimony sounds like a deposition, one that allows Fielding to impose a fairly rigorous beating and then to justify it. One has to wonder to what degree this scene was influenced by the episodes of domestic violence Fielding heard described at the Bow Street Magistrate's Office.[51] On May 4, 1752, for example, "one Patrick Moore, was brought before the Justice, for violently beating his Wife, who deposed in the following Words.—'An't please your Worship . . . he has tore me all to Pieces, he has tore me, that I have bled a Pint of Blood out of my Ears, and I have it all in my Cap here to shew. Indeed he has murdered me several Times within this Month, and . . . I shall be murdered again before To-morrow Morning.'"[52] In this case, however, as in the case of Mrs. Bennet, the wife's adultery is cited as justification, and she is given "a severe Reprimand" from the Justice. Both episodes are troubling, not only because Fielding seems to condone (in graphic detail) wife-beating as a punishment for adultery, but because the considerations of interest that led to Mrs. Bennet's predicament in the first place almost immediately reappear and are embraced by both character and narrator with minimal hesitation.

True to the world of interest, Mrs. Ellison and the Noble Lord, having taken Mrs. Bennet's advance payment (as it were), eventually deliver the goods. After Mr. Bennet's death, Mrs. Ellison is so kind as to offer Mrs. Bennet lodging. Then the Noble Lord settles on Mrs. Bennet "an Annuity of 150*l*. a Year" (302). These blandishments are enough (despite the self-loathing, the venereal disease, the vicious beating) to persuade Mrs. Bennet to grant the Noble Lord an interview, during which she says, "if he was not a real Penitent, no Man alive could act the Part better" (302). She admits to some fear—"I apprehended . . . that the Annuity was rather meant as a Bribe than a Recompence, and that further Designs were laid against my Innocence"—but luckily the Noble Lord desires novelty and Mrs. Bennet no longer qualifies. Under these circumstances, she accepts the annuity and lives in some contentment on money provided by the man who raped her in the house of the woman who set her up for rape.

This is the quotidian reality of the client system Fielding inhabited and fictionally reconstructed in *Amelia*: in a radically insecure world, the administration of such *doceurs,* no matter how exploitative or capricious the preceding usage, serves to quiet the conscience, salve the wound, and insure the primacy of interest (and accompanying gratitude) in the amalgam of human transactions we call eighteenth-century English society.

IV

Incessant grinding insecurity temporarily alleviated by the charity of self-interested (often sexually motivated) benefactors provoking fawning beneficiaries into histrionic raptures of gratitude despite what must be suspicions inculcated by years of capricious and exploitative usage: this is the ethical and emotional rhythm of *Amelia*. To the modern reader, perhaps the greatest mystery is the mental process that allows hope to spring so eternal in the battered and betrayed breast of the eighteenth-century client. Having just heard from Mrs. Bennet about the Noble Lord's duplicity, and having just experienced it herself, how can Amelia a few days later open herself so wholly to Colonel James's transparent sexual machinations? Knowing James's sexual proclivities, how can Booth, confined to a Bailiff's, listen with any patience to James's offer "to wait on [Amelia] myself . . . and give her such Assurances as I am convinced will make her perfectly easy" (335)? Yet Amelia opens herself, and Booth not only accepts James's offer, he "embraced his Friend, and weeping over him paid his Acknowledgment with Tears, for all his Goodness. In Words, indeed, he was not able to thank him; for Gratitude joining with his other Passions almost choaked him" (335).

Such a scene almost choaks the modern reader—and begs for explanation. As in the case of Mrs. Bennet and the Noble Lord, there is certainly necessity: Booth is under arrest, he and Amelia are in dire need of assistance, and their survival has long depended on taking it from any quarter. Were they at least hesitant or guarded such an explanation might suffice, but the histrionic gratitude, the utter blindness to the possible ulterior motives, seem to derive from a mentality so foreign as to seem almost inconceivable. Is it that in the sexual and economic world of eighteenth-century England (at least as constructed in *Amelia*), exploitation was so omnipresent as never to be thought of except at the moment, and for the duration, of its occurrence? Were Fielding's people blessed with instant selective memory? the ability to live wholly in the present? attention deficit disorder? The evidence from *Amelia* suggests the answer to all these questions may be yes. When in the succeeding scene Colonel James attempts to make Amelia "perfectly easy," Fielding constructs a rhapsody of mutual admiration in which the Colonel's motives seem absolutely overt and in which Amelia's seemingly "innocent" but intense flattery suggests that Fielding (if he still thinks her innocent) is not in control of his material.

Soon after the scene opens, James leads with the provocative observation that "the highest Friendship must always lead us to the highest Pleasure":

> Here *Amelia* entered into a long Dissertation on Friendship, in which she pointed several Times directly at the Colonel as the Hero of her Tale.
>
> The Colonel highly applauded all her Sentiments; and when he could not avoid taking the Compliment to himself, he received it with a most respectful Bow. He then tried his Hand likewise at Description, in which he found Means to repay all *Amelia*'s Panegyric in Kind. This tho' he did with all possible Delicacy; yet a curious Observer might have been apt to suspect that it was chiefly on her Account that the Colonel had avoided the Masquerade. (336)

The curious Observer might also have been apt to suspect that what Fielding describes is foreplay. The curious Mrs. Atkinson (formerly Bennet) certainly does, remarking, "I am sure the Colonel is in Love with somebody. I think, I never saw a more luscious Picture of Love drawn than that which was pleased to give us, as the Portraiture of Friendship" (336). She goes on to make her case so strongly that Amelia is finally forced to ask "But what would you infer from what he said? I hope you don't think he is in Love with me!" Mrs. Atkinson replies that "he fixed his own Eyes on yours with the most languishing Air I ever beheld," but Amelia's answer is interrupted by the arrival of Serjeant Atkinson with news about Booth. Then the convenience of disassociation does its work: "These Ideas [about Booth] so possessed her Mind, that without once casting her Thoughts on any other Matters, she took her Leave of the Serjeant and his Lady" (338) and went to bed.

But we already know that Amelia knows that she is beautiful, that men desire her, that her beauty may be used to advance her husband's interest, that Mrs. Bennet attempted such a maneuver and fell, that the Noble Lord is currently in similar negotiations with herself, and that she has just been told quite directly that Colonel James is in love with her. What's a poor girl to do? For Fielding, leading into set piece on innocence and desire (in the persons of Amelia and Colonel James), the solution is simple: "Innocence and chearful Hope, in spite of the Malice of Fortune, closed the Eyes of gentle *Amelia*" (338). It is hard not to agree that Amelia has her eyes closed throughout most of the novel. Fielding chooses to present such blindness as innocence, but he clearly understands that such innocence, real or not, can be more destructive than calculation. As Amelia sleeps, Colonel James is tormented by her (presumably) artless performance:

> The many kind Words she had spoken to him, the many kind Looks she had given him, as being, she conceived, the Friend and Preserver of her Husband, had made an entire Conquest of his Heart. Thus, the very Love which she bore him, as the Person to whom her little Family were to owe their Preservation and Happiness, inspired him with Thoughts of sinking them all in the lowest Abyss of Ruin and Misery; and while she smiled with all her Sweetness on the supposed Friend of her Husband, she was converting that Friend into his most bitter Enemy. (338)

This passage is difficult because Fielding seems, in effect, to be praising Amelia for the very thing that will bring her husband down. The only logical conclusion to be drawn from the equation of her innocence with his ruin is that it would have been better had she been rather more artful, more calculating, more interested in her behavior toward James. Yet she has already shown herself at least capable of *conceiving* of the power her beauty gives her to act on her husband's behalf; she clearly understands, because of the behavior of the Noble Lord, that friendship and favors can be the currency of sexual negotiation; and she has been told that James seems to be in love with her. The stark contrast between innocence and interest, which is the overt theme of the novel, here modulates into a hazy dialectic redolent of the ethical difficulties of real life. Amelia's response, however, remains consistent. When she is finally persuaded that James may be a villain, she exclaims: "'The Idea freezes me to Death: I can not, must not, will not think it'" (346).

At this point, Fielding seems to recognize the problem of willful ignorance—"we must do our best to rescue the Character of our Heroine from Dulness of Apprehension, which several of our quick-sighted Read-ers may lay more heavily to her Charge than was done by her Friend Mrs. *Atkinson*"—and at least tries to sort out the issues:

> I must inform, therefore, all such Readers, that it is not, because Innocence is more blind than Guilt, that the former often overlooks and tumbles into the Pit, which the latter foresees and avoids. The Truth is, that it is almost im-possible Guilt should miss the discovering of all the Snares in its Way; as it is constantly prying closely into every Corner, in order to lay Snares for oth-ers. Whereas Innocence, having no such Purpose, walks fearlessly and care-lessly through Life; and is consequently liable to tread on the Gins, which Cunning hath laid to entrap it. To speak plainly, and without Allegory or Fig-ure, it is not Want of Sense, but want of Suspicion by which Innocence is often betrayed. . . . In a Word, many an innocent Person hath owed his Ruin to this Circumstance alone, that the Degree of Villainy was such as must have exceeded the Faith of every Man who was not himself a Villain. (347)

Since Fielding makes no suggestion that the innocent should become more self-interested and suspicious, this analysis does not help much—and the last sentence is particularly confusing. Is Fielding suggesting that if the innocent had even more "faith" (i.e., walked even more "fearlessly and carelessly through Life") that somehow villainy might be overcome? Or that, having achieved the sublime point of felicity called the possession of being well-deceived, the truly innocent would simply no longer care?

As if to explore this thought problem further, Fielding noticeably ac-celerates the exigencies of interest in the final third of the book. At one point, Booth actually attempts to talk Amelia into moving in with Colonel James by explaining that "'it is your Interest and theirs [the children] that has reconciled me to Proposal, which, when the Colonel first made it, struck me with utmost Horror. . . . O, my dear Amelia, let me intreat you to give up to the Good of your Children; as I have promised the Colonel to give you up to their Interest and your own'" (369). Amelia, under-standing at last that the Colonel's is not a "disinterested Generosity" (370) refuses, and even exclaims to Dr. Harrison that "'all Mankind are Villains in their Hearts'" (374). Yet immediately thereafter, Mrs. James pays a visit, and negotiations return to a familiar rut. Once her former friend pledges never to "'let Mr. *James* rest till he hath got you a Commission in *Eng-land*,'" Amelia, who has conveniently "long since forgot the Dislike she had taken to Mrs. *James*," promises in turn that she "'should be eternally obliged to her if she could succeed in her kind Endeavours,'" for "'I am convinced, if his Pretensions were backed with any interest, he would not fail of Success.' They shall be backed with Interest,' cries Mrs. James, 'if my Husband hath any'" (383).[53]

The hypocrisies and confusions engendered by interest achieve something like a crescendo as the Noble Lord re-enters the game at, appropriately, a masquerade. Here social metaphors are literalized, as people in disguise drift about attempting to conceal their voices and identities as they negotiate sexual and economic exchanges. Booth is upbraided by Miss Mathews for ingratitude; Colonel James unsuccessfully stalks a person he thinks is Amelia; and, pretending to be Amelia, Mrs. Atkinson secures a commission for her husband from the Noble Lord (411–19).[54] In the middle of all these masked negotiations, a letter against adultery is read ironically by a young Buck, as Fielding prepares the ground for his examination of the ultimate form of interest trading.

In the meantime, however, two episodes are interpolated that review theoretically, as it were, the problems of the client system previously dramatized in the action of the novel. The first is Booth's meeting with an old brother officer, Bob Bound, who represents the fate of merit without interest in the military; the second is Dr. Harrison's attempt to secure for Booth the interest of a politically savvy Peer. The officer's case is straightforward enough: despite "very particular Merit," he has "gone out of the Army with a broken Heart, upon having several boys put over his Head" (450). Attempting to live "on Half-pay as a Lieutenant, a Rank to which he had risen in five and thirty Years," he has sunk into poverty and resides with his sister, "the Widow of an Officer that had been killed in the Sea Service" (448). Because the government does not pay her pension on time, he is reduced to procuring an advance at ten percent, but he will not prostitute himself to procure interest: "'I am honest *Bob Bound,* and always will be'" is his motto. Fielding seems to intend Bound as an exemplar of integrity in a world controlled by interest and as such perhaps a foil to Booth, who is in a similar financial state but willing to accept the emotional stress and problematic ethics implied by interest trading.

Immediately thereafter, these emotional and ethical conundrums are explicitly examined in Dr. Harrison's famous conversation with "a Nobleman of his Acquaintance . . . whom he knew to have very considerable Interest with the Ministers at that Time" (456). The episode has received extensive critical attention, perhaps because it seems to present in a relatively binary fashion issues and relations that elsewhere in *Amelia* seem to defy easy explanation.[55] On the one hand, the political Peer recalls Fielding at his most cynical, as his rationalization of corruption virtually duplicates Fielding's own position in *A Dialogue between a Gentleman . . . and an Honest Alderman* (1747), a defense of Pelhamite political practice. On the other hand, Dr. Harrison's denunciation of such views probably represents Fielding's highest political ideals. What we may have, then, is a dialogue be-

tween Fielding's political theory and Fielding's political practice; that is, between advancement through merit and advancement through interest.[56]

The most revealing incident of the Harrison-Peer episode, however,
does not occur within the terms of this relatively conventional argument,
but contextually when Dr. Harrison has the tables turned on him by the
object of his solicitation. For when Harrison asks the Peer for his interest
on Booth's behalf, the Peer proposes a *quid pro quo:* "'You certainly
know . . . how hard Colonel *Trompington* is run at your Town, in the Elec-
tion of a Mayor; they tell me it will be a very near Thing, unless you join
us. But we know it is in your Power to do the Business, and turn the Scale.
I heard you Name mention'd the other Day on that Account; and I know
you may have any Thing in Reason, if you will give us your Interest'"
(458). Harrison is taken aback by this offer—"'Sure, my Lord . . . you are
not in Earnest in asking my Interest for the Colonel'"—and subsequently
declines the Peer's request, only to have the Peer likewise decline to use his
interest to help Booth. Structurally, the scene suggests the exact equiva-
lence of both solicitations, and despite Fielding's attempt to shore up Harrison's request on the basis of Booth's merit, the Peer's reply ("'What is the
Merit of a Subaltern Officer?'")—followed by his unanswerable argument
that there are "'Abundance with the same Merit, and the same Qualifications, who want a Morsel of Bread for themselves and their Families'"
(459)—reduces Harrison to conventional sermonizing on the corruption
of the nation. What Harrison (and Fielding?) never seems to recognize is
that the clergyman's visit to the Peer on Booth's behalf has already corrupted the logic of any merit-based argument by injecting interest and
connection into the process: other meritorious officers do not have a Harrison to plead their case. In other words, the very conversation in which
Fielding most starkly compares the ideal of merit and the practice of interest is itself engendered by the solicitation of "Favour and Partiality" on
Booth's behalf by Dr. Harrison, the spokesman for merit.[57]

Having blurred the lines between political prostitution (in the form of
the political Peer) and deserved favors (in the form of Harrison), Fielding
in the succeeding episode further blurs the lines between physical prostitution and domesticity in his starkest portrait yet of the sexual dimension
of interest trading—what might be called "domestic prostitution."[58] In the
history of Captain Trent, Fielding describes without frills or sentiment the
practice of prostituting wives for cash, gifts, or preferment. Trent's history
is simple: after a roguish upbringing, marriage to a beautiful and moneyed
wife, a successful stint in Booth's regiment, and financial ruin, Trent discovers that the Noble Lord is attracted to Mrs. Trent and decides to secure
the Lord's interest using his wife as bait. When Mrs. Trent eventually takes
the Noble Lord to bed, Trent and a witness "burst from the Closet . . . and

unkindly interrupted the Action" (470). Swordplay is threatened, but Trent "with great Calmness" argues that "'it would be the highest Imprudence in me to kill a Man who is now become so considerably my Debtor.'" Negotiations ensue and a deal is cut: "my Lord stipulated to pay a good round Sum, and to provide Mr. *Trent* with a good Place on the first Opportunity," while "On the Side of Mr. *Trent* were stipulated absolute Remission of all past, and full Indulgence for the Time to come" (471).[59] With this agreement, Captain and Mrs. Trent complete the sexual and material transaction that the Noble Lord had attempted to negotiate with both the Bennets and the Booths: in return for the wife satisfying his sexual desires, he attends to the husband's material well-being.

In this transaction the multiple definitions of the term "interest" are superimposed upon the person of Mrs. Trent. A desirable property in which Trent possesses an interest, she arouses the Noble Lord's sexual interest (curiosity), which his material interest (influence) allows him to satisfy by paying dividends to the husband. The traditional wife-as-property metaphor ("'*Mind that, Ladies,* . . . *you are all the Property of your Husbands*'"—as Harrison's letter against adultery puts it), seems here to be adjusting to an emergent economic system: the willing wife becomes something like speculative capital generating interest or dividends for the husband. As James Thompson puts it, "In Fielding's attack on the decadent aristocracy of *Amelia,* social obligation has become explicitly financial, transformed into a kind of social capital."[60] But I would suggest that the broad application of such metaphors often obscures more than it reveals. In this case, it reduces to a set of mere financial transactions the far more complicated negotiation of clientage relationships that is at the heart of *Amelia.*

The Booths' and Bennets' relations with the Noble Lord are not simply "explicitly financial" but affective and "interested"—and their corruption is as much a matter of misguided emotion as cash-and-carry prostitution. As we have seen, Amelia really does admire the Noble Lord, and her admiration is enhanced by his sending expensive toys to the children and promising to help her husband. Mrs. Bennet, for her part, explicitly confesses to indulging her "Vanity and Interest" in toying with the Noble Lord. Miss Mathews—one of the few women temporarily in a dominant financial position—feels real affection for Booth, though she is not unwilling to bribe him to sleep with her. And even the Trents eventually develop a more flexible, human, and traditional—if no less corrupt— relationship with the Noble Lord than its purely contractual inception might suggest. It is a relationship Fielding seems to locate somewhere on the border between the cash nexus and hierarchical obligation; and one he exemplifies by playing with variations on the word "pimp."

Mrs. Trent, once she has sated her own and the Noble Lord's desire, finds it in her own interest to become something of a broker for his: "Her Passion indeed was principally founded upon Interest; so that Foundation served to support another Superstructure; and she was easily prevailed upon, as well as her Husband, to be useful to my Lord in a Capacity, which, though very often exerted in the polite World, hath not, as yet, to my great Surprise, acquired any polite Name, or indeed any which is not too coarse to be admitted in this History" (471). But the coarse Bob Bound has already named it, when earlier he called Trent a "Pimp in ordinary to my Lord" (449). These two descriptions—one a circumlocution based on architectural terms soon to become central to economic discourse; the other a blunt statement metaphorically invoking traditional service relationships—exemplify the muddle of old and new idioms that complicate the reading of social relations in *Amelia*. Obviously, Mrs. Trent's "Interest" can be read as the proto-Marxian "Foundation" upon which the "Superstructure" of domestic prostitution ("Passion") and then domestic pimping are erected. But honest Bob's unbowdlerized sarcasm—"Pimp in ordinary to my Lord"—casts Captain Trent himself in the more traditional role of an attendant at court. The Trents may at first cut a financial deal, but they seem to evolve into something resembling body servants. Their relationship with the Noble Lord has an affective component that either transcends or sinks below the objectivity implied by "explicitly financial" relations. Indeed, this seems to be Fielding's satirical point in describing the Noble Lord and Trent as "my Lord and his Setter, or (if the Sportsmen please) Setting-Dog" (473).

On the other hand, explicitly financial relations do come into play in Trent's "setting up" Booth for the Noble Lord, when acting on a "Hint" and financial "Credit" from his Lordship, he advances Booth money in a gambit that provokes the final spasm of interest in the novel (472). At the proper time, the Lord orders "that *Trent* should immediately demand his Money of *Booth*," which "must end immediately in the Ruin of *Booth*, and consequently the Conquest of *Amelia*" (473). Booth, "driven almost to Madness" (473) by Trent's demand, sets out to visit a "Man of great Interest and Consequence"—in fact, a supposed conduit to the great. Such men, writes the narrator, "use their Masters, as bad Ministers have sometimes used a Prince; they keep all Men of Merit from his Ears, and daily sacrifice his true Honour and Interest to their own Profit, and their own Vanity" (474). Nevertheless, the desperate Booth once again believes that interest will prevail and is aided in this delusion by none other than Bob Bound, who despite his earlier incarnation as "honest Bob" is shown to be as caught up in the interest game as anyone. "'I have heard,'" he tells Booth over a bottle, "'that Gentleman hath very powerful Interest,'" but "'the great Man must be touched; for that he never did any Thing without touching'" (475). By this time, Amelia has pawned her trinkets and clothes to secure enough money to discharge the debt, but predictably Booth gives this money to the great man, who of course promises much and does nothing. Fielding himself seems irritated enough by this scene to launch into an editorial:

> Here I shall stop for one Moment, and so perhaps will my goodnatured Reader; for surely it must be a hard Heart which is not affected, with reflecting on the Manner in which this poor Sum was raised, and on the Manner on which it was bestowed. A worthy Family, the Wife and Children or a Man who had lost his Blood abroad in the Service of his Country, parting with their little all, and exposed to Cold and Hunger, to pamper such a Fellow as this.
>
> And if any such Reader, as I mention, should happen to be in reality a great Man, and in Power, perhaps the Horrour of this Picture may induce him to put a final End to this abominable Practice of touching, as it is called; by which indeed a Set of Leaches are permitted to suck the Blood of the Brave and the indigent; of the Widow and the Orphan. (477)

We have routinely seen marriage, friendship, sexual fidelity, and self-esteem burnt on the altar of interest, yet Fielding's angry editorial requests "a final End" only to minor bribery. And with this request we reach the end of interest in *Amelia*.

Despite Fielding's earlier presentation of the idealized Universal Register Office as a cure for such corruption, the analysis of interest in *Amelia* does not suggest its replacement by a purely commercial system, particularly since commerce itself was routinely viewed by both eighteenth-century critics and modern ones as speculative, delusional, and chaotic in its own right.[61] Indeed, the nostalgically valorized system of moral economy, paternalism, and reciprocal vertical responsibility that Fielding found so attractive was to a great degree founded on proper relations of personal interest.[62] Yet, at the same time, personal relations could be corrupted by all manner of favoritism, and Fielding recognized that purely financial relations could sometimes supply the kind of objectivity missing from more subjective forms of interest trading. What Fielding seems to suggest in *Amelia* is that a somewhat "moral economy" has become a generally "immoral" one—in need of significant readjustment and perhaps even "amoral" correctives such as a Universal Register Office. But he does not suggest that the system of personal interest can or will be replaced by the cash nexus. He accepts implicitly what Roy Porter calls the "ties of importunity and gratitude, of begging and granting, the queue which political patronage created all the way down the scale."[63] Harold Perkin evocatively describes the hybrid quality of "vertical friendship" at mid-century as "a durable two-way relationship between patrons and clients permeating the whole of society . . . less formal and inescapable than feudal homage, more personal and comprehensive than the contractual, employment relationships of capitalist 'Cash Payment.' For those who lived within its embrace it was so much an integral part of the texture of life that they had no name for it save 'friendship.'"[64] Here Perkin adumbrates the socio-rhetorical world of *Amelia,* where the workings of interest cloaked as friendship are examined with relentless intensity.

Moreover, as is evident in the practice of the magistrate's court and the register office, the more objective mechanisms gradually replacing traditional discretionary proceedings could be themselves quickly compromised by human desires and subjectivities that had perhaps been recast but not removed.[65] No one would have understood better than Fielding the "highly vulnerable, occasionally humiliating and certainly weak position"—as John Brewer describes it—of those caught in the middle of such hybrid relations, whether they were officers on half pay, clergy, minor gentry, businessmen, or professional writers-turned-justices.[66] The end of interest in *Amelia,* then, may simply be a recognition of its excesses by one whose life had been based on negotiating for its rewards. Despite the increased significance of commerce and law to eighteenth-century modes of thought and action, the old system of interest and connection would not soon disappear; and in the last novel of Henry Fielding—lawyer, magistrate, businessman, and inveterate importuner—it seems to have achieved a graceless but still formidable middle age.

V

Having closed the book on interest, Fielding trots law back onto the scene, first in the rather obtrusive and preachy episode of little Betty's theft and then in the long description of Booth's final arrest and confinement. Fielding's judicial interest in the little Betty incident is understandable, and her story serves to reiterate his longstanding distrust of servants, but on the whole the episode seems to me ill-considered in a novel where overt theft otherwise plays so insignificant a role.[67] On the other hand, Booth's confinement allows for his conversion and the providential discovery of Murphy, and more importantly allows Fielding himself (or someone a good deal like him) to take the stage in the form of the indefatigable magistrate.[68]

Predictably we find this Fieldingesque character "just sitting down to his Dinner" which, "tho' it was then very late, and he had been fatigued all the Morning with public Business," he postpones "till he had discharged his Duty" (521). The cagey magistrate helpfully unscrambles some legal technicalities and provides a pretext for searching Murphy's house, where letters are discovered that "fully explained the whole Villainy" (523) that had deprived Amelia of her estate. Nothing now is left to do but to celebrate; and in a marvelous scene Fielding himself comes, as it were, face-to-face with his favorite and most beautiful child. His reaction tracks perfectly with all we know about him:

> *Amelia* was then in a clean white Gown . . . and was indeed dressed all over with great Neatness and Exactness; with the Glow therefore which arose in her Features from finding her Husband released from his Captivity, she made so charming a Figure, that she attracted the Eyes of the Magistrate and of his Wife, and they both agreed when they were alone, that they had never seen so charming a Creature. . . .
>
> Whether Amelia's Beauty, or the Reflexion on the remarkable Act of Justice he had performed, or whatever Motive filled the Magistrate with extraordinary good Humour, and opened his Heart and Cellars, I will not determine; but he gave them so Hearty a Welcome, and they were all so pleased with each other, that *Amelia,* for that one Night, trusted the Care of her Children to the Woman where they lodged, nor did the Company rise from Table till the Clock struck eleven. (525)

In spirit and in "spirits," Fielding inhabits his scene. The fictional magistrate's simultaneous pleasure in "Beauty, or the Reflexion on the remarkable Act of Justice he had just performed" is precisely the mixed pleasure Fielding derived from viewing and saving beautiful young prostitutes in Bow Street. Even the close focus on Amelia's dress and glow finds something of an analogy in Fielding's description of a prostitute in his court—"a young Woman remarkably handsome, genteel, well dressed," who "behaved herself with great decency" and convinced him to show "her all the Compassion in his Power" (March 9, 1752). The meeting of Fielding's fictional self and his female paragon generates a similar emotional openness. The magistrate, filled with "extraordinary good Humour," opens his "Heart and his Cellars." And Amelia, perhaps under the influence of both, for once indulges herself in unmitigated pleasure and leaves her children a little longer with the babysitter.

Such levity and indulgence—usually associated with Booth (now reformed)—serves paradoxically to foreground Amelia's final renunciation of interest-based aspiration for an asceticism founded on labor. Of course, such asceticism is already compromised by the knowledge that Amelia's inheritance will be restored. But she does not yet know this, and her willingness now to propose for herself and her husband something that has not once been mentioned during the tortuous interest-generated machinations that form the chief activity of *Amelia* seems Fielding's last nod to the work of the register office as an antidote to old interest. The morning after dinner at the magistrate's, Booth asks her, "'How then shall we live?'" (527). "'By our Labour,' answered she, 'I am able to labour, and I am sure I am not ashamed of it.'" When Booth asks her if she "'can support such a Life,'" Amelia responds with a paean to honest labor and human equality:

> "I am sure I could be happy in it," answered *Amelia*. "And why not I as well as a thousand others, who have not the Happiness of such a Husband to make Life delicious? Why should I complain of my hard Fate, while so many, who are much poorer than I, enjoy theirs? Am I of a superior Rank of Being to the Wife of the honest Labourer? Am I not a Partaker of one common Nature with her?" (527)

We seem suddenly back in the scenario that preceded the onset of the Booths' urban disasters: their experiment as farmers. Dr. Harrison had precipitated this episode by counseling Booth to eschew interest and embrace country life: "'I never think those Men wise who for any worldly Interest forego the greatest Happiness of their Lives. If I mistake not . . . a Country Life, where you could be always together, would make you both happier People'" (146). The Booths accept this idealized view without recognizing that it is Harrison's property (he rents them his Parsonage farm "which required but little Stock, and that little should not be wanting") that allows them to indulge themselves as genteel farmers. And genteel they are. In describing his life as a farmer, Booth never once mentions labor. He buys and sells property, sets up a coach, offends his neighbors, overextends his credit, goes bankrupt, comes to London, and the novel begins. In ending it, Amelia proposes a far more stringent kind of work.

We are never told what she has in mind for herself and Booth (taking in washing? driving a hackney coach? service?), and it is very difficult to ascertain Fielding's motivations in having Amelia mouth a theory of equalitarian labor that she will never have to put into practice. It does seem significant, however, that at the last moment before landed wealth allows his heroes to live happily ever after, Fielding should feel compelled to introduce labor as the acid test of Amelia's virtue. It was a subject much on his mind during this period, not only because of his experience with demobilized military men or as the proprietor of an employment agency, but because he was attempting to formulate a new scheme to aid or compel the poor to labor. A little over a year after *Amelia*'s publication, he would state his views in *A Proposal for Making an Effectual Provision for the Poor* (1753).

In the *Proposal*, Fielding recognizes two kinds of unemployed poor and distinguishes them not only psychologically but institutionally. The first are the "industrious but unemployed poor"; the second, "the idle" and "vagrants."[69] The first group is described by Fielding in terms strikingly reminiscent of the clients of the Universal Register Office: "able and industrious Persons, who are willing to get Livelihood by honest Labour" but who "are often, for want of such Labour, reduced to great Distress."[70] This is clearly the group into which Amelia putatively fits, although because of her class affiliations she would more likely have become a client of the register office than a beneficiary of the "County-house" Fielding proposes. Nevertheless, the admission procedures of both institutions are remarkably similar. At the County-house, "the Governor or Deputy shall examine in the said Person as to his Age, Ability, and Skill in Work or Manufacture, and shall then order the Receiver to enter in a Book, to be kept for that Purpose, the Name and Age of the said Person . . . together with the Kind of Labour to which he is appointed." Here, however, the similarities end, for such "volunteers" will then be set to work in the County-house and "detained" there: "a badge with these Words, '*County-house*,' in large Letters . . . sewed on the left Shoulder of the said Person, who shall be confined within the said House." Eventually such persons may be taken into service by "any Nobleman, Gentleman, Merchant, Tradesman, Farmer, or substantial Householder" and, if they remain for more than a year, released of their obligation to return to the County-house. The idle and vagrants (i.e., the "idle and disorderly" of the Covent Garden columns), on the other hand, are sent to the "County-House of Correction" where they are first confined to a "Fasting-room" on bread and water for 24 hours and then "put to hard Labour."[71]

Apparently the "honest Labourer" praised by Amelia is not much trusted by Fielding: a situation that holds true both in the *Proposal* and at the register office. While labor itself is valorized, those who labor remain suspect, and Amelia's equalitarian effusion is perhaps less a reflection of Fielding's views than a final example of her naiveté—or his inconsistent narration. But simple, honest labor, stripped of human inconsistencies, remains one of the least equivocal objects of Fielding's admiration. It is an activity that provokes the best sort of interest: merit-based, uninfluenced by considerations of beauty, birth, rank, or self. When combined with simple virtue, it becomes an almost transcendent ideal; and when astonishingly embodied in the homely form of a maid-of-all work named Elizabeth Canning, it will provide a mind-altering experience for Amelia's creator.

Chapter 4

Elizabeth Canning and
the Myths of Grub Street

I

On January 1, 1753, Elizabeth Canning was kidnapped. Even the bare circumstances of the purported crime, as presented by Fielding, are page-turners. Canning, an 18-year-old maid-of-all-work from Aldermanbury Postern, was returning home from a visit to "her Uncle and Aunt . . . who live at *Saltpetre Bank,* near *Rosemary-lane.*" When she "came opposite to *Bethlehem-gate* in *Moorfields,* she was seized by two Men who, after robbing her of half a Guinea in Gold, and three Shillings in Silver, of her Hat, Gown, and Apron, violently dragged her into a Gravel-walk that leads down to the Gate of *Bethlehem* Hospital."[1] At this point, one of the men "gave her a violent Blow with his Fist on the right Temple, that threw her into a Fit, and intirely deprived her of her Senses." Canning was used to such fits, which "were first occasioned by the Fall of Cieling [*sic*] on her Head," were "apt to return" whenever she was frightened, and sometimes continued "for six or seven Hours." When she came to, Canning found herself being dragged along a roadway, and eventually into a house "where she saw in the Kitchen an old Gipsy Woman and two young Women." The old gypsy took her hand and "promised *to give her fine Cloathes if she would go their Way,* which Expression she understanding to mean the becoming a Prostitute, she utterly refused to comply with." The gypsy woman then cut off her stays with a knife, one of the men took her cap, and about an hour later the gypsy "forced her up an old Pair of Stairs, and pushed her into a Back-room like a Hay-loft." There she would remain for four weeks, living on bread and water and "one small Minced-pye which she had in her Pocket," until on January 29 she broke a window and escaped to London (288). Described before her abduction as "fresh-colour'd, pitted with the Small-Pox, [with] a high Forehead, light Eyebrows, about five Feet high, eighteen Years of Age, well set," she was on her return, according to her mother's testimony, "black as the chimney stock, black and blue," "an apparition . . . almost double, walking sideways, holding her hands before her."[2] Eventually Canning's alleged kidnappers were arrested, Fielding was brought in as a consultant on the case, and the ensuing examinations and trials became a *cause célèbre* and publishing bonanza. As the editor of the *Genuine and Impartial Memoirs of Elizabeth Canning* put it a year later, "*MODERN History can scarce instance a Subject, that for such a Length of Time has more generally engaged the Attention of all Ranks of People, than the Affair of* ELIZABETH CANNING *and* MARY SQUIRES."[3]

The first spate of the literary productions deriving from the Canning case appeared during March–July 1753, immediately after the trials of Canning's captors and during the period of her own arrest for perjury.[4] Almost immediately the defenses, rejoinders, detections, and inspections took on the form of a paper war, as authors scribbled to fill public demand and their own pockets. This was to be Fielding's last paper war, one that put him again in conflict with his old enemy John Hill; but, more accurately, it might be described as the last phase of the series of overlapping paper wars in which Fielding had been engaged since the beginning of 1752.[5] At that time, it will be remembered, Fielding had provoked a literary free-for-all by declaring—in the voice of "Sir Alexander Drawcansir" of *The Covent-Garden Journal*—war on all of Grub Street and particularly on John Hill, with whom he thought he had arranged, during a deposition in Bow Street, a little mutually beneficial mudslinging. This battle was soon joined by Bonnell Thornton, writing as the ex-prostitute "Madam Roxana Termagant" in *The Drury-Lane Journal*, sponsored by the Fieldings' rival, Philip D'Halluin of the Public Register Office. Thornton then fictionally drafted Christopher Smart into the war by having his persona Mrs. (or Mother) "Mary Midnight" of *The Midwife; or the Old Woman's Magazine* visit Roxana Termagant at her chambers above a "rotting Chandler's shop" in Drury Lane.

As the war expanded and intensified, William Kenrick tried to produce a send-up of the whole thing called "FUN and MUSICK" at that bastion of popular entertainments, the Castle Tavern in Paternoster Row, where Smart had originated his Old Woman's Oratory. But the performance—which included a parody of *Macbeth*'s witch scene that was especially amusing at Fielding's and Hill's expense—was suppressed by a special order of the Lord Mayor. Kenrick, in his introduction to the printed version of the show, *Fun: A Parodi-tragical-comical Satire,* accused Fielding ("*excited,*" as he wrote, "to *this Piece of Barbarity, by an Old Woman's Prophecy*") of being behind the suppression.[6] The reference to "*an Old Woman's Prophecy*" seems to refer simultaneously to the witches' joke that Drawcansir would never fall until "against him rise a mighty *Hill*" (7) and to Kenrick's suspicion that Smart, who as "Mary Midnight" had disavowed any connection with "FUN and MUSICK," had colluded with Fielding to have the performance suppressed.[7]

By April 1752, then, Fielding was closely identified with Hill, Thornton, and Smart, and their personae, The Inspector, Roxana Termagant, and Mary Midnight, as a central figure in a major Grub Street melee. On April 8, 1752, this identification was finally given dramatic form when, with Fielding's tacit consent, Charles Macklin in *The Covent Garden Theatre, or Pasquin Turn'd Drawcansir,* had "Pasquin" describe London as a "Universal Rendevouz of all the Monsters produced by wagish Nature & fantastick Art," including "Panopticons, Microcosms . . . Hermaphrodites and Conjurers . . . Quacks, Turks, Enthusiasts, and Fire eaters.—*Mother Midnights, Termagants,* Clare Market, and Robin Hood Orators, *Drury Lane Journalists, Inspectors,* Fools, and *Drawcansirs"* (my emphasis).[8]

Both "Wagish Nature & Fantastick Art" continued to produce monsters in the succeeding months. Wagish Nature struck first when on May 6, 1752, Mountefort Brown "kicked, caned, and dewigged" Hill in Ranelagh Gardens in revenge for a comment in the *Inspector* column of 30 April.[9] The episode was widely and amusingly reported, and Hill responded by accusing Brown of criminal assault and reporting on his own injuries and treatment in the *Inspector* columns for the next several weeks. But worse yet, when Brown came before Fielding on May 9 to answer the "Complaint of Dr. Hill, for a supposed Assault in Ranelagh," Fielding found Hill's charges overblown enough to call them, in the Covent Garden column of May 11, "scandalous Paragraphs . . . in a common Newspaper, intending to vilify and misrepresent the Character of Mr. Brown."[10] Next, Fantastick Art had its chance when in July Hill gloated over the supposed demise of Smart and Thornton's female personae—"No more is heard of the Gossip or the Scold; the scattered Loading from each Blunderbuss has missed the Mark"—and Smart answered with a parodic *Inspector* essay in *The Midwife* (August 4, 1752) that emphasized Hill's vanity and self-promotion.[11] Hill responded by attacking Fielding, Smart, and himself (lightly) in *The Impertinent* (August 13, 1752). Fielding answered in *The Covent-Garden Journal* No. 60 (August 22, 1752) with a satire on Hill as a writer of panegyrics upon himself. Hill then performed the ultimate conjuring trick by criticizing *The Impertinent* in the *Inspector* of August 25, only to be exposed as the author of both the former and the latter works.

The exchanges of January through August 1752 illustrate the constantly transforming identities, loyalties, and tonalities that characterized the war and that presumably were expected by its audience; a war in which Fielding thought he was Hill's mock enemy only to discover the animosity was

real; in which Thornton and Smart's witch-like personae were routinely
exchanged and used to laugh at Fielding, Hill, and each other; in which
Kenrick expropriated all of the personae for a performance he believed
was suppressed by Fielding at the urging of Smart; and in which the personae were characterized by Macklin, in a play advertised by Fielding, as
"Monsters produced by wagish Nature & fantastick Art." It is a useful shift
of perspective to recognize that this was Fielding's journalistic world in the
period during which, in his magisterial role, he was attempting to adjudi-
cate and advertise confusing cases of domestic violence and prostitution
involving old women, young wives, mutually abusive spouses, browbeaten
"Shadows," and innocent runaways turned reluctant whores—the context
that would lead directly into his involvement with the Canning case.

As the Fall season began, old antagonists reappeared in new forms and
contexts. Thornton, whose *Drury-Lane Journal* had expired in April, rein-
carnated Roxana on November 16, 1752, in the form of her 18-year-old
relation "Priscilla Termagant" of *The Spring-Garden Journal*—a work addressed "to the Writers of the Age, but more particularly Sir Alexander
Drawcansir."[12] Young Priscilla is clearly intended to be recognized as a
prostitute, as she describes her age and charms in the manner of *Harris's
List of Covent-Garden Ladies* and goes on to solicit both Hill and Fielding
directly: "if so delicate a description of my Person should chance to excite
the Passions of a certain gallant Doctor, or superannuated Knight, let them
repair to my Bookseller, where they may have full Direction to me, and
(under certain limitations) amuse themselves in some innocent and necessary Exercises of the Human Body."[13] Although she coyly explains that one
of these "Exercises" is a "dance" for the knight, her description of the doctor's treat leaves little to be imagined: "I will prepare a most exquisite Muff
for the Emolument of his Fingers; and I have so much Vanity to think he
will pay me this Compliment,—*materium superabat Opus*."[14] An 18-year-
old of questionable virtue is thus added to the collection of boisterous old
women, ex-bawds, bombastic knights, and fatuous inspectors battling it out
for the entertainment of the public. But the paper war itself had already
been essentially transformed by the advent of a theater war between Garrick and Rich, one given physical form on November 10, when Thaddeus
Fitzpatrick, resenting Garrick's parody of Rich's rope-dancer and animal
acts, threw an apple from a Drury Lane stage box and hit Henry Woodward.[15] Over the next several days, "great Noise," "some blows in the pit,"
and Woodward's "saying I thank you to Fitzpatrick" punctuated Garrick's
parody.[16] *The Gentleman's Magazine* reported that "The *Inspector* espoused
the cause of the Gentleman; and the *Covent Garden Journalist* of the come-
dian," and, as Betty Rizzo has shown, the event had the effect of coalesc-
ing what heretofore had been a rather disparate group of writers into

something like an anti-Hill coalition.[17] By December, a major anti-Hill opus was in production: Smart was reading aloud excerpts from his mock epic, *The Hilliad*, "at Alehouses and Cyder Cellars."[18] The published version of Smart's *The Hilliad* (February 1, 1753), in fact, seems to have been something of a collaborative effort, with Arthur Murphy writing the *Notes Variorum*—"Mr. Smart walking up and down the room, speaking the Verses, and Mr. Murphy writing the notes to them"—and with Fielding perhaps contributing ideas as well.[19]

Into this mock-magical (or mock-mythical) Grubean world of print—in which positions, personae, papers, allegiances, and authorship could transform in kaleidoscopic fashion—was inserted on January 31, 1752, the first rendition of the story of a "young Woman . . . forcibly carried . . . to a House kept by one Mother Wells," where the "Woman of the House immediately cut off her Stays . . . and with the horridest Execrations forced her into a Room, where she was kept upon Bread and Water" for almost a month before escaping through a window.[20] This early version of the story from *The London Daily Advertiser* (which also carried Hill's *Inspector* essays) already contains elements of a dark fairy tale, which were soon supplemented on February 10 by the revelation (in the *Public Advertiser*'s summary of Fielding's examination) that Canning was "confined in a miserable Room for a Month" and (in *The London Daily Advertiser*) that her tormentor was an "old Woman."[21] On February 10 there also appeared an independently printed "Case of Elizabeth Canning" sponsored by Canning's friends, who were soliciting donations to support the prosecution of her captors: in this document her place of captivity was described as the "House of that notorious Woman, well known by the name of Mother Wells," and Wells was called "that Monster of a woman."[22] On February 17, a detailed advertisement deriving from the printed "Case" and again soliciting contributions appeared conspicuously in the middle column of the front page of *The Public Advertiser* and revealed to the public that after being struck on the head Canning had had a fit "which she by Fright is much subject to," that her place of confinement was the house of "a most notorious old Bawd," that her tormentor was not just any old woman but an "old Gipsy Woman," that this woman "robbed the Girl of her Stays; and then in a miserable naked Condition, because she would not become a common Prostitute, confined her in an old Back Room or Loft belonging to the said House, with some Hay therein, for twenty eight Days."

Thus the story took shape for the public: the kidnapping of an innocent 18-year-old servant girl (given to fits), her solicitation to prostitution by a horrifically ugly old gypsy woman, her captivity in the house of an old bawd named Mother Wells, her starvation in a hayloft, and her ghostlike reappearance in London. It was a story to warm the heart and crank up the machinery of Grub Street; all the more so, I would suggest, because it seemed almost to bring to life the characters in the long-running Fielding-Hill paper war into which it fit so well. Indeed, I intend the word "fit" in the material sense: for abutting the lower portion of the elaborate Canning announcement in the February 17 *Public Advertiser,* there is an advertisement for Smart's show featuring in large type the title "The OLD WOMAN's ORATORY"—a rubric that resonates in interesting ways with the mythic figures the "notorious old Bawd" and "old Gipsy Woman" were in the process of becoming.[23] And above the Canning announcement, in the space just below the masthead, is the long-running advertisement by "Justice FIELDING" soliciting information on robberies, burglaries, thefts, and stolen goods. Combined with the already commonplace conflation of actual persons and their literary personae—Fielding/Drawcansir, Smart/Midnight, Hill/Inspector, Thornton/Termagant—that had characterized the year-long paper war, the layout of the newspaper itself seems to contribute to the public's predisposition to read news as Grub Street fiction and Grub Street fiction as news. To the curious reader, then, this evocative blending of criminal life and journalistic allegory must have seemed complete when on March 9 Drawcansir's chief enemy, The Inspector, launched an all-out attack on Canning's truthfulness and Justice Fielding's handling of the case in two and a half front page columns of *The London Daily Advertiser.*

II

Fielding had come to the case reluctantly. On February 6, interrupted at tea by a Mr. Salt, Canning's solicitor, he had read over the case and given Salt advice, only to be asked to examine Canning and a material witness named Virtue Hall. As Fielding tells it, "This Business I at first declined, partly, as it was a Transaction which had happened at a distant Part of the County, as it had been examined already by a Gentleman . . . of whose Worth and Integrity I have . . . a very high Opinion; but principally, indeed for that I had been almost fatigued to Death, with several tedious Examinations at that Time" (298). Yet yielding to "Importunities, some Curiosity, occasioned by the extraordinary Nature of the Case, and a great Compassion for the dreadful Condition of the Girl" (298) Fielding finally agreed to examine Elizabeth Canning the following day. His response to her seems to have been immediate and profound. He found in Elizabeth Canning "a poor little Girl" (286), "virtuous, modest, sober, well-disposed" (293), "a Child . . . in Understanding, with all the evident Marks of Simplicity that I ever discovered in a human Countenance" (294). Although the opening phrase may recall Fielding's ambiguous handling of prostitutes in the Covent Garden columns, the later analysis of Canning's character, intelligence, and demeanor reveals a simple, pockmarked maid-of-all work, with no personal beauty or charm, to whom Fielding instinctively responded with strong sympathy and almost fatherly concern. The fact that the injured innocent was a servant girl—a class that provoked Fielding's habitual suspicion—only serves to emphasize the remarkable nature of his response; a response all the more surprising when we remember that in her name and stature, "Betty" Canning (at under five feet tall) must have at least fleetingly recalled to Fielding the dishonest and stereotypical "little Betty" in *Amelia*. Notably, the phrasing of his evaluation—"virtuous, modest, sober, well-disposed"—was suggested in part by the testimonials of "those with whom she hath lived in Service" and sounds like an advertisement for the antithesis of *Amelia*'s "little Betty": Elizabeth Canning was that rare kind of servant the Fieldings hoped to attract and place at the Universal Register Office. The plain servant girl represents "injured innocence" without sexual innuendo: she has no beauty and provokes no desire. Her otherworldly nature draws from Fielding an almost transcendental justification of his defense—"there is something within myself which rouses me to the Protection of injured Innocence, and which prompts me with the Hopes of an Applause much more valuable than that of the whole World" (286)—and converts his original interest ("Curiosity") into an excessive concern and later into something close to the improper application of legal influence.

After having Canning swear to the truth of her "Information," Fielding issued a warrant for the arrest of Virtue Hall and Judith Natus—both residents of Mother Wells's house—and had Hall brought to him for examination. As he tells it in *Elizabeth Canning,* Fielding began to question Hall "in the softest Language and kindest Manner I was able, for a considerable Time, till she had been guilty of so many Prevarications and Contradictions, that I told her I would examine her no longer, but would commit her to Prison" (301)—a scare tactic that caused Hall to change her story to one that confirmed Canning's account. Fielding then, unaccountably, "recommended to Mr. *Salt* to go with her and take her Information in Writing" (302).[24] Both Fielding's method of interrogation and his decision to allow Hall's information to be recorded by Canning's solicitor would come under strong criticism. His legal procedure has continued to be questioned by historians of the case and, in the absence of any other motive, seems explicable only as a confirmation of his deep belief in Canning's story and character.

For a time, public opinion ran almost unanimously in Canning's favor. Her entertainment value, even for the upper classes, was confirmed when Fielding, responding to an aristocratic request, gathered Canning, Virtue Hall, Mary Squires (the gypsy), and Susannah Wells in his chambers on February 14 and questioned them before "Lord *Montfort,* together with several Gentlemen of Fashion" (306). The pro-Canning sentiment of the moment is evident in a newspaper report of Squires's and Wells's behavior under questioning:

> Mother *Wells* expressed herself with the *Art* and *affected Innocence* of those *wicked* Wretches, who are *deliberately* and *methodically* taught the Methods of evading Justice; and the old *Gipsy* behaved as a Person *traditionally* and *hereditarily* versed in the antient *Egyptian* Cunning, making the most religious Protestations of her Innocence; though she was afterwards heard to say, *Damn the young Bitch!*[25]

This proceeding, too, would eventually be called into question and seems particularly exploitative (and, in the newspaper's rhetoric, racist) to modern sensibilities. But in the weeks leading up to the trial of Susannah Wells and Mary Squires, the press and the public were fully behind Canning, and stories of the gypsy's ugliness and brutality continued to proliferate. On February 21, a violent pro-Canning crowd gathered outside the Old Bailey, where Wells and Squires were tried and immediately convicted. Five days later they were sentenced: Wells to be branded in the hand and imprisoned for six months; Squires to be hung.[26]

Only then did the backlash begin. Sir Crisp Gascoyne, the Lord Mayor of London, and then others who found Canning's story too fantastic to believe or who claimed to know Mary Squires personally, came out in defense of the old gypsy as the real victim in the case. It was in this context that John Hill and Justice Thomas Lediard re-examined Virtue Hall on March 6, and carried her to the Lord Mayor where she recanted her testimony to Fielding, stating, according to *The Inspector* No. 623 (March 9, 1753) "that she never should have so sworn, unless she had been so frighted." On March 9, Gascoyne examined Susannah Wells in Newgate, where she supported Hall's new story. On March 13, he again examined Hall and, convinced by her and Well's testimony, ordered the arrest of Elizabeth Canning for perjury. Hill in *The Inspector* No. 627 (March 14, 1753) reported on the examination of Wells, cited affidavits claiming Squires was in Dorchester at the time of Canning's abduction, and praised the consequent "Warrant for apprehending *Elizabeth Canning.*" He closed his essay by pointedly expropriating Fielding's phrase of choice for Canning and applying it to Squires: "Such is an Instance of Resolution and Perseverance, of Address and of Impartiality, in the Cause of injured Innocence, no Age or Country can produce; and the Glory is the greater, as the Object of it is one of the lowest that could be found among the human Species." Public opinion seemed to hang in the balance, and Fielding responded on March 20, 1753, with *A Clear State of the Case of Elizabeth Canning.*

Fielding's main ambition in *Elizabeth Canning* is to demonstrate that Canning's improbable tale could be true. It is, indeed, a tale so improbable that its remarkable circumstances and arguments (including eventually hosts of witnesses swearing that Squires either was or wasn't in Dorsetshire during the time of Canning's abduction) have been debated ever since, as a host of amateur sleuths and professional historians have attempted over the years to solve the mystery.[27] One of the central issues in these debates has been the role of the press in pursuing, presenting, and promoting the case. In *Elizabeth Canning,* Fielding shows a high sensitivity to this literary or media dimension when early on he attacks the practice of establishing "a kind of Court of Appeal . . . in the Bookseller's Shop, to re-examine in News Papers and Pamphlets the merits of Causes which, after a fair and legal tryal, have already received the solemn Determination of a Court of Judicature" and then defends his own addition to such literature: "when such methods have been used to mislead the Public, and to censure the Justice of the Nation in its Sagacity at least, and grossly to misrepresent their Proceedings, it can require little Apology to make use of the same means to refute so iniquitous an Attempt" (285–86).

Fielding's tactics here are essentially the same as those used in a Grub Street paper war: a renunciation of press attacks followed by a justification for attacking through the press. (In the first issue of *The Covent-Garden Journal,* it will be remembered, Fielding had renounced "Slander and Scurrillity" and incursions into the "Land of DULLNESS," only then to declare a "PAPER WAR between the Forces under Sir ALEXANDER DRAWCANSIR, and the Army of GRUBSTREET.") But more significant, it seems to me, is Fielding's recognition that Canning's narrative is a "strange, unaccountable, and scarce credible Story" (289), not only because the facts themselves are hard to believe, but because its circumstances and motifs call to mind so strongly the productions of a troubled imagination. As he notes, it is a "very extraordinary Narrative, consisting of many strange Particulars, resembling rather a wild Dream than a real Fact" (288). And, exacerbating the whole, because of its association with commercial media (newspapers, pamphlets, broadsides) and a group of literary producers traditionally characterized by fanciful invention if not downright insanity, the Canning story threatens to be mistaken itself for a Grub Street production: it is "a Story full of Variety of strange Incidents, and worthy the invention of some Writer of Romances, in many of which we find such kind of strange Improbabilities that are the Productions of a fertile, though commonly a distempered, Brain" (293–94).

But the story is so good that Fielding can't resist retelling it twice from Canning's point of view and once from Virtue Hall's. Part of the appeal of his pamphlet is that it is structured to allow the reader to register the story

as a whole, then to consider the major objections to the story and Fielding's answers to those objections, then (thus informed) to read the story
again in the transcription of Canning's "Information" sworn before Fielding, and finally to compare both versions with Virtue Hall's variation on
the same events. Unlike *A True State of the Case of Bosavern Penlez,* the first
half of which is taken up with the discussion of the history of riot acts and
the last half with various "Informations" on the events, in *Elizabeth Canning* the events themselves—bizarre, fascinating events, worthy of Grub
Street invention—are central.

That "Elizabeth Canning" (not the person but the phenomenon) was
in great part a media creation (and subject to the usual monetary and
generic imperatives) was widely recognized by writers about the case.
There was, in fact, a tacit (and sometimes explicit) admission that the case
was a perfect excuse for writing and publishing. *Canning's Magazine: or, a
review of the Whole Evidence that has been hitherto offered for, or against Elizabeth Canning, and Mary Squires* (July 1753)—itself a stereotypical Grub
Street production in the "compendium with appendices" mode—offers
a revealing overview of the controversy as a press phenomenon, beginning with its author's complaint in the Preface, "Still *more of Canning!*
Surely these Fellows, who have nothing else to live by but Scribbling,
think they have a Right to impose a Tax upon the Publick as often as
they want Money." But the author soon justifies the practice of "Maga-
zining" on the grounds of public curiosity, convenience, and economy:
"So extraordinary a Transaction has given Birth to very many extraordinary Productions; and among the Number of Readers, there may be
some, who . . . may have been too *indolent* to travel thro' all the curious
Pieces the Publick have been furnished with upon this Topick; while
there may be others, to whom the Perusal of every Thing that has been
wrote upon it would have afforded infinite Pleasure, which Satisfaction
they may have been deprived of, by Reason of the accumulated Expence."[28] *Canning's Magazine* (comprising not only a review of the major
issues, but an appendix containing reprints of various newspaper advertisements and announcements) promises to relieve "the Fatigue of the
one, and the Pocket of the other" all for a mere six pence. Indeed, it is a
real bargain, for "a candid Observer will immediately perceive, that there
is Matter enough, exclusive of both Extracts and Appendix, which, under
proper *Typographical* Management, might easily have been spun out to a
modern *Twelve-penny worth.*"

This acute media consciousness (right down to "*Typographical* Management") recurs in the magazine's centerpiece, an anti-Canningite letter that specifically connects Justice Fielding and his written defense of
Canning to the world of fiction, print, and profits. "[W]ho could be so

proper to undertake this arduous Task," the writer asks, "as their experienced Friend, who had already so faithfully served them, in his double Capacity of Advocate and Magistrate, HENRY FIELDING, Esq. But would (you will perhaps ask) the worshipful Author of those illustrious Histories, *Joseph Andrews, Tom Jones,* and the *more celebrated Amelia,* condescend to *take up his Pen in Defence of a poor silly Girl?*"[29] As the writer notes in mock admiration, indeed Fielding would, with both rhetorical and material success:

> We have now gone through this Performance of Mr. *Fielding's,* nor did it in the least disappoint the warmest Expectations of those who interested themselves in its success: It *passed to a second Edition* in a few Days: the Wavering were confirmed, Apostates reclaimed, new Proselites gained, and *Subscriptions* were renewed, all the Parties concerned were satisfied, the Author applauded, his Employers pleased, and his Bookseller profited.[30]

Here Fielding, as justice and author, is placed (with a sneer) at the apex of commercial literary success: a quick second edition, public approbation, employer satisfaction, and profits for the bookseller.

On the pro-Canning side of the issue, similar tactics were employed. The anti-Hill pamphlet, *The Account of Canning and Squires fairly ballanc'd* by "a disinterested By-stander" (May 1753), criticized Hill's slipshod literary practice as a mockery of juridical procedure, abhorring the "Hurry he was in to pronounce his own Judgment of the whole Case (so contrary to that of the Law) and to publish it in common News-papers" and attacking on legal grounds Hill's version of the Lord Mayor's question to Virtue Hall— "whether what she had sworn the Night before were true, or whether what she had alledged upon Trial were so"—as

> a Mistake of the Terms of Art (too common in our News-papers) because every one knows, what he calls *alledged,* must have been *sworn,* upon the Trial: And, so ignorant was I, as to doubt, whether any Magistrate would administer an Oath to her, to swear the same Thing was white, which she before had sworn was black, (thereby permitting an unhappy Wretch to incur the dreadful Guilt of certain Perjury on the one Side or the other).[31]

Despite the writer's happy assumption, it is doubtful that "every one" would have been able to point out such acute distinctions between the usage of the newspapers and the usage of the law. That this writer could, makes me suspicious that he was trained not only in journalism but in law; or that, at least, he had a legal adviser, perhaps Fielding himself. A potentially revealing moment occurs when the writer addresses Hill's implication that Fielding suborned Hall:

If this be true, all honest Men will agree, that the sooner it is made *appear,* the better. I will not suppose any Magistrate to be justly suspected of so wicked and barefaced a Subornation. If the sagacious *Inspector* has discovered any such Criminal, 'tis hoped, his professed Zeal for Justice will make him as industrious to detect the guilty Person, how high soever his Quality or Station may be, as his Humanity has made him solicitous to defend some of the *lowest* and most contemptible of the *human Species* (even a notorious Bawd, and a vagabond Gypsey!) whom he supposeth innocent.[32]

The indignation here seems very real, as does the rather bitter challenge to Hill to do his worst. Even the archaic form "supposeth" echoes Fielding's usage. This is not to contend that Fielding wrote the *Account*—the absurd number of exclamation points alone make that seem impossible—but that the *Account* was perhaps prepared from his notes to Hill's columns. The pamphlet is structured as a series of quotations from Hill followed by commentary by the author. Possibly Fielding marked up Hill's columns and passed the whole along to a mediating hand, who then extracted, expanded, and revised.[33] Certainly Fielding, who had already appeared in print in his role as justice and neglected to mention Hill at all, would not have wished to parse Hill's "news-paper" prose and logic under his own name. But he might have furnished notes to someone who would. In any case, the writer of the *Account* (or his informant) clearly had been paying close attention to Hill's columns long before March 1753, because his closing gambit is to wonder why Hill would interest "himself with so much Zeal, in the Vindication of Bards, Gipsies, and Fortune-tellers," and then to answer the question by discovering that in "the *Inspector,* No. 407, published on *Friday, June* 19, 1752," Hill had addressed the "*Power of Witchcraft*" and demonstrated "his intimate Acquaintance with such Mysteries of Iniquity."[34] Perhaps there were other writers who would have remembered Hill's columns from nine months earlier, but none who would have remembered them so well as the justice/author who was Hill's chief antagonist during that period.[35]

In calling Squires and Wells "the *lowest* and most contemptible of the *human species* (even a notorious Bawd, and a vagabond Gypsey)" and emphasizing the occult associations of "Gipsies, and Fortune-tellers," the writer of the *Account* repeats a common pro-Canning tactic: the construction of Squires as culturally and physically "other." By all accounts, Squires was remarkably grotesque: "long and meagre, her nose very large, her eyes very full and dark, her complexion remarkably swarthy, and her under-lip of a prodigious size."[36] To the public eye, she looked like a witch, an identification made graphically in prints such as *Behold the Dame, whose chiromatic Pow'r* . . . (c. April 1753; BMC 3212), which depicted the witch

Squires conjuring for Hill; and *A T(rue) Draught of ELIZ: CANNING* (c. May 1753; BMC 3211), which showed Squires in witch costume riding a broomstick.[37] The pamphlet *The Truth's found out at last* (April 1753), in fact, contained Squires's "confession" that she was a witch. Squires's allusiveness was twofold. In the Grub Street culture, Squires might have reminded readers of Smart's irreverent midwife, Mary Midnight, who was described as wearing "a high crown hat and otherwise accoutered like a piece of venerable antiquity" or Kenrick's three witches in *Fun,* who prophesied that Drawcansir would never fall until "against him rise a mighty *Hill.*"[38] In the more traditional popular culture, she would surely have suggested the hybridization of "midwives and witches" into "a legendary composite figure during the seventeenth and early eighteenth centuries . . . 'the cunning woman' or the 'wise woman.'"[39] Remarkably, after Elizabeth's disappearance, Canning's mother had consulted a "fortune teller" or "cunning man," who, it was reported, "gave the afflicted Parent the comfortable Assurance, that she would soon see her Daughter again, though she was then in the Keeping of an *old Black Woman.*"[40] All of these images contributed to the popular notion of the old gypsy Squires as composite witch, cunning midwife, and bawd.

More materially, Mary Squires was said to have been a seller of smuggled goods, an association that Malvin Zirker speculates may have evoked "memory of the brutal murders committed by smugglers in 1749."[41] Not only that, but her witch-like demeanor may have called to mind the costume worn by gangs of poachers and rioters "dressed in women's clothes, with high-crowned hats and blackened faces."[42] And, of course, she was routinely described as a "gypsy," a group not only socially despised, but subject to (rarely enforced) legal penalties since Elizabethan times.[43] By early 1753 England was in the early stages of what would become a xenophobic frenzy (with accompanying riots) over the passage of the Jewish Naturalization Act or "Jew Bill."[44] Jews and gypsies were linked in the popular consciousness, and the anti-Jewish sentiment generated by the Jew Bill spilled over into representations of the old gypsy woman: the pro-Canning print, *The Commite [sic] of Ald—m-n* (BMC 3210), for example, depicts Gascoyne and his fellow aldermen as both pro-gypsy and pro-Jewish.[45] As witch, smuggler, gypsy, and Jew-by-association, Mary Squires seemed the physical, racial, and occupational manifestation of everything socially chaotic, antiproperty, and non-English in England—as the writer for *The Gazetteer* put it, a person "*traditionally* and *hereditarily* versed in the antient *Egyptian* Cunning."

In *Elizabeth Canning,* Fielding quietly exploits these associations by routinely linking cultural otherness and nonhuman behavior, as when he remarks that "to a humane and truly sensible Mind such Actions appear to want an adequate Motive, yet to Wretches very little removed, either in Sensations and Understandings, from wild Beasts" a sufficient motive for kidnapping Canning "might be a Desire of increasing the Train of Gipsies or of Whores in the Family of Mother *Wells*" (290). Later he notes ironically, "That Street-robbers and Gipsies, who have scarce even the Appearance of Humanity, should be guilty of wanton Cruelty without a Motive, hath greatly staggered the World" (292). Toward the end of his argument, rising to crescendo, Fielding deploys language evoking all of the cultural differences between the racially suspect gang world of Squires and the simple English honesty and individuality of Canning: "I am at this Time, on this 15th Day of *March* 1753, as firmly persuaded as I am by any Fact in this World, the Truth of which depends solely on the Evidence of others, that *Mary Squires* the Gypsy Woman, IS GUILTY of the Robbery and Cruelty of which she stands convicted; that the *alibi* Defence is not only a false one, but a Falsehood very easy to be practised on all Occasions, where there are Gangs of People, as Gipsies, &c. that very foul and unjustifiable Practices have been used in this whole Affair since the Tryal; and that Elizabeth Canning is a poor, honest, innocent, simple Girl, and the most unhappy and most injured of all human Beings" (310–11). In this peroration, the clannish mutuality associated with the lower classes—clearly evident in the way Squires's friends gathered to testify on her behalf—is cast as wholly negative and associated with "Gangs of People" conspiring to construct false alibis.[46] Elizabeth Canning, on the other hand, is portrayed as standing alone and inviolate—"a poor, honest, innocent, simple Girl"—although we know that Canning's friends, too, gathered to support her and apprehend Squires and Wells. Although deriving from similar class positions, the homely girl with the suspect occupation is cast as a singular monument to virtue, while her alleged tormentor takes the role of the grotesque Other.

Such tactics epitomize the two major strategies of the paper war between the Canningites and the "Egyptians" (as Squires's supporters came to be called). The first, a quasi-legal tactic, was the point by point quotation and refutation of the opposition's story.[47] The second, a more fully Grubean tactic, was the attempt to paint the opposition as a fantastic, indeed almost fictional, conglomeration of deluded, deluding, or delusional subjects. Thus Fielding's overall battle plan in *Elizabeth Canning* is to emphasize Canning's "simplicity" and carefully to list and rebut all of the major difficulties of her story in an attempt to convince readers of her truthfulness. But punctuating this effort are intermittent admissions highlighting Fielding's acute awareness of the bizarrely "literary" dimension of her experience, most remarkably his admitting that it is "a Story full of Variety of strange Incidents, and worthy the invention of some Writer of

Romances, in many of which we find such kind of strange Improbabilities that are the Productions of a fertile, though commonly a distempered, Brain" (293–94). Presumably such admissions were intended to neutralize the growing imputations that Canning's story *was* in fact the fictional production of a distempered brain. But to no avail. For by this time, both Canning and Mary Squires had become fully fictionalized entities—"monsters"—in the Grub Street show: Squires the witch, the conjurer, the old woman, the gypsy, the Jew; Canning the deluded runaway, the sexually suspect virgin, the con woman, the tale-teller, and the exploiter (in the tradition of Mary Toft) of contemporary credulity. Two months after the appearance of Fielding's *Elizabeth Canning,* a stereotypical Grub Street exposé and instruction pamphlet, called *The Imposture Detected; or, the Mystery and Iniquity of Elizabeth Canning's Story, Displayed; wherein Principles are laid down, and a method established, by which all impostures whatsoever, still prevailing in the world, may be directed; and all future ones for ever prevented from establishing themselves hereafter,* made these associations specific.[48] It described the "rabbit-woman, the adventure of the quart-bottle, and the migration of the Londoners to the fields, occasioned by the soldiers prophesizing a third earthquake" as "recent and notorious instances" in a tradition of credulity to which Canning now contributes.[49] Like all these hoaxers, Canning not only tells fantastic tales, but is the matrix for the production of further stories and commentaries by believers, skeptics, and bystanders: stories transmitted to the public by a print industry already identified with fantasy, delusion, and feminized literary production.

III

Remarkably, the pervasive Grubean metaphor of literary birth achieved something like material form as Elizabeth Canning's sexual matrix was probed, interpreted, and written about by doctors seeking signs of pregnancy, venereal disease, or salivation treatment that might cast into doubt her virtue and perhaps even expose her as the prostitute she had so famously refused to become. Such readings of Canning's body predictably generated readings of a more popular variety, as physicians contributed pamphlets expressing their professional opinions on hotly debated questions about her physical and ethical condition.

The first of these pamphlets was Dr. James Dodd's *A Physical Account of the Case of Elizabeth Canning* (April 1753), which advanced physical evidence and medical precedents to explain how Canning subsisted so long on so little food and water and how she retained "*her Ability to Escape after her suppos'd ill Usage.*"[50] As the focus of his argument suggests, Dodd was not especially interested in addressing the question of possible pregnancy, but seemed quite concerned to convince his readers that he had closely examined Canning about her physical symptoms to expose any signs of dissimulation. Like Fielding, he found none.

In May, Dr. Daniel Cox weighed in with *An Appeal to the Public, in Behalf of Elizabeth Canning,* a pamphlet far more explicit than Dodd's in its reading of Canning's body. Cox had inspected Canning's mouth for marks of salivation treatment and found none. He had employed "Mrs. Francis Oakes, first midwife to the lying-in hospital in Brown-low Street" to "examine her alone by the several usual methods" (presumably vaginal examination) to determine if she had delivered a child, and Oakes declared "as her positive judgment and opinion, that Elizabeth Canning has never had a child."[51] (Interestingly, Henry Fielding was a Perpetual Governor of the Lying-In Hospital for Married Women in Brownlow Street, though this fact seems not to have been noted by the anti-Canningites.)[52] Then Cox himself examined her breasts and abdomen—a procedure to which Canning submitted with "much reluctance." Such examinations of a battered 18-year-old under suspicion of sexual misconduct were not only in themselves sensational, but perhaps also carried a residual literary allusiveness in relation to Canning's and Fielding's chief journalistic enemy, "Dr." John Hill. For only five months before, it will be remembered, Thornton, writing as the 18-year-old temptress "Priscilla Termagant," had invited "a certain gallant Doctor" (Hill) to inspect her: "I will prepare a most exquisite Muff for the Emolument of his Fingers; and I have so much Vanity to think he will pay me this Compliment,—*materium superabat Opus.*" It is at least possible that Cox's serious examination, intended to exonerate Canning, may have called to mind earlier sexual tropes and glib references to prostitution, midwifery, and medicine from the long-running paper war.

Although the pamphlets by Dodd and Cox were the first publications by medical men to address Canning's health, her physical condition had been the subject of intense interest and discussion almost from the moment of her arrival home. Summarizing prevailing descriptions and opinion, Fielding wrote that "her Limbs were all emaciated, and the Colour of her Skin turned black, so as to resemble a State of Mortification" (291); that she survived "unprecedented Sufferings, the visible Marks of which then appeared on her Body" and that she was "almost starved to Death" (295). Predictably, Hill attempted to erase these "Marks": "She left her Mother plump: this, Sir, is your Account, and this the Partridge-Phrase by which you express it. She returned emaciated and black; this was on the 29th of *January.* . . . Never were Transitions so quick, as have been those of this miraculous Girl; for she was not black upon this 1st of *February;* a Day or two made an amazing Change; for those who were present tell me, she was at that Time red and white like other People."[53] In conducting their examinations, Cox and Oakes—translating Fielding's and Hill's journalistic practice into medical procedure—seemed to be probing for the physical foundations of Canning's alleged discursive "hysteria."[54]

By May 1753, then, Elizabeth Canning had been examined inside and out; and although she had not given birth to a child, the question of her mental, physical, and ethical state had given birth to a prodigious litter of literary offspring. Indeed, the suspicion that Canning was a victim of traditionally female disorders—hysteria, delusion, pregnancy—may have enmeshed her character in an even more complexly articulated, but less immediately evident, cultural subtext than either the immediate Grubean analogies provided by the Fielding-Hill-Smart-Thornton battle or the more traditional fascination with tales of the occult and the weird. It is a subtext at the very foundation of Grub Street myth; and to sound its composition, we must listen to Canning's story again, with particular attention to the cultural significance of its topography.

At the beginning of almost all the reports, advertisements, and informations concerning Canning's kidnapping, we are told that on the day of her disappearance Canning was visiting her aunt and uncle at "*Saltpetre Bank, near Rosemary Lane.*" What did this mean to the eighteenth-century reader? John Treherne writes that it was an area directly to the east of the Tower of London "near Wells Close Square."[55] Pat Rogers identifies an eighteenth-century print of this area by Thomas Bowles called "High Change, or Rag Fair." It shows "the eastern part of Rosemary Lane near Wells Close Square." A watercolor by Rowlandson, called simply "The Rag Fair," shows the same area. Rogers comments that both "these views show a teeming, pullulating world full of sharpers and hucksters" selling cast-off and sometimes stolen clothes.[56] Besides being equated with Rag Fair, Rosemary Lane was consistently mentioned in contemporary accounts as one of the most sordid streets in London. In the seventeenth century it was listed as a center of prostitution, and in 1767 a list of the "dirtiest and meanest parts of the town" included "Grub Street, Golden Lane, Moor Lane, Fee Lane, Rag Fair or the Mint." Rogers notes that the "eighteenth-century idea of the place is well-conveyed in an account which mentions 'lawless Petticoat Lane and Rosemary Lane,' where 'thieves run from side to side eluding officers.'"[57] And he concludes that "Rag Fair, a place infamous for crime, prostitution, poverty, and second-hand trading, makes an exact emblem for Pope's artistic point." Pope's artistic point, of course, is found in *The Dunciad Variorum:*

Where wave the tatter'd ensigns of Rag-Fair,
A yawning ruin hangs and nods in air;
Keen, hollow winds howl thro' the bleak recess,

> Emblem of Music caus'd by Emptiness:
> Here in one bed two shiv'ring sisters lye,
> The cave of Poverty and Poetry.
> This, the Great Mother dearer held than all
> The clubs of Quidnunc's, or her own Guild-hall (I. 27–34)[58]

Rosemary Lane is the site of Rag Fair, and Rag Fair is home of Dulness, Goddess of hack writing. Elizabeth Canning begins her journey into history from a street that would immediately have been recognized by all Londoners as a site associated with crime and poverty, and by literate Londoners as Pope's symbolic site of bad or mad literature.

And where did Canning go from there? After being walked partway home by her aunt and uncle, she proceeded alone up Houndsditch Street to Moorfields near Bethlehem Gate, on her way to her mother's house in Aldermanbury Postern.[59] That is, she followed the exact route of Pope's imagination when in *The Dunciad in Four Books* (1743) he moved the Cave of Poverty and Poetry from Rag Fair to a new site:

> Close to those walls where Folly holds her throne,
> And laughs to think Monroe would take her down,
> Where o'er the gates, by his fam'd father's hand
> Great Cibber's brazen, brainless brothers stand;
> One Cell there is, conceal'ed from vulgar eye,
> The Cave of Poverty and Poetry. (I. 29–34)

In short, Canning walked from the first site of the Cave of Poverty and Poetry to the second, where she "was seized by two Men" "opposite *Bethlehem-gate* in *Moorfields*" who "violently" dragged her up into the Gravel-walk that leads down to the Gate of *Bethlehem* Hospital."[60] There, near the gate upon which reclined Caius Gabriel Cibber's massive statues of Dementia and Mania, she received "a very violent Blow upon the right Temple, which threw her into a Fit, and deprived her of her Senses (which Fits she, this Informant, said she is accustomed and subject to upon being frighted, and that they often continue for six or seven Hours)." By any standard, this is an extraordinary combination of literary symbolism and alleged events. Of course, the association of Moorfields and Bedlam with all manner of mad behavior and mad literature is well-known; and Pat Rogers points out that the railings of Bedlam themselves were often used to display cheap publications "hung up like washing."[61] But it may be useful to emphasize once again the proximity of these sites to the central symbolic locale of all commercial literary production, Grub Street, which intersected Posterne Street about 200 yards west of Bedlam and was thus commonly associated in Augustan satire with the madness of the neighboring institution. Had Elizabeth Canning made it to her mother's house that fateful night (as she did several weeks later), she would have a been in Aldermanbury Postern, a small street less than 50 yards from the intersection of Grub Street and Posterne Street. In other words, Elizabeth Canning lived in, walked through, was attacked at, and eventually returned to the symbolic matrix of urban madness and fantastic literature.

A metaphorical reading of Elizabeth Canning's physical experience and media impact in many ways replicates the metaphorical conflation of physical, imaginative, and literary generation that pervades the first book of *The Dunciad*. At the threshold of the Cave of Poverty and Poetry, on New Year's Day, she is *seized,* has a *fit,* is *carried away,* eventually returning with a tale not only worthy, according to Fielding, "the invention of some Writer of Romances, in many of which we find such kind of strange Improbabilities that are the Productions of a fertile, though commonly a distempered, Brain" (293–94), but one that engenders scores of other works that, in Pope's words, "Escape in Monsters, and Amaze the Town" (I. 41). Further, Canning's story, raising questions about delusion, deception, and motivation, eventually becomes a matrix of imaginative production, a "Chaos dark and deep, / Where nameless Somethings in their causes sleep," where "hints, like spawn, scarce quick in embryo lie" and "newborn nonsense first is taught to cry" (I. 55–60). At the same time, Canning's body is literally being "read" for signs of pregnancy and profligacy.[62] The linkage of physical and literary reproduction in the person of Canning and the remarkable coincidence of the sites of her travail and the sites of the *Dunciad* suggest Dulness's "double-birthing ability": the generation of commercial writers and then, from their "fertile" imaginations, a proliferation of texts.[63] Moreover, although Canning herself—modest, sober, anal retentive—lacked the chaotic, occult qualities traditionally associated with the Magna Mater, her partners in notoriety, Mary Squires (gypsy woman and witch) and "Mother" Wells (proprietor of a "disorderly house") did share them. In the figure of Dulness, Pope had linked literary industry, traditional "female goddesses of disorder," and various "feminized" traits (delusion, deception, reproduction, chaos).[64] In the persons of Elizabeth Canning, Mary Squires, and Susannah Wells, this combination of tropes seems to achieve actualization. The symbolic bodies of Canning, Squires, and Wells are all pregnant with meaning and possessed of the power to engender popular literary production. Although Canning, Squires, and Wells do not themselves write, they, like Dulness, cause myriad others to scribble at full speed.

Yet despite these transgressive associations, Elizabeth Canning is crafted by Fielding as the bourgeois classical body. She is "modest, sober, honest, innocent, simple," impenetrable (she refuses to become a prostitute), and anal retentive (there was much discussion of her constipation, both before and after her captivity)—an almost statuesque individual standing firm against her accusers.[65] Squires and Wells, on the other hand, are grotesque, carnivalesque figures: "very foul," misshapen, loud, communal, alien. But, paradoxically, Canning as a servant girl is subject to all the suspicions of duplicity and lax sexuality popularly ascribed to her class (by no one more insistently than Fielding himself), as well as being directly accused of perjury and delusional tale-telling. Moreover, the geographical context of her ordeal (Rosemary Lane, Bedlam, Moorfields, Grub Street) puts her at ground zero in the Grubean impact zone. She seems, in effect, a closed classical body under suspicion of harboring a mind worthy of her alleged tormentors, a possibility Fielding seems to admit in his peroration, when he suddenly shifts from impassioned defense to sardonic resignation and somehow finds a means to endorse the ethical implications of Canning actually being the "Monster" her critics imagined: "In solemn Truth, so little desirous am I to be found in the right, that I shall not be in the least displeased to find myself mistaken. This indeed I ought, as a good Man, to wish may be the Case; since that this Country should have produced one great Monster of Iniquity, is a Reflection much less shocking than to consider the Nation to be arrived at such an alarming State of Profligacy, and our Laws and Government to lie in so languishing a Condition that a Gang of Wretches like these should dare form such an impudent Attempt to elude public Justice, nay rather to overbear it by the Force of associated Perjury in the Face of the whole World; and that this audacious Attempt should have had, at least, a very high Probability of succeeding" (311–12). Throughout *Elizabeth Canning,* Fielding had argued that Canning, because of her character, should be believed despite the logical improbabilities of her story. Here, at last, he admits that she may be something like the moral and journalistic equivalent of Pope's Grub Street "Monsters" that escape to "Amaze the Town"—and that one such "Monster of Iniquity" is better than a whole gang of them.

Although nowhere in the literature does there appear an overt equation of Canning and Dulness, nor a sneering reference to the fact that she had her "fit" at the very gates of Bedlam, the implication that Canning had much in common with mad writers is found everywhere, from Hill's reference to Canning as "that famous modern story-teller" ("modern" here, I would argue, is used both as a chronological and critical term) to the author of *The Imposture Detected's* opinion that Canning was a victim of her own delusions and had "long been persuaded of the truth of her own story."[66] Indeed, one critic attacked Fielding's statement that "every Fact that is not impossible to have happened at all, or to have happened in the Manner in which it is related, may be supported and ought to be believed" (291) by comparing Canning's story to a famous example of hack fiction: "According to his Way of Reasoning, the History of *Robinson Crusoe* would have had, to the full, as good a Title to Credit as the Story of *Elizabeth Canning*. Nay, even more Care seems to have been taken to preserve an Appearance of Probability in the former than in the later."[67] That Fielding was extremely sensitive to the satirical analogies implicit in the case seems evident in his repeated references to the story resembling a "wild dream" or "the invention of some Writer of Romances." Hill, in fact, was quick to turn this last statement against Fielding and to remind readers of the magistrate's Grub Street roots: "You say 'tis worthy of some Writer of Romances. I love to hear Men talk in Character: no one knows better how much Wit is necessary to the writing of such Books; and, to do Justice to your last performance, no Man has proved more fully, with how small a Share of it, they may be written."[68] The "last performance," of course, is *Amelia*. Thus does Fielding's favorite and most insulted fictional child join a simple servant girl as examples of the writer/justice's fond incompetence.

But Fielding had anticipated such attacks and tried to forestall them, not only by admitting the improbable nature of Canning's story and preemptively equating it with a romance, but by addressing the very nature of credulity itself. This impulse may have derived from Fielding's own strongly stated belief in the unbelievable—a credulity that may seem to sort oddly with his skills as a legal interrogator and sifter of evidence. But, as Zirker remarks, there "is really no doubt . . . about Fielding's belief in special providence."[69] About a year earlier he had produced *Examples of the Interposition of Providence in the Detection and Punishment of Murder,* a pamphlet designed especially for consumption by the lower orders and distributed to them gratis. In this compendium of exemplary episodes drawn from biblical and secular history, Fielding sought to demonstrate "the most unaccountable, indeed miraculous means, by which the most secret and cunning Murder's have often been detected."[70] The remarkable circumstances of Canning's confinement, near murder, and escape, in conjunction with her personal simplicity and innocent demeanor, may have predisposed Fielding to equate her improbable story with the improbable stories with which he had filled his little pamphlet—themselves precisely the kinds of miraculous stories upon which Grub Street production depended.

In *Elizabeth Canning,* his attempt to convince his readers that skepticism sometimes can be more dangerous than credulity results in a remarkable passage that seems once again to realize in a non-fictional mode the discourse of Grub Street myth:

In all cases, indeed, the Weight of Evidence ought to be strictly conformable to the Weight of Improbability; and when it is so, the wiser a Man is the sooner and easier he will believe. To say Truth, to judge well of this Conformity is what we truly call Sagacity, and requires the greatest Strength and Force of Understanding. He, who gives a hasty Belief to what is strange and improbable, is guilty of Rashness; but he is much more absurd, who declares that he will believe no such Fact on any Evidence whatever. The World are too much inclined to think that the Credulous is the only Fool; whereas, in truth, there is *another Fool* of a quite opposite character, who is much more difficult to deal with, less liable to the Dominion of Reason, and possessed of a Frailty more prejudicial to himself and often more detrimental to Mankind in general. (291–92)[71]

The diction, the sentiment, the contrapuntal phrasing—"the wiser a Man is the sooner and easier he will believe"; "to judge well of this Conformity is what we truly call Sagacity"; "The World are too much inclined to think that the Credulous is the only Fool"—eerily recalls Swift's remarkable exercise in Grubean logic in "A Digression on Madness": "In the Proportion that Credulity is a more peaceful Possession of the Mind than Curiosity; so far preferable is that Wisdom which converses about the Surface, to that pretended Philosophy which enters into the Depths of Things, and then comes gravely back with Information and Discoveries, that in the inside they are good for nothing."[72] I am not suggesting—as many anti-Canningites did—that Fielding was a fool among knaves, but that he seems in this case to have abandoned his innate skepticism and usual considerations of beauty, interest, and birth to defend a hardworking, homely maid-of-all-work against accusations and innuendoes deriving from a media "frenzy" with which she and her story were associated. Fielding's *A Clear State of the Case of Elizabeth Canning* not only draws on the deep stratum of symbolic discourse available in the myths of Grub Street, but reverses the traditional symbolic and usually feminized associations that denigrated romances, wild dreams, strange incidents, distempered brains, hysteria, and credulity, to argue in this special case that sometimes truth can replicate bad commercial fiction and that sometimes even maid servants will tell the truth. It is a rehabilitation of Grub Street techniques and motifs for a serious purpose—a rehabilitation Fielding would repeat at least once more in his life.

Given the conjunction of law and Grub Street fantasy that characterizes the Canning case, it seems symbolically fitting that the last indisputable portrait of Fielding to be executed during his lifetime should place him between the official world of Bow Street and the crazy world of Grub Street, facing his chief Grubean antagonist, John Hill, and framed by a virgin and a witch. The portrait appears in the print, *The Conjurors,* which was published on April 9, 1753, and advertised as being "Drawn from the Life by the Right Honourable the Lady Fa—K————————w" (plate 4.1).[73] It is, I think, a remarkable portrait: far more true to what we know of the subject than the magistrate in Marcellus Laroon's undated sketch, *Night Walkers before a Justice*, recently proposed by Battestin as a portrait of Fielding.[74] Moreover, the identity of that magistrate remains a matter of conjecture, while the Fielding in *The Conjurors* is indisputably Fielding. Despite the relatively crude execution of the etching, the faces of all three central figures—Fielding, Sir Crisp Gascoyne, and John Hill—accord remarkably well with their representations in other portraits. Fielding is shown in right profile, with features, a wig, and neckware that duplicate almost precisely those in Hogarth's famous left profile done eight years after Fielding's death (particularly if allowances are made for Hogarth's slight caricaturing of Fielding's nose). Some commentators feel that Hogarth depicted a younger Fielding, despite the fact that the age engraved on the frame of the portrait indicates that it represents Fielding in his last year.[75] But the evidence of *The Conjurors* would seem to prove the accuracy of Hogarth's memory of his friend in his last years and would seem as well to suggest that despite his illnesses, Fielding in 1753 still looked relatively young. He is gouty (as his wrapped legs reveal) and perhaps unsteady (is he leaning on his sword?), but he is not obese and his face does not have any of the indications of advanced age apparent in the red chalk drawing Battestin has also proposed as a portrait from about this time.[76] This is the Fielding we sense in the Canning case: weakened but still formidable, and in his early decline perhaps willing to accept the illogical in matters of both literature and law. A year later, in his final work, he would embrace even more fully the radical imaginative spontaneity associated with Grub Street, in a self-reflexive exercise produced primarily to secure a pension.

Plate 4.1 *The Conjurors* (1753) © copyright the British Museum

Chapter 5

Fielding's Tub

I

But to return to . . . England. Such an adaptation of Swift's hack's famous phrase might serve as the epigraph to Fielding's *The Journal of a Voyage to Lisbon,* not only because the departing traveler is repeatedly blown back to England's southern coast, or because during this pattern of incessant return his writing returns as incessantly to various aspects of English culture, but because the resulting narrative pattern seems as spontaneous, digressive, and associational as a stereotypical Grub Street performance and is accentuated by Fielding in allusions that vividly recall key images of Augustan antidunce satire.

Despite the sobering (and sometimes horrific) effects of disease and paralysis on his body and spirit, Fielding in the *Journal* seems incapable of sustained focus on his own plight, instead reacting to it as a kind of springboard for mental aerobatics that perhaps compensate for his physical immobility. And in opting for the freedom offered by imagination, Fielding seems at times to replicate the erratic, escapist flights of fancy ascribed to suffering hacks. Fielding's recognition that the *Journal* reconstituted the manic self-reflexivity traditionally ascribed to hack productions is notably manifested late in the *Journal* when he apologizes for allowing the epithet "pitiful" to distract him into a long digression on the food supplies, the captain's way of doing business, and the ambiguity of the word "pitiful " itself, in an episode preceded by his refusal to let bottles be stored in his cabin, which is itself preceded by a (mock?) proposal for the "hanging of all fishmongers within the bills of mortality" and a panegyric on the culinary virtues of john doree.[1] When Fielding returns to the point, his phrasing sums up (as it imitates Swift) one of the central tenets of the mythic Grub Street aesthetic:

But, to return from so long a digression to which the use of so improper an epithet gave occasion, and to which the novelty of the subject allured, I will make the reader amends by concisely telling him, that the captain poured forth such a torrent of abuse, that I very hastily, and very foolishly, resolved to quit the ship. (91)

We are close here to the rhetorical and epistemological world of *A Tale of a Tub*—a world occupied by a broken hack where the "novelty" of any subject can allure the mind into a maze of unpredictable associations. Yet, at the same time, Fielding's associational structure seems a manifestation in prose of a rehabilitated "reflexive process" style that would achieve something like genius in the mad poetry of Fielding's friend Kit Smart and in the comic and satirical poetry of the Nonsense Club, a group that formed around Fielding's journalistic enemy (and one of Smart's closest friends) Bonnell Thornton. One member of this group, Charles Churchill, would write in 1764:

> But to return—and this I hold,
> A secret worth its weight in gold
> To those who write, as I write now,
> Not to mind where they go, or how,
> Thro' ditch, thro' bog, o'er hedge and stile,
> Make it but worth the Reader's while . . .
>   But to return— . . . [2]

And so on for pages. Churchill's is a burlesque compositional strategy, but one with serious implications for literary history: by the time Churchill formulated it, the essential features—speed of composition, free association, humorous digression, self-reflexivity—had already achieved memorable expression in Laurence Sterne's *Tristram Shandy* (1759–62).[3] What I am suggesting is that this combination of characteristics also describes Fielding's narrative method (and, metaphorically, his wayward voyage) five years earlier in the *Journal*. As the ship is blown hither and yon down the southern coast, his mind scuds from subject to subject, caught up and redirected by each passing impulse. "Here I cannot pass by another observation" (34), "I now renewed a reflection" (37), "We will conclude this digression" (44), "But enough of this matter, of which I at first intended only to convey a hint" (63)—with these and other more subtle transitions, Fielding follows the unpredictable movement of his ideas in prose that structurally replicates, as it describes, his unpredictable voyage.

Such unpredictable mental trajectories inevitably lead to unpredictable combinations of ideas. Smart, for example, in *Jubilate Agno* (c. 1759) would construct an imaginative world in which, like Fielding rejoicing in the john doree, "Junia" might "rejoice with the Faber-Fish" and "Broil'd fish and honeycomb may be taken for the sacrament / *For the* GERMAN FLUTE *is an indirect—the common flute / good, bless the Lord Jesus* BENJAMIN HALLETT"[4]—a typically strange Smartian combination of fish, religion, and entertainment (Hallett was a child musician in Smart's Old Woman's Oratory) that finds a remarkable antecedent in the *Journal* as Fielding free-associates from the john doree to an entrepreneurial venture in Covent Garden:

> Unfortunately for the fishmongers of London, the doree resides only in those seas; for could any of this company but convey one to the temple of luxury under the Piazza, where Macklin the high priest daily serves up his rich offering to that goddess, great would be the reward of that fishmonger, in blessings poured down upon him from the goddess, as great would his merit be towards the high priest, who could never be thought to over-rate such valuable incense. (84)

Just as Smart's associational mania somehow linked fish with the sacrament and the sacrament with instruments and thus entertainment, so Fielding's extemporizing on the culinary luxuries of the doree reminds him of Macklin's "temple of luxury"—a Covent Garden establishment opened by the actor in March 1754 and advertised as "the most elegantly fitted up of any place of public entertainment in Europe"[5]—where Macklin *acted* (in both senses) as the maitre d' (or "high priest") serving up luxurious dinners (or, by implication, sacraments) to his paying guests. As Macklin's friend Fielding presumably would have known, this dining extravaganza was intended as the first phase of a larger plan to present "The British Inquisition"—a public lecture and debating society preceded by "a public ordinary every day at four o'clock, price three shillings"—the newest example of what Walpole would call the "new madness" for "Oratorys."[6] As a fledgling oratory and full-fledged eatery, the temple of luxury joined Smart's parodic Old Woman's Oratory, Henley's long-running Clare Market Oratory (already associated with butchers' shambles), and the venerable Robin Hood Society (which Macklin frequented) in a contra-Augustan economy of jumbled literary, theatrical, culinary, and performative innovation. Fielding's ludicrous imagery of religious sacrifice applied to the delivery and serving up of fish not only anticipates the transgressive combinations of Smart's seriously "mad" poem but recalls Augustan versions of duncean culinary/religious transformation—from Swift's hack's tale of Peter proclaiming bread to be as "*true, good, natural mutton as any in* Leadenhall *Market*" to Pope's vision of "a Priest succinct in amice white" (IV. 549) who turns "hares to Larks, and Pigeons into

Toads" (IV. 554).[7] The latter examples, however, are clearly satirical—if sometimes self-subverting—renditions of the Augustan nightmare of perceptual and genre confusion.[8] *Jubilate Agno* and Fielding's *Journal*, on the other hand, seem more like manifestations of the Augustan nightmare come to life: literary forms without clear or sustained satirical agendas in which the preferred mode of perception and composition is spontaneous and associational, creating bizarre hybrids of the sacred, the material, and the mundane.[9]

Fielding's playfulness with the john doree and in the spontaneous digressions that succeed it are representative examples of the ways the contemporary emphasis on literary spontaneity inform and structure the *Journal*. Recently, Tom Keymer has emphasized the "unsettling" or "uneasy" irony evident in episodes such as Fielding's proposal to hang "all fishmongers" or his praising public executions and the building of Blenheim as sensible acts of policy (to which he hopes his being granted a pension will be added). Keymer, in fact, has gone as far as to suggest of the *Journal* that a "uniquely noncommittal mode of irony unsettles the whole."[10] In what follows, I would like to examine the sources of that noncommittal irony and to propose that the unsettling or relativistic effects of the *Journal* are the pervasive byproduct of Fielding's compositional strategy—one that adapts the ricocheting trajectories of antidunce satire and reflexive process style to the production of an ostensibly "serious" work.

II

Certainly the *Journal* is, in the traditional formulation, a compendium of Fielding's "opinions about the traditions, laws, people, and customs of his own society."[11] And, just as certainly, it is a work peppered with ironies and contradictions: what Claude Rawson has called an "increased intensity of *oscillation* among [Fielding's] attitudes, which are no longer held together by the old poise and inclusiveness of view."[12] But there is another kind of "inclusiveness of view": the omnivorous, universalizing, "anti-encyclopedic" principle of heterogeneous combination so familiar to the Grub Street pseudo-genres: miscellanies, magazines (serious or parodic), doggerel, advertisers, and self-fixated extravaganzas written for "the Universal Improvement of Mankind" (not to mention Plans of a "Universal Register-Office" and various "mad" and satirical mid-century poems).[13] The inclusiveness of Fielding's *Journal* is of this second type: not poised and premeditated, but spontaneous and indiscriminate. It does indeed contain Fielding's opinions—but opinions delivered in a medium so redolent of "modern" indeterminacy and so pervaded with "dunce" tropes that the historical Fielding's rhetorical and psychological status seems elusive at best. In effect, Fielding's repeatedly aborted or misdirected voyage on the quite real *Queen of Portugal* becomes a material simulacrum for the discontinuous, digressive trajectory of his mind in the *Journal*—a trajectory he seems consciously to emphasize by invoking traditional Grub Street motifs. Ludicrously and sadly "hoisted" into the ship "by a chair lifted with pullies" (a late addition to Swift's "edifices in the air"?), no longer held down by the responsibilities of magistracy, and near death, the unencumbered "journalist" constructs a disconcertingly relativized vehicle to contain his wide-ranging, contradictory, and final thoughts on whatever comes to mind.

The *Journal* begins with a Dedication, Preface, and Introduction—the only work of entertainment by Fielding to boast such a proliferation of introductory matter.[14] Whether or not there is any consciously parodic intent in this literary delaying and padding tactic is difficult to ascertain, but only one day after Fielding is hoisted aboard the *Queen of Portugal* on June 26, 1754 (after four previous delays), Captain Veale arrives to announce a fifth delay and attempt to pad his fee, by dropping "several hints of the presents which had been made him for his cabin, of 20, 30, and 40 guineas . . . over and above the sum for which they had contracted" (24). Given that a similar if more deserved present, in the form of a pension, is just what Fielding has been requesting in his Introduction, a parallel pattern of importunity and delay is at least structurally apparent. In any case, after retrospectively describing the "disagreeable . . . confines of Wapping and Redriffe," Fielding begins to contemplate "the conveyance of goods and passengers from one place to another" and launches into his first burlesque digression on matters of real import to himself and his family, a paradox that seems to me to sum up the bewildering tone of the *Journal* as a whole:

> Now there is no such thing as any kind of knowledge contemptible in itself; and as the particular knowledge I here mean is entirely necessary to the well understanding and well enjoying this journal; and, lastly, as in this case the most ignorant will be those very readers whose amusement we chiefly consult, and to whom we wish to be supposed principally to write, we will here enter somewhat largely into the discussion of this matter; the rather, for that no antient or modern author (if we can trust the catalogue of Dr. Mead's library) hath ever undertaken it; but that it seems (in the stile of *Don Quixote*) a task reserved for my pen alone. (25)

Here, as Keymer notes, Fielding adopts "exactly the role mocked in his Preface"—the role of a travel writer "obsessed by trifles which have 'no other right of being remembered, than they had the honour of having happened to the author.'"[15] But more than that, the passage overthrows the

Augustan tradition of attacking "useless knowledge" and seems—in its insistence that a "particular knowledge" is "entirely necessary" to understand and enjoy the journal—to validate the archetypally "modern" obsession with the topical and immediate: an obsession famously represented by Swift's hack's "general maxim" that "whatever Reader desires to have a thorow Comprehension of an Author's Thoughts, cannot take a better Method, than by putting himself into the Circumstances and Postures of Life, that the Writer was in upon every important Passage as it flow'd from his Pen; For this will introduce a Parity and strict Correspondence of Idea's between the Reader and the Author."[16] Indeed, when Terence Bowers calls the *Journal* "self-centered, uninformative, and downright petty," he sounds remarkably like an Augustan describing negatively the chief characteristics of a dunce literary production.[17] That Fielding had such satirical precedents in mind seems evident in his prominent mention of "antient or modern" authors (a phrase sure to recall the Scriblerian enterprise), followed by the citation of Dr. Mead's library (the enormous collection of the great physician and virtuoso, who throughout his career was a major figure at Gresham College), and finally a wink to those in the audience who might still not have got it, in the self-aggrandizing reference to the fictitious chronicler of Quixote, Cid Hamet: an indication, perhaps, that Fielding's journal will also contain some tilting at windmills.[18]

And yet "the conveyance of goods and passengers" is also a subject quite central to Fielding's personal well-being (particularly because in his debilitated state he was often conveyed more like a "good" than a "passenger"). Moreover, it is a topic that had seriously engaged his thoughts when writing *A Plan of the Universal Register-Office,* where he proposed to offer information on "Conveniencies for Travelling in all Manners by Sea or Land. Ships, whither bound, and when depart, with the Terms for Passengers. Stage Coaches; the Inns they put up; the Days and Hours they depart and arrive at, with their Prices. . . . Likewise all Methods of conveying Goods, either by Land or Water Carriage; Companions for Post-Chaises, &c."[19] In the first edition of *Amelia,* it may be remembered, Mrs. Bennet, who "had seen something of this Matter in the Plan of the Register-Office," advised her husband to go there for a post-chaise, "where he found a Companion registered to go within a few Miles" of his destination (553).

Fielding, in short, had a serious material investment in the topic of his digression, but at the same time a literary investment in the traditionally satirical and entertaining connotations of both useless knowledge and universalizing discussions.[20] In the case of "conveyance" (as so often in the *Journal*), literary entertainment takes precedence, as Fielding imagines creating an opus "enquiring into the antiquity of travelling": "I flattered myself that the spirit of improving arts and sciences, and of advancing useful and substantial learning, which eminently distinguishes this age, and hath given rise to more speculative societies in Europe than I can at present recollect the names of; perhaps indeed than I or any other besides their very near neighbours ever heard mentioned, would assist in promoting so curious a work" (25). "A work!" he continues, that might even gain him membership in one of those unrecollected societies. Reveling in the vortex of anti-antiquarian satire, Fielding spirals onward, promising himself "the communication of such valuable manuscripts and records as they must be supposed to have collected from those obscure ages of antiquity" (25–26); and referencing the discovery of "a curious and learned member of the young society of antiquarians," a "young antiquarian, who from the most antient record in the world (tho' I don't find the society are at all agreed in this point) one long preceding the date of the earliest modern collections, either of books or butterflies" proves that Adam and Eve were the first travelers, because they "scarce settled in Paradise before they disliked their own home and became passengers to another place" (26). Philip Edwards, missing the elaborate invocation of anti-antiquarian/antivirtuoso themes, has read this passage as an example of Fielding's turning people "into myth": "Travel itself (in a remarkable passage) becomes a symbol for fallen humanity. He thought of including in his work a history of travel, until he heard of the discovery of a 'young antiquarian' that 'the first man was a traveller.' . . . This discovery greatly shortened his labours."[21] But of course Fielding has his tongue firmly in cheek here, in the tradition of antivirtuoso satirists from Pope right up to Colman and Thornton in *The Connoisseur* (1754–56), a position he makes completely evident in distinguishing between the historian (who "shews you how things are") and the antiquary (who "shews you how things were"): "The former receives the thanks of mankind, the latter of that valuable part, the virtuousi" (26). Although the notion that travel is a symbol of fallen humanity is an intriguing one, Fielding steeps it so thoroughly in anti-antiquarian imagery that any serious intention is rendered ambiguous at best.

Fielding has now written several pages without returning to his original and presumably serious topic. He has elaborately embellished and relativized his "history of travel" by framing it within the tradition of antivirtuoso and anticuriosity satire perfected by the Augustans, and he has done so in a digression that formally replicates the central characteristic of the "modern" style. Luckily, he has also finally made the distinction that will allow him to return to "conveyance"—"we shall pursue the historical method, and endeavour to shew by what means it [e.g., travel] is at present performed"—and, in fact, the succeeding catalogues of vehicles, goods, and conveyers are characterized by a new economy of imagery and sharpening of tone: a "stage-coachman . . . carries you how he

will, when he will, and whither he will, provided it be not much out of
the road; you have nothing to eat, or to drink, but what, and when, and
where he pleases" (28). But the residual tropes of mock-scholarship won't
go away, and they sometimes combine with "serious" indignation to produce the wry comprehensiveness often associated with Fielding's earlier
prose. Thus, as the digression on conveyance returns circularly to the present, Captain Veale, Fielding's current tormentor, is approached through a
kind of mock semantic analysis of all who affect that title: "he is called the
captain; a word of such various use and uncertain signification, that it
seems very difficult to fix any positive idea of it: if indeed there be any
general meaning which may comprehend all its different uses, that of the
head, or chief, of any body of men, seems to be most capable of this comprehension; for whether they be a company of soldiers, a crew of sailors,
or a gang of rogues, he who is at the head of them is always stiled the captain" (29). Here we apprehend fleetingly the poise, detachment, and inclusiveness of view so often absent in the disjunctive conjunctions of the
Journal.

Having established a narrative pattern in which present occurrences
spawn rambling digressions characterized by mixed topics and tonalities,
Fielding repeats it incessantly, although each recurrence varies in duration
and significance. The spectacle of the *Royal Anne* (31) inspires a digression
on the necessity of military ostentation (32); the placement of houses along
the Thames (33) sparks a bizarrely ambiguous rhapsody on (of all things)
recreational sailing (34); a nautical collision (35) provokes a lecture on why
sailors swear, which ends by referring the whole matter "to form a question in the Robin Hood society, or to be propounded for solution among
the aenigmas in the *Woman's Almanack* for the next year" (36); the rude-
ness of customs officers (36) "renewed a reflection, which I have oft seen
occasion to make" on the relation of power and degree (37), which segues
into a subsidiary digression on trade (38); the exorbitance of transporting
food from shore (41) provokes an angry tirade against those "who live on
the sea-shore" (42); another nautical collision (43) inspires a digression on
hierarchy (44), which ends with Fielding quite specifically identifying his
method: "We will conclude this digression with one general and short observation, which will, perhaps, set the whole matter in a clearer light than
the longest and most laboured harangue."[22] Until Fielding gets ashore at
Ryde—and thus into the abundant material provided by his misadventures
at Mrs. Francis's inn (48)—such digressions and general observations dom-
inate the text, occupying nearly twice as much space as specific descriptions of the voyage itself.

We know Fielding felt alone during much of his time on board ship
and that this loneliness provoked "the first serious thought which I ever

entertained of enrolling myself among voyage writers" (98). Indeed, he implies that the journal was specifically begun to provide a distraction from his "own thoughts." Not surprisingly, digressions seem to abound when Fielding is onboard and become less frequent when, on shore, he has new and provoking human beings to write about. The digressions, in effect, are Fielding's tub, but a tub intended to "divert" himself, rather than "the wits of the present age." To a remarkable degree, they do seem to chart with minimal mediation (and seemingly no revision) his spontaneous mental processes. But it is important to remember that the adoption of such a compositional strategy was itself a self-conscious decision in favor of the reflexive process mode. In 1754, the young William Cowper, a Nonsense Club member, would write to Robert Lloyd:

> Sure so much labour, so much toil,
> Bespeak at least a stubborn soil:
> Theirs be the laurel-wreath decreed,
> Who write both well, and write full-speed!
> Who throw their Helicon about
> As freely as a conduit spout![23]

And Lloyd himself, in an epistle to Churchill, would choose to focus on "simple thoughts," "just as they rise from head or heart, / Not marshall'd by the herald Art."[24] In the *Journal's* most interesting digressions (more interesting, I think, than the political segments that traditionally have received the most critical attention), Fielding is impelled by spontaneous, self-conscious literary freedom into amusing and unpredictable associational trajectories.

Perhaps the most remarkable of these is the digression on recreational sailing that develops from Fielding's rather confusing observations about the placement of houses on the Thames shore (and the various ships that can be seen from those locales) into an emotional simulacrum of sailing itself. After denigrating both the houses and the taste of those who find pleasure in viewing small craft as "very mean and contemptible," Fielding suddenly tacks: "And here I cannot pass by another observation on the deplorable want of taste in our enjoyments, which we shew by almost totally neglecting the pursuit of what seems to me the highest degree of amusement: this is, the sailing ourselves in little vessels of our own, contrived only for our ease and accommodation, to which such situations of our villas, as I have recommended, would be so convenient and even necessary" (34). This amusement, Fielding admits, would be expensive, but "would fall very short of the prices which are daily paid of pleasures of a far inferior rate":

> The truth, I believe, is, that sailing in the manner I have just mentioned, is a pleasure rather unknown, or unthought of, than rejected by those who have experienced it; unless, perhaps, the apprehension of danger, or sea-sickness, may be supposed, by the timorous and delicate, to make too large deductions; insisting, that all their enjoyments shall come to them pure and unmixed, and being ever ready to cry out,
>
> —*Nocet empta dolore voluptas*
>
> This, however, was my present case; for the ease and lightness which I felt from my tapping, the gaiety of the morning, the pleasant sailing with wind and tide, and the many agreeable objects with which I was constantly entertained during the whole way, were all suppressed by the single consideration of my wife's pain. (34)

Whether or not Fielding knew the slightest thing about sailing, he seems in this passage to become momentarily caught up in the idea of such activity, finding in it "the highest degree of amusement," amusement that, it seems to me, comes to represent his own amusement in writing such a passage. As a kind of spontaneously occurring metaphor, "sailing ourselves in little vessels of our own, contrived only for our ease and accommodation" suggests not merely an imagined nautical activity, but Fielding's emotional and rhetorical elevation, especially as he rhapsodizes that it must be "a pleasure rather unknown, or unthought of, than rejected by those who have experienced it." But it is at precisely this moment that Fielding seems associatively to sail a point too close to the wind. For in seeking reasons people might not enjoy sailing, he discovers fear and seasickness, attempts to dismiss them as problems only for the "timorous and delicate" who insist that "all their enjoyments shall come to them pure and unmixed" and suddenly, in the midst of a quotation from Horace, finds his own little vessel overturned by the sad recognition that this is his "present case." Then, in a poignant act of self-consciousness, he reconstructs the stimuli that made him susceptible to the unmitigated, but momentary, pleasures of "sailing": "the ease and lightness which I felt from my tapping, the gaiety of the morning, the pleasant sailing with wind and tide, and the many agreeable objects with which I was constantly entertained during the whole way." Here, in retrospect, he and the ship are one: well-drained, light, easy, gay in the morning wind and tide—a set of characteristics he seems symbolically to have embodied in the "little vessels" he so enthusiastically imagined sailing.

The point of my analysis is that Fielding's digressions in the *Journal* call into serious question Battestin's categorical statement that "one of the most remarkable facts about the *Journal*—a fact perhaps symptomatic of the sobering effects of his years at Bow Street—is that it represents Fielding's repudiation of the pleasantries and indirections of mere literature."[25]

On the contrary, I would argue that the *Journal* is steeped in "the pleasantries and indirections of mere literature": pleasantries and indirections
incorporating, as early as the entry for the second day, a broad range of literary (and, more specifically, Augustan) fictions and techniques—burlesque
digression, anti-antiquarian satire, mock-scholarship, indeterminate
irony—and built upon the self-indulgent, reflexive process style that is itself in the process of aesthetic transformation from "duncean" to "progressive" at mid-century.[26] In Fielding's *Journal,* it seems to me, such
disjunctive conjunctions of mirth and misery, reportage and whimsy, official distance and personal engagement result in a work that far from ful-
filling the requirements of what Fielding calls "a true history of his own
times in humble prose" (a phrase Battestin uncritically accepts as representing "the reordering of Fielding's literary and intellectual values")[27] is
more like the culminating example of the imbrication of Bow Street and
Grub Street, of officialdom and entertainment, of fact and fiction, that is
the defining characteristic of Fielding's late literary production.

But as in much of the late literary production, the question of authorial intent remains murky. I am not proposing that Fielding, in the manner
of Swift, followed a consistent or conscious satirical program; nor do I believe that all the duncean characteristics of the *Journal* derive from Fielding's losing control of his material or his mind. My sense is that Fielding's
conscious decision to engage in a spontaneous, reflexive process of composition carried him into questionable ethical, critical, and emotional ter-
ritory. Sometimes he recognized and ironically emphasized his folly;
sometimes he didn't. At mid-century, we must remember, such unpremed-
itated "flow" of thought and attendant excesses were considered by many
professional writers to be the very soul of "genius." In 1763, William Kenrick would tellingly connect the ideas of genius, spontaneity, and "vagaries": "There is something so peculiar even in the extravagancies of true
genius, something so seductive in its wildest flights and vagaries, that the
fruits of its very dissipation are more esteemed by Readers of taste, than
the most elaborate lucubrations of plodding industry."[28] This, in effect, is a
positive restatement of the dunce aesthetic—and, it must be said, a convenient excuse for professional writers to write fast without thinking. It was
a paradox recognized and laughed at even by those who advocated such an
aesthetic. George Colman, whom Boswell called one of the "London Ge-
niuses," wrote satirically of the mid–eighteenth-century Genius: "he runs
round the whole circle of his pleasure. . . . Almost every man is an adept
in every art; acquires learning without study; improves good sense without
meditation; writes without reading; and, being full as well acquainted with
one thing as another, is unquestionably a GENIUS."[29] With some allowances for ironic intent, this description sounds rather like Fielding's

method in the *Journal*. He comments spontaneously, in varying tonalities, and in short order on (among other things) modern conveyances, the history of travel, antiquarian societies, military ostentation, recreational sailing, sailors' swearing, power and degree, trade, shore-folk, hierarchy, and, eventually, fishmongers, john doree, and Macklin's temple of luxury. In short, Fielding's authorial performance in the *Journal* enacts the mid-century theory of "spontaneous genius" that was then under development by his colleagues in the world of professional writing.

III

Given the lack of order and direction (besides bare chronological divisions) that characterizes the *Journal,* one has to sympathize with Fielding when, safe in Lisbon at last, he is forced to explain in a Preface just what he thought he'd been doing. In confronting what he had wrought, Fielding seems to have become aesthetically and generically disoriented. At first, he prudently attempts to aggrandize his own travel book by denigrating others. But in so doing, he equates good "voyage-writing" with "true history" and Homeric epic with "romance" to arrive at the bizarre conclusion that he "should have honoured and loved Homer more had he written a true history of his own times in humble prose, than those noble poems that have so justly collected the praise of all ages" (8)—precisely the kind of oxymoronic "dunce-narrator" comment one might expect in an Augustan parody. For if, as Fielding admits, Homer's *"noble* poems" have indeed *"justly* collected the praise of *all ages"* (my emphasis)—that is, completely fulfilled the grand desiderata of elevation and staying power that form the very core of Augustan humanist aesthetics—who but a dunce could desire that they had been exchanged for "a true history of his own times in humble prose"?

Fielding continues his ironically indeterminate but ostensibly anticlassical theme by attacking Pliny (and others) for not even "taking the pains to adapt their lies to human credulity." Such lies he compares to religious fallacies, only to raise against himself, as it were, the obvious objection that "whole nations have been firm believers in such most absurd suppositions," an objection he then answers bombastically: "I reply, the fact is not true. They have known nothing of the matter, and have believed they know not what. It is indeed, with me, no matter of doubt, but that the Pope and his clergy might teach any of those Christian heterodoxies, the tenets of which are the most diametrically opposite to their own; nay, all the doctrines of Zoroaster, Confucius, and Mahomet, not only with certain and immediate success, but without one catholick in a thousand knowing he had changed his religion" (9). How Fielding's demonstration that Catholics will believe anything answers the objection that "whole nations have been firm believers in such most absurd suppositions" is unclear and calls into question Fielding's intent in this passage has a whole. He had, we must remember, recently argued in *Elizabeth Canning* that "The World are too much inclined to think that the Credulous is the only Fool; whereas, in truth, there is *another Fool* of a quite opposite character . . . and possessed of a Frailty more prejudicial to himself and often more detrimental to Mankind in general." In the *Journal,* however, the credulous are once again despised, but in an anticlassical, tautological argument that rhetorically self-destructs.

Such egregious contradiction is likewise evident in Fielding's subsequent attack on the kind of author "to whom nothing seems trivial that in any manner happens to himself," which seemingly misses the fact that (as Keymer suggests) his *Journal* is shot through with trivia born of self-absorption. Or perhaps Fielding knows this is the case and is trying to mislead his audience. Or perhaps he is ironically separating from his narrator, as when Swift's hack proclaims in *his* Preface that it is "a great ease to my Conscience that I have writ so elaborate and useful a Discourse without one grain of Satyr intermixt"[30]—a sentiment echoed in the final defense of this whimsical, digressive journal of a trip through Fielding's brain:"One hint, however, I must give the kind reader; which is, that if he should be able to find no sort of amusement in the book, he will be pleased to remember the public utility which will arise from it" (11). Although great pains have been taken to argue that the *Journal* fulfills this pledge, such claims, it seems to me, radically distort the experience of reading the book.

I would suggest, on the contrary, that there is strong evidence that Fielding's tongue was even more firmly in his cheek than is usually recognized. For after making the claim to "public utility," Fielding backpedals rapidly into a remarkable series of tropes that evocatively locate the *Journal* within the richly self-conscious tradition of English parodic satire:

> But perhaps I may hear, from some critic of the most saturnine complexion, that my vanity must have made a horrid dupe of my judgment, if it hath flattered me with an expectation of having any thing here seen in a grave light, or of conveying any useful instruction to the public, or to their guardians. I answer with the great man [Addison], whom I just now quoted, that my purpose is to convey instruction in the vehicle of entertainment, and so to bring about at once, like the revolution in *The Rehearsal,* a perfect reformation of the laws relating to our maritime affairs: an undertaking, I will not say more modest, but surely more feasible, than that of reforming a whole people, by making use of a vehicular story, to wheel in among them worse manners than their own. (11)

The conventional conjunction of entertainment and instruction with which the Preface opened resurfaces here, but intricately metaphorized. After first worrying that the reader will find "no sort of amusement in this book" and offering in its place "public utility," Fielding now worries the reader will find no "useful instruction" in the book and hurriedly engages a "vehicle of entertainment" to "convey instruction" in the service of "revolution"—a travel metaphor followed by an image that recalls Swift's ship "mythologiz'd" to represent "Schemes of Religion and Government": "hollow, and dry, and empty, and noisy, and wooden, and given to Rotation."[31] In a sense, then, Fielding's literary vehicle is allusively conflated with the ship (the material conveyance) that inspires it: one conveys instruction as the other conveys Fielding—in the same desultory, unpredictable way. As if to emphasize the ironic quality of grandiose schemes of instruction, Fielding then shifts into the hyperbolic and universalizing mode: he will "bring about at once, like the revolution in *The Rehearsal,* a perfect reformation of the laws relating to maritime affairs." This absurd promise surely signals either deep skepticism or incredible naiveté about the entire "instruction" enterprise, but the "revolution" it references does more: it steeps instruction in the context of burlesque acting and burlesque acting in the context of absurdist literary parody. For the "revolution" Fielding touts is from the most famous "Mock-play" ever written, one intended to expose the pretentious idealism and bombast of heroic drama, and one that arguably had more influence on Fielding's own dramatic work than any other single piece of literature: Buckingham's *The Rehearsal.*

The "revolution" Fielding alludes to is the short-lived one carried out by the Physician and the Gentleman Usher when they momentarily occupy the thrones of the two Kings of Brentford. Fielding was particularly enamored of this scene, which, as he wrote in *The True Patriot* No. 16 (February 11–18, 1746), is "the most striking Ridicule of all worldly Greatness drawn from its Instability": "the Gentleman Usher and Physician dethrone the two Kings of *Brentford* by a Whisper. . . . These two Usurpers therefore, who are always personated by *two very ridiculous Actors,* having sat a little while in their Places, to the great Diversion of the Spectators, *sneak off* as comically and as absurdly as they enter'd."[32] This is not exactly the action one would choose as a serious model of "perfect reformation," but certainly one that emphasizes all the hyperbolic bluster of Fielding's promise. Fielding's succeeding hit at Richardson reactivates the conveyance metaphor, by parodying the epistolary novelist's reference to his own instructional vehicle.[33] But the parallelism of endeavor (and result?) implied by Fielding's description of the *Journal* as a "vehicle of entertainment" to "convey instruction" that will "bring about at once . . . a perfect reformation," and then laughing at Richardson's ambition "of reforming a whole people, by making use of a vehicular story, to wheel in among them worse manners than their own" has the same subversive effect as the allusion to *The Rehearsal:* both tropes emphasize the pretension, ambiguity, and ironic potential of all such schemes of literary and social reformation.[34]

The simultaneously bombastic and self-exposing spirit of *The Rehearsal* lingers in the *Journal* itself, as it seems to have lingered in Fielding's life. Not only was Fielding's dramatic work strongly influenced by the play, but more significantly for present purposes he took the name of *The Covent-Garden Journal's* persona from its blustering warrior, "Sir Alexander Drawcansir."[35] Drawcansir's burlesque swagger and mock military prowess seem the obvious reasons for this choice, but I would like to suggest one more. Sir Alexander Drawcansir is a drunk. "He that dares drink, and for that drink dares dye, / And, knowing this, dares yet drink on, am I" are his initial lines in the play.[36] The dying Fielding, though no longer a drunk, still loved his bottle. He was dying of multiple ailments, chief among them cirrhosis of the liver.[37] And despite a stomach swollen with fluid, unusable legs, emaciated flesh, he would "dare" to eat and drink prodigiously throughout his final voyage. Drawcansir's lines—hedonistic, defiant, self-satirizing, self-destructive—could serve as a motto for the *Journal* and for Fielding's life.[38] But, more importantly, they direct our attention to Fielding's daring, drinking, dying body—a body that embodies the contradictions of the text.

IV

The state of Fielding's body and its relation to his last discourse have become the focus of much recent critical discussion of the *Journal*. The verdict seems to be that his diseased body—in keeping with the conventional employment of the body politic metaphor in his earlier work—must symbolize the degenerating "social body" of England and thus stand as a personal simulacrum of the social ills Fielding intermittently rails against as he makes his digressive way along the southern coast of England. In the most sustained analysis of this kind, Terence Bowers writes:

> All the personal physical problems Fielding chronicles—vomiting, paralysis in the legs, and swelling of the stomach—are bodily transgressions that reflect social transgressions. In the same way that his head seems to have little control over his limbs, Fielding has little control over those below him on whom he depends to serve as his limbs. Thus, just as Fielding's paralyzed legs refuse to carry him, watermen and dock workers repeatedly refuse to carry him or fetch provisions. Servants and inn-keepers either ignore or disobey his commands, leaving Fielding without hands to perform basic tasks for

him. . . . More disturbingly, just as Fielding's swelling stomach recurrently threatens to burst, servants and a mob of sailors on different occasions verbally abuse him and threaten to explode into violence. All the bulges, protrusions, and disorders on and within Fielding's body represent a body politic that has itself lost all shape, form, and order.[39]

Abstracted from the shifting tonalities of the text as a whole, this is a compelling argument. But, put in context, most of these episodes (and other related ones) are more rhetorically complex and usually less sombre than the "bodily/social ills" model implies. Moreover, the conclusions and analogies generated by body politic model often fail to take into account the contradictory or supplemental patterns of body imagery within the *Journal* and, for that matter, Fielding's own contravening attitudes and practices outside of it.

The most memorable body image in the *Journal* must certainly be Fielding's belly: filling with quarts of fluid, being surgically tapped, filling again. This pattern begins in the Introduction and serves as a link to the voyage that follows. Fielding tells of being tapped three times (14 quarts, 13 quarts, and 10 quarts) before embarking, when he "had more urgent cause to press our departure, which was, that the dropsy, for which I had undergone three tappings, seemed to threaten me with a fourth discharge" (24). Bowers compares the swelling, rather impressionistically, to servants and sailors threatening to "explode into violence." Keymer suggests that Fielding "taps the poison away from the body of the state, even as he neglects his own; it is as though he acts, indeed, as some healing leech, who drains it into himself."[40] But both of these interpretations leave questions unresolved: if the lower classes are a belly ready to explode, what does tapping represent? if Fielding is tapping the "body of the state" and filling up with its poisons, where do the poisons go when he is tapped? As long as the body politic metaphor is restricted to images of disease, all swelling must be bad and all tapping symbolically meaningless.

If, however, we expand the metaphor to include a more positive notion of fullness or perhaps even repletion, it becomes evident that Fielding fills up with a great deal that is not the product of illness, venom, or disgust. In a sensitive assessment of the *Journal,* but one that unfortunately neglects its parodic and satirical elements, Albert Rivero writes that "Fielding struggles to 'glut' and 'feed' on the world around him, to incorporate what is outside into his body, to assert his own embodiment in the world as he approaches death."[41] Fielding fills up with food; he fills up his senses with the multiplicity of England; he fills up his loneliness with digressions; and he fills the pages of his *Journal* with all three. At Woolwich, the "ostentation" of the dry-docked *Royal Anne* represents "the flourishing state of our trade" (31); and, in a resonant phrase, "the King's body yacht" is celebrated as "unequalled in any country, for convenience as well as magnificence; both which are consulted in building and equipping her with the most exquisite art and workmanship" (32–33). In the catalogue of ships that follows, Fielding fills a paragraph with hierarchized and geographically symbolic vehicles that embody England's affluence and commercial health:

> We saw likewise several Indiamen just returned from their voyage. There are, I believe, the largest and finest vessels which are any where employed in commercial affairs. The collier's, likewise, which are very numerous, and even assemble in fleets, are ships of great bulk; and, if we descend to those used in the American, African, and European trades, and pass through those which visit our own coats, to the small craft that ply between Chatham and the Tower, the whole forms a most pleasing object to the eye, as well as highly warming to the heart of an Englishman, who has any degree of love for his country, or can recognize any effect of the patriot in his constitution. (33)

Here the bulk, variety, and richness of the ships take the form of a luxurious meal: "pleasing . . . to the eye," "warming to the heart," good for the "constitution." Passages like this, in which Fielding fills up with English goodness, recur: even the region that houses the odious Mrs. Francis is done "impartial justice" by being called "the most pleasant spot in the whole island" (68). In this locale, too, the paean to shipping recommences with the enthusiastic observation that "fleet of ships is . . . the noblest object which the art of man hath ever produced" (68), followed by a comparison of men of war to merchant-men that expands into a rhapsodic panorama ranging through the power and beauty of naval vessels to the abundance of industry and trade:

> [H]owever the ship of war may, in its bulk and equipment, exceed the honest merchant-man, I heartily wish there was no necessity for it; for tho' I must own the superior beauty of the object on one side, I am more pleased with the superior excellence of the idea, which I can raise in my mind on the other; while I reflect on the art and industry of mankind, engaged in the daily improvements of commerce, to the mutual benefit of all countries, and to the establishment and happiness of social life. (69)

The cultural repletion implied by the inclusiveness and sweep of the three parallel phrases charting "the art and industry of mankind" is an impressive example of Fielding's continuing ability to find satisfaction in the richness of English commercial strength and energy. It is a satisfaction that is echoed in his succeeding paean to the natural luxuriance of the English landscape, "apparent from its extraordinary verdure . . . which in the regularity of its plantation vies with the power of art, and in its wanton exuberancy exceeds it" (69). Indeed, what Fielding says of his physical condition may be said of the relationship between images of disease and repletion in the imaginative constitution of the *Journal:* the "distemper was not of the kind which entirely deprives us of appetite" (40).

In relation to the political and natural state of England, then, Fielding's swelling and shrinking body does not exclusively represent disorder and illness, but paradoxically also a kind of abundance and appetite. And although Bowers suggests "the bulges, protrusions, and disorders on and within Fielding's body represent a body politic that has itself lost all shape, form, and order," I would suggest that such bodily transformations more evocatively recall the difficult negotiations of luxury and labor that muddled Fielding's own relationship to the ethics of the class system. Indeed, in the eighteenth century such negotiations were often embodied in two metaphorical bodies: the "Somebody" and the "Nobody." As early as 1730, Fielding had written a song for *The Author's Farce* that characterized the latter as the potentially subversive nonconformist, the "Jolly Nobody," who frequents taverns and "does nothing at all / But eat and snore / And drink and roar / From whore to tavern / From tavern to whore."[42] The term "Nobody" specifically denoted the underfed, the underclass: a "Figure . . . all Head, Arms, Legs and Thighs" (i.e., no body). Conversely, the "Somebody" was the well-fed, well-heeled carcass, encased in expensive clothes, represented by Hogarth as a body without a head, and in Bonnell Thornton's Sign Painter's Exhibition as "a rosy Figure, with a little Head, and huge Body, whose Belly swags over, almost down to his Shoe-Buckles."[43] When Fielding wrote this song for *The Author's Farce,* he was himself a bit of a Nobody—a rakish, irreverent, ne'er-do-well playwright, accused by his enemies of being a "mad and drunken plagiarist."[44] Later, as a scribbling quasi-Somebody in *The Covent-Garden Journal,* he composed a humorous letter from "EVERY-BODY" that constructed the "Nobody" as something like an allegorical personification of sarcastic negation. Explaining his withdrawal from public affairs, Everybody writes that "I have long declined doing any Service to my Country, the Consequence of which is, that No-body takes upon him to regulate and reform all Manner of public Grievances and Nuisances." Fielding even references his own accusations (in the *Enquiry into the Causes of the Late Increase of Robbers)* of national misconduct in providing for the poor, accusations that cause Everybody to produce "a vast number of Schemes for redressing this Evil, when my old Antagonist began to put in his Claim, and all his Party cried out, that No-body was equal to the Task."[45] Nobody, in effect, acts as the rhetorical and figural equivalent of underclass or duncean irreverence: that combination of cynicism and *ressentiment* that disengages people from the system and, in Nietzche's phrase, preserves them "from harm through the exercise of imaginary vengeance."[46]

Yet the figural and cultural relationship between the two symbolic bodies, and their realization in eighteenth-century negotiations of class and status, are hardly as binary as these traditional descriptions imply. Indeed, the Somebody's and the Nobody's respective physical characteristics and class affiliations precisely reverse Bakhtin's well-known categories of the idealized "classical" body and the popular "grotesque" body. As Stallybrass and White point out, the "classical" body is, in a sense, "disembodied": elevated, static, with "no openings or orifices, . . . it appears indifferent to a body which is 'beautiful,' but which is taken for granted." Its locus is the reasoning head. The grotesque body, on the other hand, is "multiple, bulging, over- or under-sized, protuberant and incomplete. . . . It is an image of impure corporeal bulk with its orifices (mouth, flared nostrils, anus) yawning wide and its lowers regions (belly, legs, feet, buttocks and genitals) given priority over its upper regions (head, 'spirit,' reason)."[47] So the Nobody and the classical body emphasize the head at the expense of the body; and the Somebody and grotesque body emphasize the body at the expense of the head.[48] Here is ontological fluidity with a vengeance, a fluidity perhaps sensed by Bonnell Thornton when he titled the renditions in the Sign Painter's Exhibition "Somebody, alias Nobody" and "Nobody, alias Somebody."[49]

Fielding, as he is socially, physically, and rhetorically constructed in the *Journal,* is also a "Somebody, alias Nobody." A once-powerful magistrate, he finds himself powerless aboard ship. A once-striking physical specimen, he has lost the use of his legs, and his body swells and collapses in a rhythmic alternation of repletion and tapping. He is sick and emaciated, but constantly eating and drinking. He is a Somebody in decline and a living embodiment of the grotesque body—"bulging, over- or under-sized, protuberant and incomplete." Just as episodes detailing the indignities of the flesh debilitate Fielding's lingering sense of himself as gentleman and censor, so the irreverent tonalities and digressiveness of duncean style infect and deform grandiose pronouncements of ethical and social reformation.

In keeping with this pattern, the most sustained series of body references in the *Journal* appear in the Introduction when Fielding presents himself as a self-sacrificing magistrate of unprecedented honesty and effectiveness in order to grovel one last time for a favor to be conferred upon his family.[50] Fielding's determined campaign against street gangs and its nearly fatal consequences—fatigue, lameness, "a severe cold," "a jaundice, a dropsy, and an asthma" (12–14)—are presented as alternating focal points in an episode triggered by the highly unusual occurrence of "five different murders, all committed within the space of a week, by different gangs of

street robbers" (12). Aided by the Bow Street runners—"a set of thief-takers whom I had enlisted into the service, all men of known and approved
fidelity and intrepidity" (13)—and relentlessly carried to completion by a
badly ailing Fielding, the campaign is presented as a heroic endeavor, but
at the same time a chance to plead for interest: "an opportunity, as I apprehended, of gaining such merit in the eye of the public, that if my life
were the sacrifice to it, my friends might think they did a popular act in
putting my family at least beyond the reach of necessity, which I myself
began to despair of doing" (15). In this narrative, Fielding appears initially
as a powerful and effective public figure, deploying all the powers at his
command to "demolish the then reigning gangs, and to put the civil policy
into such order, that no such gangs should ever be able, for the future, to
form themselves into bodies, or at least to remain any time formidable to
the public" (13). Yet in the end he seems a pitiable and rather self-serving
spendthrift who, even though he worked himself to death, left his family
"very slenderly provided for" (15) and in need of public assistance.[51]

But this contrast is only the beginning. For having built his case for a
pension in an effective story of alternating heroic and pathetic detail,
Fielding suddenly recodes the pension as a salutary public "Example," and
inexplicably compares it to hanging a horse thief or building Blenheim:

> Example alone is the end of all public punishments and rewards. Laws never
> inflict disgrace in resentment, nor confer honour from gratitude. "For it is
> very hard, my lord," said a convicted felon at the bar of the late excellent
> Judge Burnet, "to hang a poor man for stealing a horse." "You are not to be
> hanged, Sir," answered my ever-honoured and beloved friend, "for stealing a
> horse, but you are to be hanged that horses may not be stolen." In like man-
> ner it might have been said to the late Duke of Marlborough, when the par-
> liament was so deservedly liberal to him, after the battle of Blenheim, 'You
> receive not these honours and bounties on account of a victory past, but that
> other victories may be obtained.' (16)

Whatever one may think of the theory that such "examples" encourage
public emulation, the practical effect of the passage is a ludicrously inap-
propriate conjuring up of the chaos of Tyburn (where the "example"
would be given) and the excesses of Blenheim Palace (that notorious architectural manifestation of "bounties") applied to a previously sober pe-
tition.[52] In the first chapter I suggested that Fielding's rhetorical and
behavioral inconsistencies were significantly affected by his simultaneous
interest in "what was true, what was right, and what would sell" and that
although exploitation from a position of authority was possible, "so was,
through an audience's recognition of this exploitation, a backlash that
transgressed the very authority Fielding sought to uphold." Fielding's

bizarre endorsement of Burnet's callousness and Parliament's excess seems a late example of this phenomenon, in that while presumably extolling the authority of both "courts," Fielding does so for self-interested reasons and in a rhetorical mode that seems to undercut the very pension-granting authority he seeks to validate. His rhetorical performance, in fact, seems to replicate the actions of Burnet and Parliament: the glib manipulation of authority exposing to ridicule the arbitrary behavior of those in power.

In crucial ways, this incongruous mixture of sobriety and irreverence anticipates the *Journal's* disturbing effect on contemporary readers. Thomas Edwards, for example, was amazed that Fielding "should trifle in that manner when immediate death was before his eyes."[53] And Arthur Murphy applied a most critically illuminating metaphor to Fielding's last performance, when he conjured up the very vision that Fielding himself had so often contemplated:"In his last sketch he puts us in mind of a person, under the sentence of death, jesting on the scaffold."[54] Although Murphy's image is meant only to point up the disturbing incongruity of tone and situation in the *Journal,* it should also remind us that, as Fielding well knew, last dying speeches often occurred in the context of carnivalesque celebrations verging into irreverent protest and sometimes even riot, while at the same time they became in printed form ("Tyburn's elegiac lays") part of Pope's "Grub-Street race": literary products sold and recited in the streets by men and women who, in Linebaugh's rich catalogue, "rubbed shoulders with bear-wards, buffoons, charlatans, clowns, acrobats, fencers, mountebanks, showmen, tumblers, puppeteers, quacks and rope-dancers, who in turn were part of an ancient urban culture of street-sellers of fruits, fish, vegetables, game, potions, medicines, drugs, toys, buttons, etc."[55] Perhaps at the jumbled crossroads where death, entertainment, commerce, and irreverence meet stands the critical signpost that will direct us to a better understanding of the contradictions of Fielding's last dying journal. Although laced with serious observations about his own and his nation's situation, the *Journal's* more pervasive impression on the reader is of a Grub Street Tub: a "floating," associational, omnivorous distraction from pain and dissolution; and, turned on end, an edifice in the air from which mountebanks, pitchmen, itinerant entertainers, cranks, scribbling magistrates, and those-about-to-die could indulge in often irreverent and not terribly effective harangues.

Conclusion

Appropriately, when Fielding at length "returns" rhetorically from the madcap digression on "pitiful" and then "very hastily and very foolishly" resolves to quit the ship, his former powers as a magistrate and man seem suddenly (and for the last time) to reconstitute themselves in a threat of legal action that brings Captain Veale to his knees:

> The most distant sound of law thus frightened a man, who had often, I am convinced, heard numbers of cannon roar round him with intrepidity. Nor did he sooner see the hoy approaching the vessel, than he ran down again into the cabin, and, his rage being perfectly subsided, he tumbled to his knees, and a little too abjectly implored for mercy.
>
> I did not suffer a brave man and an old man, to remain a moment in this posture; but I immediately forgave him. (91)

Here we find Fielding in a familiar posture, looking down in judgment on a supplicant, then graciously granting mercy. And like so many other of Fielding's "legal" judgments, this one too would find its way into print. But in this singular case, it is accompanied by Fielding's arch analysis of his own motivations:

> And here, that I may not be thought the sly trumpeter of my own praises, I do utterly disclaim all praise on the occasion. Neither did the greatness of my mind dictate, nor the force of my Christianity exact this forgiveness. To speak truth, I forgave him from a motive which would make men much more forgiving, if they were much wiser than they are; because it was convenient for me so to do. (91)

In this slightly cynical and eminently clear-eyed formulation may lie a key to understanding the man. "Convenience" has not been a usual heuristic in Fielding studies, but it is of some utility in attempting to understand his behavior in his last offices because its etymology and diverse allusiveness fairly canvass the range of human responses to ethical and emotional decision-making. Despite differing modern usage, a now obsolete meaning of "convenient" was "morally or ethically suitable or becoming," and it is this definition that seems to hover over Fielding's last judicial decision as he weighs its motivation and potential outcome.[1] When Fielding disclaims greatness of mind and religion as motives for forgiving Veale, he rejects precisely the ideals that so often confuse our evaluation of his performance in court, in business, and in print. In great part, he is to blame for such confusion, because as a "sly trumpeter" of his own praises (in the service of interest or sales or pleasure or reform) he himself invokes such ideals time and again to justify or aggrandize his practice. In admitting, in this case, that convenience was his foremost consideration, he humanizes his quasi-judicial judgment without attributing it wholly to self-serving expedience. In the end, he opts for what is "convenient" not only for himself, but for Captain Veale: that is, what is suitable or proper to the old man's trespass. In so doing, Fielding responds in completely human terms, unaided by the laws or transcendental concepts that elsewhere he cites only to ironize or contradict by his own less than transcendental practice.

Of course, this is not the definition of "convenient" that Fielding chiefly intends in this passage. What he does intend, with a slight smirk, is the predominant modern usage—"favorable to one's comfort, easy condition, or the saving of trouble"—and his implication seems to be that if men did not rigidly adhere to high-flown principles or theories they would be more forgiving because they would consult their own pleasure first. The divergence and convergence of convenient as "morally or ethically suitable" and as "favorable to one's comfort" seems to me to replicate the boundaries and intersections of Fielding's practice as they have been developed in this study. Remarkably, the last example of obsolete usage in the *Oxford English Dictionary* (and one that I would argue also slyly references modern usage) comes from Swift's send-up of religious and political bigotry in *Gulliver's Travels*—"And which is the convenient end seems, in my humble opinion, to be left to every man's conscience, or at least in the power of the first magistrate to determine." The magistrate here is placed in the same equivocal position in which we so often find Fielding: determining the "convenient" end in matters already corrupted by doctrine and interest and probably best left to individual conscience. Indeed, if the evidence of his last offices is any indicator, finding the "convenient" end seems to have been Fielding's predominant ethical imperative in his day-to-day interactions with human beings in all circumstances, public and private. This is not to say that Fielding did not make difficult decisions—decisions that sometimes worked against his own interest, health, and reputation, and sometimes against our sense of his own ethical or authorial fitness—but that convenience explains more immediately than, say, latitudinarian doctrine the crux of his everyday thinking in the venues and texts considered in this study.[2]

Again and again those critics who have looked at Fielding most dispassionately have found in him a tendency to consult his own convenience. Contextualizing Fielding's decisions as a playwright in the commercialized theatrical world of London, Hume sweeps away years of conjecture about shifting or conflicted political loyalties to write that the "plain dull truth is that Fielding was a freelance writer who peddled his plays wherever he could get them accepted."[3] Lockwood notes that the heroic conception of Fielding's "dignified, manly, uncomplaining" demeanor after being abruptly silenced by the Licensing Act is "the merest fancy," and argues instead that "Fielding, despite his long-lived reputation as an opposition wit who tormented Walpole upon the stage for years, in truth was a young writer who from the first had adopted or been willing to adopt Walpolean interest, according to the custom and convenience of patronage."[4] The convergence here of "interest" and "convenience" is rich in implication not only because it reminds us of Fielding's tendency to tolerate (and textually explore) corruption mediated by benevolence or exploitation mediated by sympathy, but also because it recalls the more practical intersections of institutional authority and literary transgression, commercial idealization and irreverent innuendo, professions of virtue and considerations of interest, which characterize his quotidian engagement with the changing circumstances of his life and times. It is the particular and unpredictable mixture of these elements that makes Fielding uniquely human—neither a flat construction of pronouncements about himself nor an (I had almost said, "convenient") embodiment of the dominant historical conditions of the period.

I have attempted to focus on Fielding's *practice:* what the texts of the last offices perform rather than what they say they are performing or what the most current theory of textual and cultural production insists we should find them performing. This method will stand in marked contrast to critical approaches to eighteenth-century literature that seem to equate on the basis of analogy various forms of written discourse while excluding or minimizing the role of the author. The theory that "the public sphere—the market in ideas, in literature—and the market constituted by commercial paper (both developing during this period) generate a mutually inflecting discursive field around the notion of 'fiction,'" for all its value in suggesting relations between various forms of paper credit, has been particularly abused in homogenizing generalizations that flatly assume the lack of individual motivation, human difference or, remarkably, human presence: "if texts are perceived as nodes of discourse, outworkings of a depersonalized market, then the 'author' of potential fiction cannot be identified, interrogated, held to account . . . the market disperses authorship as it does genre: fiction proliferates fiction to hide fictionality, palimpsest promises pile up against no visible originary Fund."[5] This might be called the "cash machine" version of literary history: no teller. Similarly, broad analogical syntheses constructed single-mindedly around, for example, the notion of the individual as a function of law—the "juridical subject"—have a tendency to exaggerate the centrality of legal relations in texts concerned far more intensely with the emotional politics of human interaction and its effect on the material condition of those who interact. Indeed, if Fielding's practice is any indication, even the overtly "legal" reportage and pamphleteering of the period must be seen as a hodge-podge of personal interests, ambiguous feelings, and mixed agendas masquerading as objective analysis. Certainly, law and commerce were developing cultural forms amenable to depersonalization, but, if anything, eighteenth-century commercial, legal, and literary relations were far more personal, practical, and messy than comparable institutional forms today.

Even at moments of existential crescendo, Fielding's vision, too, seems most often to turn to personal and practical rather than theoretical or transcendental matters. At the end of *The Journal of a Voyage to Lisbon* (that is to say, at the end of a work Fielding surely knew would be the last he ever wrote), the weary traveler is transported "to a kind of coffee-house, which is very pleasantly situated on the brow of a hill, about a mile from the city and hath a very fine prospect of the river Tajo from Lisbon to the sea" (107). There we are poised for the grand overview of the writer's life: his ideas on death, his feelings at the end of his final work. But what we get is dinner:

> Here we regaled ourselves with a good supper, for which we were as well charged, as if the bill had been made on the Bath road, between Newbury and London:
>
> And now we could joyfully say,
>
> > *Egressir optata Troes potiuntur aerena.*[6]
>
> Therefore in the words of Horace,
>
> > *—hic Finis chartaeque viaeque.*[7]

Fielding died in Lisbon on October 8, 1754.

Appendix I

Fielding's Bow Street Clientele,
January 3–November 24, 1752

The following tables contain a partial record of the clientele and cases to come before Henry Fielding in the Bow Street Magistrate's Office between January 3 and November 24, 1752. The Alpha table sorts persons alphabetically by surname. The Criminal Activity table sorts crimes alphabetically. The Stolen Property table focuses exclusively on crimes against property and sorts stolen items alphabetically.

In the Alpha table, I have included all persons who at least *possibly* appeared before Fielding. Because of the ambiguous phrasing employed by Brogden—"George Upton was committed to Clerkenwell Bridewell, for stealing several Pewter Pots the Property of Thomas Lucas" (February 17)—it is sometimes impossible to tell whether, in this case for example, the said Thomas Lucas actually appeared in court as an accuser or was merely named by a law officer as the victim. As Beattie notes, private prosecution played a crucial role in the administration of the criminal law: "the pursuit and apprehension of suspects, the gathering of evidence, and the preparation of cases . . . these matters were left largely to the private initiative of the victim" (35). Nevertheless, agents could and did act for victims, and I remain reluctant automatically to assume their presence in cases such as the one cited above. In all such ambiguous cases, I have included the victim's name in the table. I have also included the names of murder victims, although obviously the dead would not have physically appeared in court. I have not, however, listed persons whose names appear in secondary descriptions of legal or criminal events not under the jurisdiction of Fielding's court. Thus, for example, Mary Blandy's name will not be found in the table, although an incident from her trial is mentioned in the column of March 27.

Cross-referencing and certain problems engendered by it are exemplified by the cases of the two Mary Andersons appearing in the Alpha table. The Mary Anderson accused of theft is cross-referenced under "theft" in the Criminal Activity table and under "halfpence" in the Stolen Property table. It seems improbable that she is the Mary Anderson who is the victim/witness in a case of linen theft on May 11. The second Mary Anderson also appears in the Stolen Property table, bracketed (as a victim) after "linen." When hard evidence exists that multiple listings refer to the same person, I have simply indicated recurrent dates of appearance in the date column (e.g., the poisoner, Rachael Davis, in the Criminal Activity table).

Sometimes, however, even though it is evident that the reference is only to one person I have had to cite the same person twice for crime tabulation purposes. The double listing of Sarah Rock, for example, is based on my inability to prove she is the same woman, although the evidence points to that conclusion. Likewise, I am convinced that Mary "Brown" is a slip by Brogden for Mary Parkington, but again I have been forced by a lack of hard evidence to list both names. In the case of the Halwyn family, the only way to convey the reversal of positions described above was to list Catherine and Thomas Halwyn as being both accused of domestic violence and as being victims of it.

I have combined certain crime categories for easier sorting: "idle & disorderly" standardizes a number of different wordings used by Brogden; crimes described as "larceny" have been tabulated as "theft." The parenthetical inclusion of "pp" after a theft case indicates pickpocketing. Under "unrecorded" in the Alpha table, I have listed only those cases that included particularizing details (e.g., name, occupation, etc.). "Unrecorded" in the Crime table, however, includes all crimes reported.

Last name	First name	Activity	Additional Information	Age	Date
Adams	Ann	victim	washerwoman		2/17
Addis	Thomas	theft (pp)			8/07
Agnew	Bernard	forgery			1/06
Agnew Mrs.		victim			1/06
Ainsworth	Elizabeth	theft			1/20
Akers	Mary	victim			10/20
Albani	Christopher	victim			1/26
Alderidge	Judith	theft			3/20
Allen	John	defrauding			5/22
Allen	Alice	witness			4/24
Anderson	Alexander	embezzlement	hackney-coachman		2/21
Anderson	Mary	theft			10/27
Anderson	Mary	victim/witness			5/11
Anderton	Benjamin	victim			10/20
Andrews	Jeremiah	theft			1/03
Archer	Robert	bigamy			4/10
Arthur	Mr.	victim			3/27
Ash	Elizabeth	theft			10/13
Ashley	Thomas	perjury			2/21
Baitin	(Batin) Mary		theft	13	4/17
Baker	Robert	robberies/felonies			3/20
Baldwin	Lucey	theft			10/20

(continues)

Last name	First name	Activity	Additional Information	Age	Date
Banks	William	theft (pp)			3/06
Barber	Thomas	robberies/felonies			11/10
Barker	George	felonies			1/26
Barker	Jeremiah	receiving stolen goods			5/11
Barkerville	John	embezzlement	hackney-coachman		2/14
Barlow	John	theft			9/29
Basset	Elizabeth	victim			7/3
Bath	Mr.	policework	thief catcher		1/24
Baxter	Richard	murder			2/17
Baylis	William	theft		18	1/03
Beckett	Richard	robbery			2/07
Bedford	Sarah	victim			10/13
Bedwin	William	victim/witness			7/10
Beezley	Richard	burglary			11/24
Bennitt	John	theft	soldier		1/13
Benstead	Mary	idle & disorderly			1/26
Bentley	Henry	victim			5/22
Bertin	Mathieu	victim	Frenchman		3/30
Bewley	Elizabeth	victim		60	3/27
Bignal	James	vagabond			1/13
Bishop	Susannah	prostitution			8/21
Blackwell	James	victim			4/13
Blake	Mary	victim			4/10
Blasdale	Alexander	kidnapping	bailiff	(?)	3/30
Blasdale	Elling	victim			7/31
Blinkcoe	Mary	theft			6/15
Boldock	Joseph	victim			10/27
Bounk	Alexander Agustus	robbery			10/20
Bowden	Thomas	victim	clothier		5/11
Boyle	Lord	witness			5/11
Bradford	John	theft			6/01
Breach	Benjamin	burglary			6/19
Brooks	Anne	idle & disorderly			1/26
Brown	Susanna	idle & disorderly			1/26
Brown	Elizabeth	larceny			1/10
Brown	Anne	prostitution			8/21
Brown	Peter	victim			9/22
Brown	James	victim/witness			2/07
Brown	Mary	witness	servant		1/03
Brown Esq.	Mountefort	assault			5/11
Brown	Mary	prostitution	prostitute		1/24
Buchanan	Paul	felonies			1/17
Buchanan	Paul	receiving stolen books			11/03
Buchanan	Mary	theft			11/03

(continues)

Last name	First name	Activity	Additional Information	Age	Date
Buckhout	Martha	theft			7/31
Buddle	George	theft	hackney-coachman		1/10
Burton	Richard	theft			5/08
Butler	Judith	theft			3/20
Caister	Mr.	victim/witness			6/19
Callder	Robert	theft			6/15
Calverley	John	victim			10/13
Calvert	Francis	victim			10/06
Campbell	Judith	theft			4/24
Carey	George	victim	higgler		1/26; 4/06
Carlton	Judith	larceny			1/10
Carne	Mr.	policework	constable		1/10
Carne	Mr.	policework	constable		1/24
Carney	William	prison break out			4/3
Carr	Daniel	robberies/felonies			3/20
Carroll	Ann	theft			3/06
Carter	Martha	theft			7/03
Cawley	Mary	theft			11/17
Chandler	Anne	idle & disorderly			1/26
Chandler	John	victim	carpenter		3/23
Chapman	Sarah	theft			11/03
Child	John	burglaries/felonies			3/06
Child	Henry	theft			5/25
Church	Philip	keeping a bawdyhouse			1/24
Churchill	Colonel	witness			5/11
Clark	John	victim			9/29
Clarke	John	robbery/felonies			11/10
Clarke	William	theft (pp)			3/06
Clavering	Capt.	victim	soldier		1/10
Cole	Sarah	assault			6/01
Cole		theft			7/10
Cole	Mary	theft			7/10
Coleman	Stephen	riding upon dray	drayman		4/24
Coles	Mary	victim			10/13
Connor	David	theft			1/24
Cooper	David	embezzlement	labourer		1/13
Cooper	Christopher	victim			7/31
Cope	John	victim			2/10
Copeland	Mr.	judicial	magistrate		1/20
Cordwell	John	victim			10/13
Crane	Francis	assault			7/03
Cranford	Anna Maria	felonies			1/26
Curtis		threatening murder			4/17

(continues)

Last name	First name	Activity	Additional Information	Age	Date
Daily	Mary	victim/witness			1/17
Dakin	John	victim			3/20
Dale	Richard	rape			10/20
Daniel	Isaac	felonies			1/17
Darby	William	robbery/accessory			4/06
Darnell	Thomas	idle & disorderly			1/26
Davies	Matthew	theft (pp)			10/13
Davis	John	fraud			3/09
Davis	Rachael	poisoning			4/24, 27
Delaheus	Elizabeth	idle & disorderly			1/26
Dennis	Richard	victim	newsboy		11/24
Dingle	Ann	theft			3/06
Dobies	Monsieur	witness			3/30
Dodd	Edward	victim			9/15
Doharty	Matthew	theft			3/09
Dollison	Anne	theft			9/29
Drake	James	idle & disorderly			1/26
Duff	Sarah	receiving stolen money			11/03
Duncomb	Zachariah	theft (pp)			10/13
Dupie		theft	servant		5/25
Dupree	Anne	theft			7/31
Dust	Samuel	theft (pp)			10/27
Dust	Francis	theft (pp)			11/17
Emero	Christopher	theft (pp)			4/10
Emners	Christopher	theft (pp)			1/24
Errington	George	judicial	magistrate?		1/24
Errington	George	judicial	magistrate		6/19
Etch	Samuel	idle & disorderly			1/26
Evans	Joshua	idle & disorderly			1/26
Evans	John	theft			10/20
Evans	Joshua	victim	farmer		8/21
Eyres Esq.	Richard	victim			11/17
Fagen	Mary	theft (pp)			10/27
Falkner	Mary	witness			6/01
Farey	Samuel	victim			5/22
Favre	Priscilla	theft			8/07
Field	Mrs.	assault			6/08
Finch	Ann	theft			7/03
Finch	William	victim	hosier		6/12
Fisher	Anne	receiving stolen goods			1/24
Fitzer	John	victim	farmer		7/03
Flowers	Elizabeth	keeping a bawdyhouse prostitute			1/03
Flowers	Anne	theft			6/01
Forrester	David	victim			3/09

(continues)

Last name	First name	Activity	Additional Information	Age	Date
Fox	Ann	theft			10/27
Frances	Abigail	theft			7/10
Francis	Thomas	victim			2/07
Franklin		victim	printer		8/07
Franklyn	Job	vagabond			1/13
Frazer	Anne	theft			9/29
Freeman	William	idle & disorderly			1/26
Furness	Honor	theft			9/22
Gallant	Henry	victim			10/27
Gardiner	Elizabeth	victim			11/17
Garnidge	Mary	idle & disorderly			1/26
Garway	John	idle & disorderly			1/24
Gascoigne	Counselor	victim	barrister		6/19
Gerardini	Joseph	murder	Italian		1/26
Gibbon	George	idle & disorderly			1/26
Gibbons	Michael	victim			6/19
Gilbee	Mary	victim			9/22
Good	Thomas	victim			10/06
Goodburn	Mr.	victim			6/08
Goodey	Anne	felonies			1/26
Gooding	Mary	prostitution			8/21
Goodwin	Anne	theft			2/10
Gordon	Daniel Hugh	victim			4/10
Gordon Esq	Lockhart	victim			10/27
Gough	George	idle & disorderly			1/26
Grange	Margaret	victim			7/03
Gray	Joseph	victim			3/09
Grayham	George	burglary			4/13
Grear	Thomas	victim			10/20
Green		witness			2/17
Greensmith	Thomas	victim		18	4/24
Griffin	Margaret	theft			5/04
Groves	Bess	witness			6/01
Guilliam	Thomas	theft			4/27
Haines	William	idle & disorderly			1/26
Hains	Hannah	theft			1/26, 31
Haley	Jane	theft			3/20
Hall	William	felonies			3/09
Hall	Robert	swindling			4/20
Hall	Joseph	theft			3/09
Hall	James	theft			5/11
Hall	James	theft (pp)			3/09
Hall		uttering counterfeit money			1/24
Hall	Thomas	victim			11/10

(continues)

Last name	First name	Activity	Additional Information	Age	Date
Halwyn	Benjamin	domestic violence			1/24
Halwyn	Catherine	domestic violence	housewife		1/24
Halwyn	Catherine	victim	housewife		1/24
Halwyn	Samuel	domestic violence			1/24
Halwyn	Thomas	domestic violence			1/24
Halwyn	Thomas	victim			1/24
Hamilton	Mr.	witness			5/11
Hammond	James	returned from transportation			2/17
Hammond		victim			5/25
Harbins	Mary	theft			2/14
Harris	Henry	victim/witness			11/17
Harrison	Samuel	chance-medley carman		5/08	
Hart	Rebecca	theft			4/06
Hart	John	victim			6/01
Harvey	William	assisting breakout			4/03
Hatter	Diana	exposing body of an abortive child			9/29
Hawes	Isaac	theft (pp)			11/17
Hawkins	George	victim	salesman		9/22
Hayley	Jane	theft			3/20
Haynes	William	theft			6/01
Head Sir	Francis	victim			1/13
Heyerd	Thomas	cheating & defrauding			6/12
Hicleton	George	victim			7/10
Hide	Elizabeth	witness, wife of Edward Hide, turnspit at the King's Kitchen			2/17
Hill	John	victim	doctor/writer		5/11
Hill	John	witness	doctor/writer		1/10
Hilton	Mary	theft			6/08
Hinton	Jane	larceny			1/10
Hogg	Joseph	theft			7/31
Holland	Mary	theft			10/06
Holland	Mary	theft (pp)			8/07
Holland	Dorothy	victim			10/20
Holland	Henry	victim			11/24
Holmes	Thomas	idle & disorderly			1/26
Holmes	Mr.	victim			6/12
Holmes	Nathan	witness	porter		6/15
Holwell	Mr.	victim			1/20
Hook		murder & deerstealing			1/26
Humphreys	Elizabeth	victim			3/30
Incleton	Henry	theft			6/15
Ireland	Mary	theft			7/31

(continues)

Last name	First name	Activity	Additional Information	Age	Date
Jacobs	Benjamin	idle & disorderly			1/26
James	Thomas	robberies/felonies			11/10
James	Thomas	theft			11/03
Jarvis	William	victim			4/10
Jenkins	Henry	victim			6/19
Jessett	John	policework	constable		1/26
Johnson	Esther	theft	maid		5/04
Jolley	Samuel	theft			10/06
Jones	Simon	assaulting constable			1/26
Jones	Mary	theft			5/01
Jones	John	theft			8/21
Jones	Mary	theft			9/29
Jones	Mary	theft (pp)			3/06
Jones	Daniel	victim	merchant		1/03
Jones	Thomas	victim			2/14
Jones	Rice	victim			10/27
Kendall	Edward	idle & disorderly			1/26
King	Margaret	theft			10/13
King	Alice	victim			4/20
Kirby	Richard	victim			5/01
Kircham	Anne	theft			1/13
La Fortune	Antony	witness			1/26
Labrosse	Mr.	rape	coffeehouse keeper		1/24
Lacan	Mr.	witness	jeweler		1/26
Lake	Robert	theft			3/16
Lancaster	Elizabeth	idle & disorderly			1/26
Langenfilder	John	theft			10/27
Langston	John	theft			10/13
Laxton	Thomas	idle & disorderly			1/26
Lewis	John	theft			2/07
Lister	Penelope	theft			11/10
Llewin	Jane	witness			6/19
Lloyd	Anne	theft			6/01
Lloyd	William	victim			10/06
Lory	James	theft		16	5/29
Lucas	Thomas	victim			2/17
Lynch	Bridget	theft			2/17
Lyres	Edward	victim	linen-draper		4/17
Macculloh	Jane	domestic violence			4/27
Macculloh	Mary	domestic violence			4/27
Macculloh	Elizabeth	victim			4/27
Mackenzie		abusing & assaulting servant	master	6/19	
Macklin	Charles	victim			11/17

(continues)

Last name	First name	Activity	Additional Information	Age	Date
Mariston	Mary	uttering false coin			2/21
Marsh	John	perjury			1/24
Marshal	Thomas	victim			6/01
Marshall	Elizabeth	theft			4/24
Marshall	Martha	theft (pp)			3/02
Mascall	Mary	theft			3/20
Matthews	Sarah	victim		80	3/09
Meadows	John	burglary			6/19
Mears	Thomas	breaking the peace			1/17
Mears	James	victim			11/03
Meiers	William	idle & disorderly			1/24
Meredith	Margaret	victim			6/01
Merryfield	William	idle & disorderly			1/24
Miller	Samuel	victim			2/17
Miller	James	victim			5/15
Mills	Elizabeth	theft			5/01
Minett		victim	farmer		4/20
Mitchell	Thomas	robberies/felonies			11/24
Mooney	Joyce	theft			3/20
Moore	Patrick	domestic violence			5/4
Moresley	Isack	victim			10/13
Morris Esq.	John	victim			3/06
Mullier	Cicely	theft			4/17
Murphy	David	theft			2/17
Murphy	Arthur	theft			9/22
Murray	David	theft			6/15
Neal	William	theft			1/24
Neale	William	theft			1/13
Newman	Maria	theft	prostitute (?)		6/19
Newsom	Thomas	victim			2/17
Noble Rev.	William	victim			3/16
Norris	Sarah	prostitution			8/21
Norton	William	policework			6/05
Nowland	Patrick	victim			6/15
Oglevey	George	burglary			5/15
Orme	Richard	victim/witness			10/13
Osborne	Sarah	theft			7/03
Page	John	burglary	soldier		6/19
Pagget	William	victim			9/15
Pallin	William	victim			3/02
Panthen	Elizabeth	idle & disorderly			1/26
Parkington	Mary	prostitution	prostitute	16	1/24
Parnham	Mary	theft			11/10
Paterson	Samuel	victim			11/03
Payne	William	victim			3/09

(continues)

Last name	First name	Activity	Additional Information	Age	Date
Perry	William	victim/witness	waterman		6/15
Pierce	Judith	theft			4/20
Pierce	Mrs.	charity			5/01
Pierce	William	charity	baker		5/01, 04, 08, 11, 15, 18, 22
Pitt Esq.	George	victim			5/25
Plimpton	Richard	victim			3/09
Porter	Jane	victim			7/03
Pouch	Esther	receiving stolen goods			1/24
Powell	William	victim			11/17
Presser	Thomas	theft			3/09
Price	Margaret	theft			3/30
Priestman	Mark	idle & disorderly			1/26
Purser	John	defrauding			5/15
Quinn	Patrick	victim			10/27
Randall	William	theft			7/10
Read	Hannah	theft			9/22
Redman	Samuel	disorderly/mad			5/11
Redman	Samuel	charity	madman		2/10, 2/14
Revill	John	idle & disorderly			1/24
Reynolds	Thomas	victim			3/06
Richards	John	victim			9/29
Richardson	Mary	theft			9/29
Roberts	Philip	theft			4/10
Roberts	Elizabeth	theft			10/06
Roberts	Edward	victim	brewer		7/03
Roberts	Humphry	victim			9/29
Robinson	Barbara	theft			11/17
Robley	Nathan	victim			4/06
Rock	Sarah	theft			3/06
Rock	Sarah	theft		old	6/12
Rogers	Robert	theft			9/15
Rogers	Thomas	victim			5/08
Rolfe		murder			2/17
Rolte	Mr.	victim			1/24
Rompster	Mary	theft			2/21
Room	John	assault			11/24
Rose	Elizabeth	idle & disorderly			1/26
Rosse	John	theft			4/10
Row	Elizabeth	theft			5/08
Russel	John	theft			1/24
Sainsbury	John	victim			11/03

(continues)

Last name	First name	Activity	Additional Information	Age	Date
Salisbury	John	robbery	soldier		2/21
Sandford	Col.	victim	soldier		1/24
Sawler	John	idle & disorderly			1/24
Scott	Elizabeth	domestic violence			5/18
Scott	William	victim			5/08
Seers	Barnard	burglary			4/13
Sewell	Joseph	victim			4/13
Sheffield	Samuel	felonies			1/17
Shepherd	William	victim	brewer		1/13
Sheppard	Mary	victim			5/04
Simon	John	theft			10/20
Smith	John	idle & disorderly			1/24
Smith	John	rape/robbery			1/10
Smith	John	returned from transportation			4/17
Smith	Thomas	theft			10/06
Smith	William	theft			10/13
Smith	John	theft (pp)			3/02
Smith	William	policework	constable		1/26
Smith	Matthew	victim			3/09
Smith	David	victim/witness	sailor		3/30
Sneesby	Richard	theft			2/17
Spencer	John	victim			5/01
Squires	William	victim			3/02
Stagg	Jane	felony			5/29
Stamford	Richard	victim	mercer		3/20
Stevens	John	robbery/rape	ostler at the White Hart		3/30
Stewart	Mr.	witness			5/11
Stocker	John	theft			11/17
Stratford	Edward	victim			6/15
Studd	John	theft			8/21
Stuffs	Eleanor	idle & disorderly			1/26
Sturges		assault/attempted rape			5/04
Sundell	William	theft			5/11
Sutherwood	Samuel	cheating & defrauding	gambler		5/22
Swain	Arthur	victim			11/10
Swanson	Elizabeth	theft (pp)			11/17
Tate	Jane	rape			1/10
Tate	Jane	witness			1/10
Taylor	Francis	victim			1/03
Theed	Counsellor	victim			3/09
Thompson	William	theft			8/07
Thompson	John	victim	turnpike collector		2/21

(continues)

Last name	First name	Activity	Additional Information	Age	Date
Thrift	Mrs.	victim			6/08
Tittley	John	victim			3/06
Tomkyns	Packington	victim			6/01
Townshend Col.	George	victim			1/26
Tremman	Joseph	breaking the peace			8/07
Trequet	Stephen	victim			1/13
Turner	William	theft			4/17
Turner	Mary	theft			5/01
Turner	Edward	victim			4/27
unrecorded		acting	a Set of Apprentices		4/03
unrecorded		acting	Barbers Apprentices, Journeyman Staymakers, Maid-Servants, &c		4/13
unrecorded		assault		25	3/09
unrecorded		assault	2 labourers		7/31
unrecorded		assaulting a young gentlewoman	watchman of this Parish		3/02
unrecorded		attempted murder	woman in man's clothing		6/26, 7/10
unrecorded		breaking the chariot of noble carter			5/22
unrecorded		breaking the peace	bricklayer		3/02
unrecorded		domestic violence	Cook's shop keeper		2/10
unrecorded		domestic violence	Bewley niece	25	3/27
unrecorded		embezzlement	porter	old	10/13
unrecorded		enticing to murder	enticed woman in man's clothes to murder wife		6/26, 7/10
unrecorded		exercising trade on the Lord's Day	barber		5/18
unrecorded		exercising trade on the Lord's Day	barber		5/18
unrecorded		exercising trade on the Lord's Day	barber		5/18
unrecorded (30)		gaming	Apprentices, Journeymen and Gentle-mens Servants		6/19

(continues)

Last name	First name	Activity	Additional Information	Age	Date
unrecorded ("a great Number")		idle & disorderly	"taken at a Mob DRUM or ROUT"		5/01
unrecorded		idle & disorderly		17	5/08
unrecorded		idle & disorderly		20	5/08
unrecorded		idle & disorderly		14	5/08
unrecorded		idle & disorderly		>13	5/08
unrecorded		idle & disorderly		>13	5/08
unrecorded (5)		idle & disorderly	"notorious Vagabond Wenches"		6/26
unrecorded		insulting noble	servant		5/22
unrecorded		prostitution	bawdyhouse, backside of St. Clements	>17	1/10
unrecorded		prostitution	bawdyhouse, backside of St. Clements		1/10
unrecorded		prostitution	bawdyhouse, backside of St. Clements		1/10
unrecorded		prostitution	bawdyhouse, backside of St. Clements		1/10
unrecorded		prostitution	persons of ill fame		3/09
unrecorded (9)		prostitution	loose, idle, and disorderly Persons, and common Night-Walkers		11/10
unrecorded		rape	staymaker		5/15
unrecorded		sodomitical practices			8/21
unrecorded		theft	urchin	12	2/03
unrecorded		theft		10	7/10
unrecorded		theft	apprentice		8/14
unrecorded		theft		13	9/15
unrecorded		theft (pp)		13	4/03
unrecorded		unlawful assembly (acting)	apprentices & milliner		8/14
unrecorded		uttering counterfeit money	soldier of the guards		1/24
unrecorded		witness	Bewley niece's husband		3/27

(continues)

Last name	First name	Activity	Additional Information	Age	Date
unrecorded		victim assaulted by woman in man's clothes			6/26, 7/10
unrecorded		victim	silversmith		7/31
unrecorded		victim	nurse, Covent Garden workhouse		2/14
unrecorded		victim	secretary of war		3/23
unrecorded		victim	Bewley niece husband		3/27
unrecorded		victim	farmer		7/31
unrecorded		victim	tradesman		8/14
unrecorded		victim	oilman		9/15
unrecorded		victim	tradesman		10/13
unrecorded		victim	infant		6/05
unrecorded		witness	tailor (foreigner)		3/02
unrecorded		witness	apothecary's journeyman		4/24
unrecorded		witness	pawnbroker		6/05
Upton	George	theft			2/17
Utridge	John	victim			6/15
Vain	Charles	theft			7/03
Vale	William	victim	haberdasher		3/06
Valle	Gaspar	victim			1/20
Vaughan	Elizabeth	victim			11/17
Walker	Isaac	theft			11/10
Walker	Mrs.	victim	milliner		2/07
Walker	George	victim			8/07
Wallis	Peter	theft (pp)			11/17
Ward	Catharine	idle & disorderly			1/26
Ward	Edward	idle & disorderly			1/26
Warner	Thomas	theft, assault, robbery			3/23
Warren	Catharine	idle & disorderly			1/26
Watson	Francis	victim	linen-draper		3/06
Welch	Saunders	policework	constable		1/06, 24, 26; 4/03, 13; 5/01, 04, 08; 6/19
Welsh	Mary	theft			2/14
West	John	theft			8/21
White		murder & deerstealing			1/26
Wickham	Cath.	theft			5/11
Wilford	Thomas	murder of wife		17	5/25
Wilford	Sarah	victim			5/25

(continues)

Last name	First name	Activity	Additional Information	Age	Date
Williams	Mary	accessory to murder			2/17
Williams	Ralph	felonies			1/26
Williams	Anne	larceny			1/10
Williams	Mary	theft			9/1
Williams	John	victim			10/06
Willis	Rebecca	prostitution			8/21
Wilson	James	victim			10/13
Winterton	Thomas	victim			11/10
Wood	Elizabeth	theft (pp)			10/13
Wood	Joseph	victim			2/21
Worth	Mary	felonies			1/26
Yardley	Mary	theft			4/10
Young	William	victim	silversmith		5/15

Criminal Activity

Crime	Last name	First name	Additional Information	Age	Date
abusing & assaulting master	Mackenzie		servant		6/19
accessory to murder	Williams	Mary			2/17
acting unrecorded	a Set of Apprentices				4/03
acting unrecorded	Barbers Apprentices, Journeyman Staymakers, Maid-Servants, &c				4/13
acting (unlawful assembly)	unrecorded		Apprentices & milliner		8/14
assault	Brown Esq.	Mountefort			5/11
assault	Cole	Sarah			6/01
assault	Crane	Francis			7/03
assault	Field	Mrs.			6/08
assault	Room	John			11/24
assault	unrecorded			25	3/09
assault	unrecorded		2 labourers		7/31
assault/attempted rape	Sturges				5/04
assaulting a young gentlewoman	unrecorded		watchman of this Parish		3/02
assaulting constable	Jones	Simon			1/26
assisting breakout	Harvey	William			4/03
attempted murder	unrecorded		woman in man's clothing		6/26, 7/10
bigamy	Archer	Robert			4/10
breaking the chariot of noble	unrecorded		carter		5/22
breaking the peace	Mears	Thomas			1/17

(continues)

Crime	Last name	First name	Additional Information	Age	Date
breaking the peace	Tremman	Joseph			8/07
breaking the peace	unrecorded		bricklayer		3/02
burglaries/felonies	Child	John			3/06
burglary	Beezley	Richard			11/24
burglary	Breach	Benjamin			6/19
burglary	Grayham	George			4/13
burglary	Meadows	John			6/19
burglary	Oglevey	George			5/15
burglary	Page	John	soldier		6/19
burglary	Seers	Barnard			4/13
chance-medley	Harrison	Samuel	carman		5/08
cheating & defrauding	Heyerd	Thomas			6/12
cheating & defrauding	Sutherwood	Samuel	gambler		5/22
defrauding	Allen	John			5/22
defrauding	Purser	John			5/15
disorderly/mad	Redman	Samuel			5/11
domestic violence	Halwyn	Benjamin			1/24
domestic violence	Halwyn	Catherine	housewife		1/24
domestic violence	Halwyn	Samuel			1/24
domestic violence	Halwyn	Thomas			1/24
domestic violence	Macculloh	Jane			4/27
domestic violence	Macculloh	Mary			4/27
domestic violence	Moore	Patrick			5/4
domestic violence	unrecorded		Cook's shop keeper		2/10
domestic violence	unrecorded		Bewley niece	25	3/27
embezzlement	Anderson	Alexander	hackney-coachman		2/21
embezzlement	Barkerville	John	hackney-coachman		2/14
embezzlement	Cooper	David	labourer		1/13
embezzlement	unrecorded		porter	old	10/13
enticing to murder	unrecorded		enticed woman in men's clothes to murder wife		6/26, 7/10
exercising trade on the Lord's Day	unrecorded		barber		5/18
exercising trade on the Lord's Day	unrecorded		barber		5/18
exercising trade on the Lord's Day	unrecorded		barber		5/18
exposing body of an abortive child	Hatter	Diana			9/29
felonies	Barker	George			1/26

(continues)

Crime	Last name	First name	Additional Information	Age	Date
felonies	Buchanan	Paul			1/17
felonies	Cranford	Anna Maria			1/26
felonies	Daniel	Isaac			1/17
felonies	Goodey	Anne			1/26
felonies	Hall	William			3/09
felonies	Sheffield	Samuel			1/17
felonies	Williams	Ralph			1/26
felonies	Worth	Mary			1/26
felony	Stagg	Jane			5/29
forgery	Agnew	Bernard			1/6
fraud	Davis	John			3/09
gaming	unrecorded (30)		Apprentices, Journeymen and Gentle-men's Servants		6/19
idle & disorderly	Benstead	Mary			1/26
idle & disorderly	Brooks	Anne			1/26
idle & disorderly	Brown	Susanna			1/26
idle & disorderly	Chandler	Anne			1/26
idle & disorderly	Darnell	Thomas			1/26
idle & disorderly	Delaheus	Elizabeth			1/26
idle & disorderly	Drake	James			1/26
idle & disorderly	Etch	Samuel			1/26
idle & disorderly	Evans	Joshua			1/26
idle & disorderly	Freeman	William			1/26
idle & disorderly	Garnidge	Mary			1/26
idle & disorderly	Garway	John			1/24
idle & disorderly	Gibbon	George			1/26
idle & disorderly	Gough	George			1/26
idle & disorderly	Haines	William			1/26
idle & disorderly	Holmes	Thomas			1/26
idle & disorderly	Jacobs	Benjamin			1/26
idle & disorderly	Kendall	Edward			1/26
idle & disorderly	Lancaster	Elizabeth			1/26
idle & disorderly	Laxton	Thomas			1/26
idle & disorderly	Meiers	William			1/24
idle & disorderly	Merryfield	William			1/24
idle & disorderly	Panthen	Elizabeth			1/26
idle & disorderly	Priestman	Mark			1/26
idle & disorderly	Revill	John			1/24
idle & disorderly	Rose	Elizabeth			1/26
idle & disorderly	Sawler	John			1/24
idle & disorderly	Smith	John			1/24
idle & disorderly	Stuffs	Eleanor			1/26
idle & disorderly	Ward	Catherine			1/26

(continues)

Crime	Last name	First name	Additional Information	Age	Date
idle & disorderly	Ward	Edward			1/26
idle & disorderly	Warren	Catherine			1/26
idle & disorderly	unrecorded ("Upwards of Twenty")				1/31
idle & disorderly	unrecorded (30)				2/3
idle & disorderly	unrecorded ("a great Number of Persons")		"taken at a Mob DRUM or ROUT"		5/01
idle & disorderly	unrecorded			17	5/08
idle & disorderly	unrecorded			20	5/08
idle & disorderly	unrecorded			14	5/08
idle & disorderly	unrecorded			>13	5/08
idle & disorderly	unrecorded			>13	5/08
idle & disorderly	unrecorded (5)		"notorious Vagabond Wenches"		6/26
insulting noble	unrecorded		servant		5/22
keeping a bawdyhouse	Church	Philip			1/24
keeping a bawdyhouse	Flowers	Elizabeth	prostitute		1/03
kidnapping	Blasdale	Alexander	bailiff (?)		3/30
larceny	Brown	Elizabeth			1/10
larceny	Carlton	Judith			1/10
larceny	Hinton	Jane			1/10
larceny	Williams	Anne			1/10
murder	Baxter	Richard			2/17
murder	Gerardini	Joseph	Italian		1/26
murder	Rolfe				2/17
murder & deerstealing	Hook				1/26
murder & deerstealing	White				1/26
murder of wife	Wilford	Thomas		17	5/25
perjury	Ashley	Thomas			2/21
perjury	Marsh	John			1/24
poisoning	Davis	Rachael			4/24, 27
prison break out	Carney	William			4/3
prostitution	Bishop	Susannah			8/21
prostitution	Brown	Anne			8/21
prostitution	Brown	Mary	Mary Parkington?		1/24
prostitution	Gooding	Mary			8/21
prostitution	Norris	Sarah			8/21
prostitution	Parkington	Mary	prostitute	16	1/24
prostitution	unrecorded		bawdyhouse, backside of St. Clements	>17	1/10

(continues)

Crime	Last name	First name	Additional Information	Age	Date
prostitution	unrecorded		bawdyhouse, backside of St. Clements		1/10
prostitution	unrecorded		bawdyhouse, backside of St. Clements		1/10
prostitution	unrecorded		bawdyhouse, backside of St. Clements		1/10
prostitution	unrecorded		persons of ill fame		3/09
prostitution	unrecorded		loose, idle, and disorderly Persons, and common Night-Walkers		11/10
prostitution	Willis	Rebecca			8/21
rape	Dale	Richard			10/20
rape	Tate	Jane			1/10
rape	unrecorded		staymaker		5/15
rape	Labrosse	Mr.	coffeehouse keeper		1/24
rape/robbery	Smith	John			1/10
receiving stolen goods	Fisher	Anne			1/24
receiving stolen goods	Pouch	Esther			1/24
receiving stolen goods	Barker	Jeremiah			5/11
receiving stolen books	Buchanan	Paul			11/03
receiving stolen money	Duff	Sarah			11/03
returned from transportation	Hammond	James			2/17
returned from transportation	Smith	John			4/17
idling upon dray	Coleman	Stephen	drayman		4/24
robberies/felonies	Baker	Robert			3/20
robberies/felonies	Barber	Thomas			11/10
robberies/felonies	Carr	Daniel			3/20
robberies/felonies	James	Thomas			11/10
robberies/felonies	Mitchell	Thomas			11/24
robbery	Beckett	Richard			2/07
robbery	Bounk	Alexander Agustus			10/20
robbery	Salisbury	John	soldier		2/21
robbery/accessory	Darby	William			4/06
robbery/felonies	Clarke	John			11/10

(continues)

Crime	Last name	First name	Additional Information	Age	Date
robbery/rape	Stevens	John	ostler at the White Hart		3/30
sodomitical practices	unrecorded				8/21
swindling	Hall	Robert			4/20
theft	Ainsworth	Elizabeth			1/20
theft	Alderidge	Judith			3/20
theft	Anderson	Mary			10/27
theft	Andrews	Jeremiah			1/03
theft	Ash	Elizabeth			10/13
theft	Baitin (Batin)	Mary		13	4/17
theft	Baldwin	Lucey			10/20
theft	Barlow	John			9/29
theft	Baylis	William		18	1/03
theft	Bennitt	John	soldier		1/13
theft	Blinkcoe	Mary			6/15
theft	Bradford	John			6/01
theft	Buchanan	Mary			11/03
theft	Buckhout	Martha			7/31
theft	Buddle	George	hackney-coachman		1/10
theft	Burton	Richard			5/08
theft	Butler	Judith			3/20
theft	Callder	Robert			6/15
theft	Campbell	Judith			4/24
theft	Carroll	Ann			3/06
theft	Carter	Martha			7/03
theft	Cawley	Mary			11/17
theft	Chapman	Sarah			11/03
theft	Child	Henry			5/25
theft	Cole				7/10
theft	Cole	Mary			7/10
theft	Connor	David			1/24
theft	Dingle	Ann			3/06
theft	Doharty	Matthew			3/09
theft	Dollison	Anne			9/29
theft	Dupie		servant		5/25
theft	Dupree	Anne			7/31
theft	Evans	John			10/20
theft	Favre	Priscilla			8/07
theft	Finch	Ann			7/03
theft	Flowers	Anne			6/01
theft	Fox	Ann			10/27
theft	Frances	Abigail			7/10
theft	Frazer	Anne			9/29
theft	Furness	Honor			9/22

(continues)

Crime	Last name	First name	Additional Information	Age	Date
theft	Goodwin	Anne			2/10
theft	Griffin	Margaret			5/04
theft	Guilliam	Thomas			4/27
theft	Hains	Hannah			1/26, 31
theft	Haley	Jane			3/20
theft	Hall	Joseph			3/09
theft	Hall	James			5/11
theft	Harbins	Mary			2/14
theft	Hart	Rebecca			4/06
theft	Hayley	Jane			3/20
theft	Haynes	William			6/01
theft	Hilton	Mary			6/08
theft	Hogg	Joseph			7/31
theft	Holland	Mary			10/06
theft	Incleton	Henry			6/15
theft	Ireland	Mary			7/31
theft	James	Thomas			11/03
theft	Johnson	Esther	maid		5/04
theft	Jolley	Samuel			10/06
theft	Jones	Mary			5/01
theft	Jones	John			8/21
theft	Jones	Mary			9/29
theft	King	Margaret			10/13
theft	Kircham	Anne			1/13
theft	Lake	Robert			3/16
theft	Langenfilder	John			10/27
theft	Langston	John			10/13
theft	Lewis	John			2/07
theft	Lister	Penelope			11/10
theft	Lloyd	Anne			6/01
theft	Lory	James		16	5/29
theft	Lynch	Bridget			2/17
theft	Marshall	Elizabeth			4/24
theft	Mascall	Mary			3/20
theft	Mills	Elizabeth			5/01
theft	Mooney	Joyce			3/20
theft	Mullier	Cicely			4/17
theft	Murphy	David			2/17
theft	Murphy	Arthur			9/22
theft	Murray	David			6/15
theft	Neal	William			1/24
theft	Neale	William			1/13
theft	Newman	Maria	prostitute (?)		6/19
theft	Osborne	Sarah			7/03
theft	Parnham	Mary			11/10

(continues)

Crime	Last name	First name	Additional Information	Age	Date
theft	Pierce	Judith			4/20
theft	Presser	Thomas			3/09
theft	Price	Margaret			3/30
theft	Randall	William			7/10
theft	Read	Hannah			9/22
theft	Richardson	Mary			9/29
theft	Roberts	Philip			4/10
theft	Roberts	Elizabeth			10/06
theft	Robinson	Barbara			11/17
theft	Rock	Sarah			3/06
theft	Rock	Sarah		old	6/12
theft	Rogers	Robert			9/15
theft	Rompster	Mary			2/21
theft	Rosse	John			4/10
theft	Row	Elizabeth			5/08
theft	Russel	John			1/24
theft	Simon	John			10/20
theft	Smith	Thomas			10/06
theft	Smith	William			10/13
theft	Sneesby	Richard			2/17
theft	Stocker	John			11/17
theft	Studd	John			8/21
theft	Sundell	William			5/11
theft	Thompson	William			8/07
theft	Turner	William			4/17
theft	Turner	Mary			5/01
theft	unrecorded		urchin	12	2/03
theft	unrecorded			10	7/10
theft	unrecorded		apprentice		8/14
theft	unrecorded			13	9/15
theft	Upton	George			2/17
theft	Vain	Charles			7/03
theft	Walker	Isaac			11/10
theft	Welsh	Mary			2/14
theft	West	John			8/21
theft	Wickham	Cath.			5/11
theft	Williams	Mary			9/15
theft	Yardley	Mary			4/10
theft (pp)	Addis	Thomas			8/07
theft (pp)	Banks	William			3/06
theft (pp)	Clarke	William			3/06
theft (pp)	Davies	Matthew			10/13
theft (pp)	Duncomb	Zachariah			10/13
theft (pp)	Dust	Samuel			10/27
theft (pp)	Dust	Francis			11/17

(continues)

Crime	Last name	First name	Additional Information	Age	Date
theft (pp)	Emero	Christopher			4/10
theft (pp)	Emners	Christopher			1/24
theft (pp)	Fagen	Mary			10/27
theft (pp)	Hall	James			3/09
theft (pp)	Hawes	Isaac			11/17
theft (pp)	Holland	Mary			8/07
theft (pp)	Jones	Mary			3/06
theft (pp)	Marshall	Martha			3/02
theft (pp)	Smith	John			3/02
theft (pp)	Swanson	Elizabeth			11/17
theft (pp)	unrecorded			13	4/03
theft (pp)	Wallis	Peter			11/17
theft (pp)	Wood	Elizabeth			10/13
theft, assault, robbery	Warner	Thomas			3/23
threatening murder	Curtis				4/17
uttering counterfeit money	Hall				1/24
uttering counterfeit money	unrecorded		soldier of the guards		1/24
uttering false coin	Mariston	Mary			2/21
vagabond	Bignal	James			1/13
vagabond	Franklyn	Job			1/13

Stolen Property

Item	Thief		Date
	Last name	First name	
apparel (wearing) and other things [Henry Holland]	Beezley	Richard	11/24
blanket	Yardley	Mary	4/10
books (several) [Samuel Paterson]	Buchanan	Mary	11/03
books (several) [Samuel Paterson]	Buchanan	Paul	11/03
box (silver) [Henry Harris]	Swanson	Elizabeth	11/17
box containing valuable things [Nathan Homes; Edward Strafford]	Murray	David	6/15
brass belonging to coaches	Lory	James	5/29
burgundy, champagne & other liquours (great quantity) [Richard Plimpton]	Doharty	Matthew	3/09
cap, muslin apron, a sack	Johnson	Esther	5/04
carpenter's tools	Russel	John	1/24
china (several large pieces) and other goods [Mr. Caister; Jane Llewin]	Page	John	6/19

(continues)

| Item | Thief | | |
	Last name	First name	Date
china (several large pieces) and other goods [Mr. Caister; Jane Llewin]	Meadows	John	6/19
china plates (several), spoon (silver) [Mr. Goodburn]	Hilton	Mary	6/08
cloaths and linen (in a box)	Hogg	Joseph	7/31
coals (several quantities) [Nathan Robley]	Hart	Rebecca	4/06
coat (cloth) [George Hawkins, a salesman]	Read	Hannah	9/22
coat (great) [Richard Eyres, Esq.]	Stocker	John	11/17
coat, iron (great quantity), other things [Samuel Miller]	Sneesby	Richard	2/17
coats (2) [John Calverley]	Langston	John	10/13
coats (6 great) [Michael Gibbons]	Breach	Benjamin	6/19
copper (a large) [Esther Roberts; Henry Canham]	Studd	John	8/21
copper (a large) [Esther Roberts; Henry Canham]	West	John	8/21
diamonds (3) [Hon. Col. George Townshend]	Hains	Hannah	1/26
dishes (several out of the King's Kitchin]	Burton	Richard	5/08
ducape (great quantity), Irish stuff, other goods (value of 10 pounds) [Richard Stamford, Mercer]	Haley	Jane	3/20
Dutch Cocks and hens (several), bantam cocks and hens (several) [Right. Hon. the Secretary of War]	Warner	Thomas	3/23
frocks (10 long-Lawn), napkins (3 children's, marked A.), aprons (5 white), handkerchiefs (2 coloured) [Mr. Arthur, of White's Chocolate House]	unknown		3/27
furniture, household (several pieces)	Mullier	Cicely	4/17
gown	Baitin (Batin)	Mary	4/17
guinea (1)	Welsh	Mary	2/14
guinea (gold), shillings (13 silver) [James Mears]	Chapman	Sarah	11/03
guinea (gold), shillings (13 silver) [James Mears]	Duff	Sarah	11/03
guinea (gold), shoe-buckles (pair of silver), shillings (5), sixpence (silver) [Thomas Grear]	Simon	John	10/20
guinea (half gold), shillings (9 silver), metal watch [Rev. Mr. William Noble]	Lake	Robert	3/16
guinea (half) [Thomas Francis]	Lewis	John	2/07
guinea [Alice King]	Pierce	Judith	4/20
guineas (2 1/2 gold), ring (gold) & other things [Patrick Quinn]	Fox	Ann	10/27

(continues)

| Item | Thief | | |
	Last name	First name	Date
guineas (10), shillings (4) and sixpence, gold ring [Henry Jenkins]	Newman	Maria	6/19
guineas (2) [Thomas Good]	Jolley	Samuel	10/06
guineas (60) [George Pitt, Esq.]	Dupie		5/25
hair (cut off in alley)	unrecorded		4/24
halfpence (great quantity), spoons (3 silver), table cloths (3) & several other things [Joseph Boldock]	Anderson	Mary	10/27
handkerchief	unrecorded		4/03
handkerchief (linen) [William Squires]	Smith	John	3/02
handkerchief (silk) [Charles Macklin]	Dust	Francis	11/17
handkerchief (silk) [Daniel Hugh Gordon]	Emero	Christopher	4/10
handkerchief (silk) [John Morris]	Banks	William	3/06
handkerchief (silk) [Lockhart Gordon, Esq.]	Dust	Samuel	10/27
handkerchief (silk) [Rice Jones]	Fagen	Mary	10/27
handkerchief (silk) [Rolte]	Emners	Christopher	1/24
handkerchief (silk) [William Powell]	Wallis	Peter	11/17
handkerchief (silk) [William Powell]	Hawes	Isaac	11/17
handkerchief [Col. Sandford]	Connor	David	1/24
handkerchief [Isack Moresley]	Davies	Matthew	10/13
handkerchief [Richard Orme]	Duncomb	Zachariah	10/13
handkerchief [George Walker]	Holland	Mary	8/07
handkerchiefs (2 linen) [William Payne & David Forrester]	Hall	James	3/09
handkerchiefs (2 silk) [William Lloyd]	Smith	Thomas	10/06
handkerchiefs, (3 silk) [Francis Calvert]	Holland	Mary	10/06
hat [Gaspar Valle]	Ainsworth	Elizabeth	1/20
hat [John Saintsbury]	James	Thomas	11/03
housebreaking [Francis Taylor]	Baylis	William	1/03
household goods (quantity) [George Hicleton]	Cole	Mary	7/10
household-furniture (great quantity) [James Miller]	Oglevey	George	5/15
iron (quantity of)	Haynes	William	6/01
iron grate	Sundell	William	5/11
iron grate [Mary Gilbee]	Murphy	Arthur	9/22
iron-rails [Sir Francis Head]	Neale	William	1/13
iron-rails [Sir Francis Head]	Neal	William	1/24
jewels (quantity), watch (gold repeating)	Cole		7/10
knife (silver handled), two pair of shoes, three shirts, and several other things [John Cope]	Goodwin	Anne	2/10
lawn (quantity flowered) [Francis Watson]	Carroll	Ann	3/06

(continues)

| Item | Thief | | Date |
	Last name	First name	
lawn and muslin (quantity of) [Edward Lyres, Linnen-Draper]	Turner	William	4/17
lead (300 lb.) [Edward Turner]	Guilliam	Thomas	4/27
lead (great quantity) [Counsellor Theed]	Hall	Joseph	3/09
lead (quantity of) [Wm. Jarvis]	Roberts	Philip	4/10
lead (quantity of) [Wm. Jarvis]	Rosse	John	4/10
lead (quantity) [John Fitzer, farmer]	Vain	Charles	7/03
linen	Favre	Priscilla	8/07
linen & wearing apparel (great quantity) [John Richards]	Dollison	Anne	9/29
linen & wearing apparel (great quantity) [John Richards]	Jones (aka Merrit)	Mary	9/29
linen (bundle of) [William Pagget]	Rogers	Robert	9/15
linen (child bed) [Elling Blasdale]	Buckhout	Martha	7/31
linen (great quantity)	Mascall	Mary	3/20
linen (great quantity)	Butler	Judith	3/20
linen (great quantity)	Alderidge	Elizabeth	3/20
linen (great quantity) & other things [M. Anderson]	Wickham	Cath.	5/11
linen (great quantity) [Elizabeth Gardiner]	Cawley	Mary	11/17
linen (quantity of) [Ann Adams]	Lynch	Bridget	2/17
linen (quantity) [Thomas Hall]	Lister	Penelope	11/10
linen (quantity) [Thomas Reynolds]	Dingle	Ann	3/06
linen (quantity), other things [Edward Roberts, brewer]	Osborne	Sarah	7/03
linen and other goods [Christopher Cooper]	Ireland	Mary	7/31
linen, wearing apparel, money [Joseph Sewell; from house of James Blackwell, grocer]	Grayham	George	4/13
linen, wearing apparel, money [Joseph Sewell; from house of James Blackwell, grocer]	Seers	Barnard	4/13
loaves	Thompson	William	8/07
money and other things [William Bedwin]	Randall	William (aka Shock)	7/10
money out of till [Daniel Jones]	Andrews	Jeremiah	1/03
muslin aprons (3)	Turner	Mary	5/01
petticoat, shoes (pair), caps (several), handkerchiefs & other things [Elizabeth Vaughan]	Ronison	Barbara	11/17
pewter (great quantity) [John Tittley]	Rock	Sarah	3/06
pewter (quantity of) [Thomas Winterton]	Parnham	Mary	11/10
pewter plates (several) [Mr. Hammon]	Child	Henry	5/25
pewter pot [Thomas Newsom]	Murphy	David	2/17

(continues)

Item	Thief		
	Last name	First name	Date
pewter pots (several) [Thomas Lucas]	Upton	George	2/17
picking pocket [Mr. Franlkin, the Printer]	Addis	Thomas	8/07
pins that fasten shutters	boy		9/15
pistols (pair) [Capt. Clavering]	Buddle	George	1/10
plate (quantity of) [Edward Dodd]	Williams	Mary	9/15
plate (silver)	Dupree	Anne	7/31
plough irons [Joshua Evans]	Jones	John	8/21
promissory note of five pounds [Thomas Jones]	Harbins	Mary	2/14
ring (gold) & linen (quantity of) [Richard Kirby]	Mills	Elizabeth	5/01
ring (gold) [John Cordwell]	Smith	William	10/13
scarlet cloth (11 pieces) [Thomas Bowden]	Hall	James	5/11
sheet, apron, handkerchief [Elizabeth Basset]	Finch	Ann	7/03
sheet, brass candle stick, pewter dish, pewter plate out of ready furnished lodgings [Patrick Nowland]	Blinkcoe	Mary	6/15
sheet, quilt, curtains out of ready furnished lodging [John Utridge]	Incleton	Henry	6/15
sheets (pair) & other things [John Hart]	Lloyd	Anne	6/01
sheets (pair) and other things [Arthur Swain]	Walker	Isaac	11/10
sheets (pair), tea kettle, other things [Margaret Grange]	Carter	Martha	7/03
shilling pieces, (36 gold) [James Wilson]	Wood	Elizabeth	10/13
shillings (20) [David Smith, sailor}	Price	Margaret	3/30
shillings (26) [William Scott]	Row	Elizabeth	5/08
shillings (40) [William Perry, waterman]	Callder	Robert	6/15
shillings and sixpences (several) [Benjamin Anderton]	Evans	John	10/20
shirt, napkin, several other goods [John Dakin]	Mooney	Joyce	3/20
shirts (2), neck cloth (muslin) [Sarah Bedford]	Ash	Elizabeth	10/13
spoon (silver) [John Clark]	Frazer	Anne	9/29
spoons (2 large silver) [Packington Tomkyns, at Shakespeare's Head]	Bradford	John	6/01
spoons (2 silver)	lad of 10		7/10
spoons (2 silver) [Humphry Roberts]	Richardson	Mary	9/29
spoons (2 silver) [Mathew Smith]	Presser	Thomas	3/09
stays (pair), pettycoat, shift (holland), handkerchief (silk), caps (2 linen), & other things [Mary Coles]	King	Margaret	10/13
stockings (several pair) [William Finch, hosier in Covent-Garden]	Rock	Sarah	6/12

(continues)

Item	Thief		Date
	Last name	First name	
tankard (silver, from Eagle and Child in St. Martin's Le Grand) [Henry Gallant]	Langenfilder	John	10/27
watch (gold) [Peter Brown]	Furness (aka Geary)	Honor	9/22
watch (silver)	Frances	Abigail	7/10
watch (silver) [William Pallin]	Marshall	Martha	3/02
watch (silver), watch (gold)	Barlow	John	9/29
watch case (gold set with diamonds) [Stephen Trequet]	Bennitt	John	1/13
watch [Thomas Marshal]	Flowers	Anne	6/01
wearing apparel (great quantity) [Dorothy Holland]	Baldwin	Lucey	10/20
wearing apparel (great quantity) [John Williams]	Roberts	Elizabeth	10/06
wearing apparel [John Spencer]	Jones	Mary	5/01

Appendix II

Plan of the Public Register-Office

The following plan of Philip D'Halluin's Public Register Office appeared in *The London Daily Advertiser* on November 23, 1752.

PLAN *of the* PUBLIC REGISTER-OFFICE,
in King-street, Covent-Garden, very commodiously situated and conveniently fitted up;

WHERE

I. Gentlemen wanting to buy or sell Estates, may, by Registering in this Office, have the greatest Probability either of laying out their Money to the most Advantage, or of readily meeting with a Purchaser.

II. Clergymen may expeditiously be acquainted of what Livings or Advowsons are to be disposed of, and those who have Livings or Advowsons to dispose of, may speedily be informed of Clergymen or others, who are willing to contract for them, by entering their Names timely in this Office.

III. By Registering in this Office, those who want Money on Mortgage, or who have Money to advance on Mortgage, may have their mutual Purposes answered.

IV. Any who have the Power to dispose of Places in State and Army, or who have Leave to resign any Employment, by applying here, may immediately hear of Purchasers; and those who are desirous of laying out their Money in that Manner, may find it the shortest Way of meeting with a Purchase.

V. Annuities on Lives, either of the Buyer or Seller, being much sought after, this Office registers both; and there is no Method calculated to serve the respective Ends of both Buyers and Sellers, so well as by entering in this Office.

VI. If those who have Houses or Lodgings to lett, register here, they can take no Method so likely to fill their Houses or Lodgings; nor can persons wanting either, be accommodated with so little Trouble as above.

VII. All who have Curiosities to sell, or such who are fond of buying Curiosities, may find their Account in this Office; as the former, by exposing their Goods, need not doubt of having a quick Sale, nor the latter of being suitably accommodated.

VIII. Persons qualified to collect rents, settle Accounts, Book-keeping, &c. are Register'd in this Office, and by Registering provided for, according to their several Capacities.—Merchants, Tradesmen. &c. who want Persons or Servants, in the above Capacities, by so doing, will undoubtedly be provided according to their Expectations. Tradesmen and handicrafts may be supplied with Journeymen; and Journeymen, of any Trade or Handicraft, are readily got into Employment at this office of universal Benefit.

IX. Curacies, Curates, Chaplainships, or other Ecclesiastical Preferments, are Register'd here; and those wanting to be supplied in either of the said Particulars, may almost depend upon being served in the most expeditious Manner, by giving their Names and Respective wants.

X. As there are few Articles in Life more material than the Education of Youth, so no better Method can be taken to be provided with proper Tutors and Instructors, than by applying to the Register-office, where Men of the Best Character and Recommendation are to be heard of, well skilled in most Languages, and in most of the Sciences; and such who are qualified to take on them the Charge of instructing Youth, cannot hope to pursue a more proper Method, in order to be employed, than by Registering themselves there. Gentlemen and Ladies wanting to place out Children to reputable Boarding-Schools; and such Schools wanting Ushers, Governesses, or any Sort of Teachers, of the best Qualities and Qualifications, may constantly be supplied.

XI. For the Benefit of those who want, and those who have Money, the Office undertakes to advance Money upon Plate and Jewels; where both Parties may, with the greatest Reason, hope to find their Account, by making this Office a Medium of their Dealings, as the greatest Secrecy and Punctuality may be depended upon.

It would be needless to particularize every Branch of Business this Office undertakes; but that the Public may have a general Idea of the Plan of it, we must inform them, that there is nothing which depends on the mutual Assistance of Man and Man, but is comprehended in it. As every Person, one way or other, must rely on the Aid and Service of somebody else, so there can be nobody but may really and rationally become a Correspondent of this Office. To mention an Instance, almost every Man, whose Condition is above Servitude, cannot be very happy without a Servant; and all whose Circumstances oblige them to be Servants, can subsist but poorly without Masters. Now as the Office registers Masters of all Ranks, in any Trade or Occupation, and Servants of all Kinds, from Steward and Housekeeper to the most inferior of both Sexes (and these never Register'd but with the same Caution and Care that any Gentleman would use when he chuses a Servant himself) it is plain and evident, that great Benefit and Ease must accrue to both Master and Servant, by making the Office a Means of giving them reciprocal Information.

We have one more thing to allege in our Favour, and to induce Gentlemen and Ladies who want Servants, as well as any of the above-cited Articles, and servants of all Degrees, who want Masters, to favour this Office with their Applications, that all the above Particulars, as well as Masters and servants, are Register'd gratis, provided no such are upon the Books; so whoever applies, and is not served, can be at no Expence, which the Proprietors hope will be sufficient to keep them from the Imputation of having a Design to impose on the Thoughtless and Unexperienced.

For the better Conveniency of Ladies and Gentlemen, distinct Offices are provided for treating with them, or for taking their Directions or Commands; so that when any Lady or Gentleman has Business to do, there will be no Necessity of discovering the Particulars of their Business to a Number of Servants and other Persons who may be in a Public Room; but here they will be quite free, and not incommoded in any Sense whatever.

As this Metropolis has a great Number of Foreigners resorting to it, many of whom not having Friends or Acquaintance to apply to, and those, who have Acquaintance, may not always be able to procure satisfactory Accounts, in abundance of Instances, if they apply to the Office, they will meet with Gentlemen qualified to give them the most punctual Information in any Particular whatsoever.—And every one may be informed of the Residence, both in Town and Country, of any Nobleman, Member of Parliament, or other Person of Distinction, whether Gentleman, Merchant, or Tradesman: Of all Ships going out; Stage-Coaches, Stage-Waggons, their Days of coming in, going out, and where they Inn in London. For which Purpose, all Masters of Stage Coaches, and Stage-Waggons, may find their account by making this Office an Instrument of furnishing them with Passengers.

In short, this Office is designed as a General Mart or Exchange, where the whole World may converse and become acquainted: Where any Person who wants to sell an Estate, may meet with one who wants to buy: Where he who has occasion to borrow Money, may be brought to him who is ready to lend: Where the Scholar, who stands in need of a Patron, may find a Patron who wants his Assistance. Thus we may go on and rehearse Examples through all the above-cited Articles. Thus every Want may meet with its Opposite: Thus Men may bring hither Abilities, good Qualifications, and good Qualities, as well as their Goods, Money, and Merchandize, in order to procure by them the greatest Advantages.

The Scholar, the Mechanic, and persons of the most inferior Rank, from such an Establishment as this, may equally hope Benefit; and People of an elevated Station and Condition in Life, will find it a better Method of accommodating themselves with such Persons and Things, which their Fortune makes necessary for them, than has been hitherto pursued. And though the general Good, which may result to the Community from the present Undertaking, is apparent; yet, unless the Community join in the Attempt, and support what is so evidently contrived for the mutual Advantage or Advancement of all Men, this good Design will naturally produce no very good Effect.

We must conclude with saying, that what every Man has an Interest in, either immediate or remote, we hope every Man will endeavor to encourage.

Notes

Introduction

1. Although Fielding took oaths for the Westminster magistracy on October 25, 1748, I date the beginning of his service as magistrate from November 2, 1748, when he began holding court in Bow Street. For the complexities of his appointments to the magistracy, see W. B. Coley, "Fielding's Two Appointments to the Magistracy," *Modern Philology* 63 (1965): 144–49.
2. For example, Colin Nicholson, *Writing and the Rise of Finance: Capital Satires of the Early Eighteenth Century* (Cambridge: Cambridge Univ. Press, 1994); Sandra Sherman, *Finance and Fictionality in the Early Eighteenth-Century: Accounting for Defoe* (Cambridge: Cambridge Univ. Press, 1996); Brean S. Hammond, *Professional Imaginative Writing in England 1670–1740: 'Hackney for Bread'* (Oxford: Clarendon Press, 1997); Paula McDowell, *Women of Grub Street: Press, Politics and Gender in the London Literary Marketplace* (Oxford: Clarendon Press, 1998); Catherine Ingrassia, *Authorship, Commerce, and Gender in Early Eighteenth-Century England: A Culture of Paper Credit* (Cambridge: Cambridge Univ. Press, 1998); John Bender, *Imagining the Penitentiary: Fiction and the Architecture of the Mind in Eighteenth-Century England* (Chicago: Univ. of Chicago Press, 1987); James Thompson, *Models of Value: Eighteenth-Century Political Economy and the Novel* (Durham: Duke Univ. Press, 1996).
3. For example, Alexander Welsh, *Strong Representations: Narrative and Circumstantial Evidence in England* (Baltimore: Johns Hopkins Univ. Press, 1992); John P. Zomchick, *Family and the Law in Eighteenth-Century Fiction: Public Conscience in the Private Sphere* (Cambridge: Cambridge Univ. Press, 1993). For a somewhat dated overview of relationship of law and literature in Fielding's work, see B. M. Jones, *Henry Fielding: Novelist and Magistrate* (London: George Allen & Unwin, 1933).
4. Martin C. Battestin with Ruthe R. Battestin, *Henry Fielding: A Life* (London: Routledge, 1989), 460.
5. Battestin, *Fielding,* 542–43.
6. Bender, for example, does not once mention the existence of the Universal Register Office; see Bender, *Imagining the Penitentiary,* 139–98, passim. Linebaugh discusses the Universal Register Office, but does not mention *The Covent-Garden Journal.* See Peter Linebaugh, *The London Hanged:*

Crime and Civil Society in the Eighteenth Century (Cambridge: Cambridge Univ. Press, 1992), 252.

7. Henry Fielding, *The Covent-Garden Journal and A Plan of the Universal Register-Office,* ed. Bertrand Goldgar (Middletown, CT: Wesleyan Univ. Press, 1988), xv–xvi. Hereafter cited as Goldgar, *CGJ.*

8. Pat Rogers, *Henry Fielding: A Biography* (London: Paul Elek, 1979), 176; Linebaugh, *Hanged,* 252.

9. Battestin, *Fielding,* 498.

10. For a useful overview of Fielding's biographers and critics prior to 1918, see Wilbur L. Cross, *The History of Henry Fielding,* 3 vols. (New Haven: Yale Univ. Press, 1918), 3:125–257. For an overview of more recent criticism, see Albert J. Rivero, ed., *Critical Essays on Henry Fielding* (New York: G. K. Hall & Co., 1998), 1–9. As Ronald Paulson remarked in 1962, "the effect of twentieth-century Fielding criticism has been to prove him moral," a development Paulson found reductive; see *Fielding: A Collection of Critical Essays* (Englewood Cliffs, NJ: Prentice-Hall, 1962), 1–2. Over the past 35 years a more conflicted Fielding has emerged, particularly in the work of Claude Rawson and J. Paul Hunter, but this work has not in the main addressed Fielding's performance as a magistrate and its relation to his business and journalistic interests. See Rawson, *Henry Fielding and the Augustan Ideal under Stress* (London: Routledge & Kegan Paul, 1972); Hunter, *Occasional Form: Henry Fielding and the Chains of Circumstance* (Baltimore: Johns Hopkins Univ. Press, 1975). Interestingly, Cross, reviewing Austin Dobson's 1883 monograph on Fielding, credits Dobson with initiating the idea that Fielding possessed "'a curious dual individuality.' The reader is led to surmise that if he knew all there would emerge a sort of Dr. Jekyll and Mr. Hyde" (3:250). It is a view Cross dismisses—"To explain him in this way is to resort to a crude psychology. Fielding was merely human like the rest of us" (3:251).

11. The three were *The Covent-Garden Journal* (1752), *Have At You All: or, The Drury-Lane Journal* (1752), and the *Public Ledger: or, The Daily Register of Commerce and Intelligence* (1760).

12. Cf. Roland Barthes: "Denotation is not the first sense, but it pretends to be. Under this illusion, in the end, it is nothing but the last of connotation (where the reading is at the same time grounded and enclosed), the superior myth, thanks to which the text pretends to return to the nature of language." Barthes, *S/Z* (Paris: Sueil, 1970). Variations on Barthes's (as well as Althusser's, Veron's, Baudrillard's) analyses of the ideological dimension of language have become a staple of cultural and media studies in the "politics of signification," but as yet have had no impact on the study of Fielding's register office, court, and the texts that preserve and encode them. See, for example, Marina Camargo Heck, "The ideological dimension of media messages," and Stuart Hall, "Encoding/decoding," in *Culture, Media, Language,* ed. Stuart Hall et al. (London: Hutchinson, 1980), 122–29.

13. I use the term "Grub Street" to designate simultaneously the production of commercialized literature and its fictional mapping and mythologizing

in Augustan satire. As Paula McDowell writes of Pat Rogers's work and her own: "Rogers's study emphasizes 'Grub Street' as a 'constructive fiction of satire' in the works of Augustan cultural elites and as a mappable literary locus. My own study emphasizes the democratic possibilities inherent in the new literary marketplace" (*Women of Grub Street,* 10). In Fielding's work, both principles seem to compete for precedence.

14. Although historical "realities" are necessarily mediated through individual consciousness (and none more than Fielding's), we would do well to remember Pocock's observation that we "are studying an aspect of reality when we study the ways in which it appeared real to the persons to whom it was more real than to anyone else." See J. G. A. Pocock, *Politics, Language, and Time: Essays on Political Thought and History* (New York: Atheneum, 1973), 38. On the problems of reconstructing historical contexts, see Robert D. Hume, *Reconstructing Contexts: The Aims and Principles of Archaeo-Historicism* (New York: Oxford Univ. Press, 1999), passim; cf. Leo Damrosch, *Fictions of Reality in the Age of Hume and Johnson* (Madison: Univ. of Wisconsin Press, 1989), 11–13. The ascendancy of materialist explanations of cultural change has had the tendency to emphasize the importance of developing political or economic systems at the expense of both residual cultural practices and individual agency. In recent eighteenth-century literary criticism, this tendency has manifested itself in the "new economic criticism" and its fascination with the "financial revolution" and "cash nexus" as controlling heuristics for the explication of the literature of the period. The theory that the gradually evolving use of bills and notes by merchants, as it was incorporated into common law, led to the increasing abstraction of the form of money (and thus of other forms of social interaction) has been invoked in myriad ways as a symbol and enabling condition for the dynamics of modern literary production and modern models of behavior. But as John O'Brien has recently pointed out, literary critics would do well to heed the argument of legal historian James Stevens Rogers that "the incorporation theory tends to flatten the landscape of this period's commercial practices in order to emphasize the end result of the process: the pale, bloodless, and undifferentiated styles of exchange characteristic of mature capitalism." See O'Brien, "Union Jack: Amnesia and the Law in Daniel Defoe's *Colonel Jack,*" *Eighteenth-Century Studies* 32 (1998): 67–69. It is crucial to remember that during the eighteenth century, more traditional, local, and personal practices continued to coexist with and penetrate developing forms of "modern" legal and economic procedure, and that in order to avoid reductiveness the literature of the period must be read with this reciprocal influence constantly in mind. The classic discussion of dominant, emergent, and residual forms remains Raymond Williams, *Marxism and Literature* (Oxford: Oxford Univ. Press, 1977), 115–27.

15. See Frank Donoghue's discussion of the importance of biography to criticism in *The Fame Machine: Book Reviewing and Literary Careers* (Stanford:

Stanford Univ. Press, 1996), 11–14. As Donoghue observes, it has become commonplace for scholars privately to chide biographers for "old-fashioned critical methods" while relying "upon these biographies anytime they write as thematic critics" (13).

16. Bender, *Imagining the Penitentiary,* 165–66.

17. Welsh, *Strong Representations,* 43–76.

18. Zomchick, *Family and the Law,* 130–53.

19. For example, Susan Sage Heinzelman, "Guilty in Law, Implausible in Fiction: Jurisprudential and Literary Narratives in the Case of Mary Blandy, Parricide, 1752," in *Representing Women: Law, Literature and Feminism,* ed. Susan Heinzelman and Zipporah Batshaw Wiseman (Durham: Duke Univ. Press, 1994), 309–36; Arlene Wilner, "The Mythology of History, the Truth of Fiction: Henry Fielding and the Cases of Bosavern Penlez and Elizabeth Canning," *The Journal of Narrative Technique* 21 (1991): 185–202.

20. Battestin, *Fielding,* 498; Rogers, *Henry Fielding,* 176; Linebaugh, *Hanged,* 252.

21. Cross, *History of Henry Fielding,* 3:267.

22. Angela J. Smallwood, *Fielding and the Woman Question: The Novels of Henry Fielding and Feminist Debate 1700–1750* (Hemel Hempstead: Harvester Wheatsheaf, 1989), 1. The phrase "misogynist monster" is Rivero's, *Critical Essays on Fielding,* 7.

23. Jill Campbell, *Natural Masques: Gender and Identity in Fielding's Plays and Novels* (Stanford: Stanford Univ. Press, 1995).

24. On the messy contingency of the eighteenth-century moment, see Clement Hawes, "Introduction," in *Christopher Smart and the Enlightenment,* ed. Clement Hawes (New York: St. Martin's Press, 1999), 2–17.

25. On the mixed nature public and private spheres in the eighteenth century, see, for example, Hawes, "The Utopian Public Sphere: Intersubjectivity in *Jubilate Agno," Smart and the Enlightenment,* 197–99; Kathleen Wilson, *The Sense of the People: Politics, Culture and Imperialism in England, 1715–1785* (Cambridge: Cambridge Univ. Press, 1995), 44; Lisa Forman Cody, "The Politics of Reproduction: From Midwives' Alternative Public Sphere to the Public Spectacle of Man-Midwifery," *Eighteenth-Century Studies* 32 (1998): 478–79. On the public sphere, see Jürgen Habermas, *The Structural Transformation of the Public Sphere: An Inquiry into a Category of Bourgeois Society,* trans. Thomas Burger (Cambridge, MA: MIT Press, 1991).

26. Rawson, *Henry Fielding and the Augustan Ideal,* 23.

Chapter 1

1. See Martin C. Battestin with Ruthe R. Battestin, *Henry Fielding: A Life* (London: Routledge, 1989), 440, 448–50, 460, passim.

2. For a succinct overview of the magistracy in eighteenth-century England, see J. M. Beattie's *Crime and the Courts in England, 1660–1800* (Princeton: Princeton Univ. Press, 1986), 59–67. For a more detailed study, see Norma

Landau, *The Justices of the Peace, 1679–1760* (Berkeley: Univ. of California Press, 1984). On the "court JP," see John H. Langbein, "Shaping the Eighteenth-Century Criminal Trial: A View from the Ryder Sources," *University of Chicago Law Review* 50 (1983): 57–60.

3. Battestin, *Fielding*, 459.

4. Ibid., 462.

5. Other significant sources include *A Clear State of the Case of Elizabeth Canning* for Fielding's handling of that case, and *The Journal of a Voyage to Lisbon* for Fielding's description of his anti-gang campaign of December 1753. For both, see below.

6. For legal historians, the journalistic record of Fielding's court has been of primary interest as a source for understanding how, through the magistrate's gathering of evidence and investigation of charges at the level of the pretrial hearing, evidence began to be shaped with regard to the requirements and strategies of the potential criminal trial to follow. See Langbein, "Shaping," 55–67; cf. Beattie, *Crime*, 273–76.

7. Henry Fielding, *The Journal of a Voyage to Lisbon,* ed. Tom Keymer (Harmondsworth, UK: Penguin, 1996), 13. David Low quotes this entire episode, but includes not a single journalistic account of the daily goings-on at Bow Street. See "Mr. Fielding of Bow Street," in *Henry Fielding: Justice Observed,* ed. K. G. Simpson (London: Vision, 1985), 24–28. Battestin, 576–81, examines this episode at length, emphasizing Fielding's "selfless exertions on behalf of the public." One must remember, however, that in this Introduction Fielding is asking for a pension and would have had cause to highlight his self-sacrifice and success. On Fielding and the Bow Street runners generally, see Gilbert Armitage, *The History of the Bow Street Runners* (London: Wishart, 1932), 37–59.

8. Linebaugh's generally negative view of Fielding's behavior in the Penlez case provokes Battestin to caricature his work as ""the jaundiced view of a modern historian of these events" (475). See, Peter Linebaugh, "The Tyburn Riot Against the Surgeons," in *Albion's Fatal Tree: Crime and Society in Eighteenth-Century England,* ed. Douglas Hay et al. (New York: Pantheon, 1975), 89–98.

9. Peter Linebaugh, *The London Hanged: Crime and Civil Society in the Eighteenth Century* (Cambridge: Cambridge Univ. Press, 1992), xvii.

10. Joanna Innes and John Styles, "The Crime Wave: Recent Writing on Crime and Criminal Justice in Eighteenth-Century England," *Journal of British Studies* 25 (1986): 388. See also E. P. Thompson, *Whigs and Hunters: The Origin of the Black Act* (New York: Pantheon, 1975), 219–69; John Langbein, "*Albion's* Fatal Flaws," *Past and Present* 98 (1983): 96–120; John Brewer and John Styles, eds., *An Ungovernable People: The English and their Law in the Seventeenth and Eighteenth Centuries* (New Brunswick, NJ: Rutgers Univ. Press, 1980).

11. V. A. C. Gatrell comments that the debate on class interest, criminal law, and mercy is "now more than a little tired" and remarks that "whether or

not the claims of class are disproven . . . depends on how literally you read class." See Gatrell, *The Hanging Tree: Execution and the English People 1790–1868* (Oxford: Oxford Univ. Press, 1994), 613.

12. Linebaugh, *Hanged*, 252.

13. Martin Battestin, unfortunately, confounds the issue by loosely calling it "Fielding's paper" (Battestin, *Fielding*, 574). John Bender also exaggerates in calling *The Public Advertiser* (along with, more accurately, *The Covent-Garden Journal*) "[n]ewspapers that Fielding operated" (171). Although Fielding held shares in the *Public*, his was not a controlling interest. Moreover, his reports from Bow Street had already been running in *The General Advertiser* prior to its being renamed (Battestin, 460–61). For Fielding's connection with the *Public*, its editorial policy, and its role in informing pawnbrokers of stolen goods, see *The Covent-Garden Journal*, No. 72 (November 25, 1752), in which Fielding prints the proprietors' announcement.

14. Although, as I will argue below, the relationship between Henry Fielding's simultaneous activities as an author of periodical literature, magistrate in Bow Street, and proprietor of the Universal Register Office is complicated and disturbing, it scarcely points to the surveillance-crazed caricature Linebaugh suggests—an interpretation perhaps inspired by John Bender's characterization of Fielding's judicial practice as an anticipation of the invention of panoptical penitentiaries (170) and by the more general interest in "surveillance" as a topic of critical discussion provoked by Michel Foucault's *Discipline and Punish: The Birth of the Prison* (New York: Vintage, 1979).

15. The Covent Garden columns are usually dated one day earlier than the issue date of *The Covent-Garden Journal*. Archibald Shepperson argues that *The Whitehall Evening Post* was the paper in which "the greatest number of [Fielding's cases] were reported and reported with the greatest detail and liveliness," but all of the cases he reprints from that paper are simply slightly altered versions of the reports in *The Covent-Garden Journal*, which he does not mention as a source. See Archibald Bolling Shepperson, "Additions and Corrections to Facts about Fielding," *Modern Philology* 51 (1954): 217–24.

16. This is a summary of the Criminal Activity table (Appendix I), which is divided into categories by crime and covers accused persons exclusively. The determination of the exact percentage of each category in relation to the whole is impossible because of the statistical generalizations discussed above and because of Brogden's related habit of describing groups of offenders in such phrases as "a set of Barbers Apprentices, Journeymen Staymakers, Maid-Servants, &c." (April 13) or "several lewd Women" (January 24). But even limiting the entries to specific individuals and assigning a value of one to groups described collectively, we still have a record of 42 categories of crime comprising over 300 alleged perpetrators.

17. Fielding, *Journal*, 12.

18. For the definition of author, see Hannah Arendt, *Between Past and Future: Six Exercises in Political Thought* (New York: Viking Press, 1961), 121. To

date, the columns have been of primary interest when Fielding's hand is clearly evident or when they "make editorial comments or . . . include such features as narrative sketches or humorous dialogue" (Goldgar, *CGJ*, 389). On the basis of such criteria, Bertrand Goldgar has reprinted some but not all of the Covent Garden columns in Appendix I of *CGJ*. A reading of this selective appendix, however, is not wholly satisfactory if we desire a somewhat more complete source from which conclusions may be forthcoming concerning the frequency of various types of crimes or numbers and kinds of criminals. Even then clear conclusions are not easy to derive from the columns. Brogden will sometimes make comprehensive or vague statistical statements—"Above twenty have been committed for various Misdemeanours and Breaches of the Peace" (August 7)—while specifically naming or describing only a few of the actual cases. After the above generalization, for example, only one misdemeanor is fully described, but it is an especially interesting one for a number of reasons. First, it indicates that the volume of Fielding's cases was much larger than the numbers that can be derived by merely counting specific crimes and named individuals. Second, the case appears in a column excluded from Goldgar's edition although it clearly fulfills his criteria that columns either "make editorial comments or . . . include such features as narrative sketches or humorous dialogue." Third, it indicates that "entertainment value" criteria similar to Goldgar's was already being imposed by Brogden (or Fielding) as he sorted through more than 20 cases to find one worth recording in detail. In this case, it was the commitment of "one Joseph Tremman, for biting a Piece out of his Wife's Arm; at the same Time declaring he loved her well enough to eat her" (August 7). The journalistic precedent for such selectivity had been set by the *Old Bailey Sessions Papers,* in which, as Langbein writes, "the tastes of the lay readership appear to have guided the editors' selection of which cases to report more fully and which to treat as squib reports. Sensationalism prevailed." On the *OBSP,* see Langbein, "Shaping," 3–18. Quotations from columns not included in Goldgar's appendix are from the microfilm version of *The Covent-Garden Journal* (London, 1752), in Early English Newspapers (Woodbridge: Research Publications, Inc.), reel #1134.

19. Goldgar, *CGJ,* xxxvii.

20. These figures would tend to confirm Battestin's sense that "the sad drudgery issuing warrants to settle the vagrant poor in their country parishes, or of binding over the contentious to keep the peace, or of examining and correcting prostitutes" made up "the great majority of cases which occupied" Fielding. See Fielding, *Amelia,* ed. Martin Battestin (Middletown, CT: Wesleyan Univ. Press, 1983), xxv.

21. 147 thefts; 12 robberies; 6 burglaries; 2 housebreakings. I have excluded indirect crimes against property such as embezzlement and fraud.

22. For a cogent discussion of all such distinctions and their practical application, see Beattie, *Crime,* 140–98.

23. On the general nature of women's crime, see J. M. Beattie, "The Criminality of Women," *Journal of Social History* 8 (1975): 80–116.

24. In statistically summarizing the tables, I have therefore used the category "theft" to describe all crimes against property that are not specifically denoted as robbery, burglary, or housebreaking.

25. Battestin, *Fielding*, 551–53; Bertrand Goldgar, "Fielding and the Whores of London," *Philological Quarterly* 64 (1985): 270–71.

26. Beattie, *Crime*, 36.

27. Ibid., 274.

28. Fielding, *Journal*, 14. Welsh writes that "Fielding's services have to be regarded as mainly prosecutorial" in Bow Street, although they are exercised mainly "on behalf of the defense" in *Tom Jones;* see Alexander Welsh, *Strong Representations: Narrative and Circumstantial Evidence in England* (Baltimore: Johns Hopkins Univ. Press, 1992), 47. I would suggest that Fielding was perhaps less consistently prosecutorial in Bow Street than Welsh implies.

29. Goldgar, "Whores," 269.

30. The Act (25 Geo. II, c.36) had gone into effect on June 1; Goldgar ("Whores," 267) summarizes its provisions.

31. Goldgar, *CGJ,* 276. Wilbur L. Cross, *The History of Henry Fielding,* 3 vols. (New Haven: Yale Univ. Press, 1918), 2:370, attributes the letter to Fielding; Goldgar and Battestin reject it.

32. Goldgar, *CGJ,* 276, includes the letter among the leaders.

33. Goldgar, "Whores," 268; Battestin, 550–51.

34. Goldgar, *CGJ,* 307.

35. *The Gentleman's Magazine* 22 (1752), 27; cf. Goldgar, *CGJ,* xxxvi.

36. Quoted by Goldgar, *CGJ,* xxxvi.

37. Battestin, *Fielding,* 551–52.

38. Goldgar, "Whores," 271.

39. *The Gentleman's Magazine* 22 (1752), 27. This writer summarized the January 10 prostitute episode in a footnote as an example of Fielding's "penetration and sagacity."

40. Although this argument was developed before the appearance of Cheek's article, it finds interesting parallels in a French context in Pamela Cheek's "Prostitutes of 'Political Institution,'" *Eighteenth-Century Studies* 28 (1994–95): 193–219. Cheek notes "that the mode of narration in police and sexualized writing was striking for the atmosphere of entertainment surrounding the attitude of surveillance. One could argue that the police reports strove for what we identify now as a bureaucratic voice: a normativizing and objective tone. And indeed, many of Inspector Meusenier's reports were barely developed beyond note form. Yet a number of his reports and most of his successor's show a consciousness of how their material might entertain" (202).

41. As will be suggested below, the interrogation of young prostitutes, with Fielding taking the role of questioner, judge, and reporter, also interacts suggestively with the business of the Universal Register Office. The fran-

chise provided by both venues is the similar: a sanction to view, to enquire, and to command a subordinate object. In a relevant passage, Toril Moi points out that for Freud the act of seeing is linked "to anal *activity*, which he sees as expressing a desire for *mastery* or for the exercise of *power* over one's (libidinal) objects, a desire that underlies later (phallic or Oedipal) fantasies about phallic (masculine) power. Thus the *gaze* enacts the voyeur's desire for sadistic power, in which the object of the gaze is cast as its passive, masochistic, feminine victim." See *Sexual/Textual Politics: Feminist Literary Theory* (London: Routledge, 1991), 180, n. 8. Fielding's "gaze" seemed particularly suited to this kind of domination: James Harris noted that he had "an Eye peculiarly penetrating [and quick] and which during the Sallies of Wit or anger never failed to distinguish it self." See "Essay on the Life & Genius of Henry Fielding Esq," MS, dated Bath, 5 February 1758; quoted Battestin, 48–49. Nancy Armstrong observes that in eighteenth-century sexual politics the "work of the pen is rivaled only by that of the eyes." See *Desire and Domestic Fiction: A Political History of the Novel* (New York: Oxford Univ. Press, 1987), 122.

42. Fielding's habitual linkage of beauty and innocence, unattractiveness and guilt, is strikingly enacted in a report in the Covent Garden column of March 27 concerning an incident during the trial of Mary Blandy for parricide: "A Gentleman who was present at the Trial of Miss Blandy, and who had his Eyes on her when the Hon. Mr. Bathurst . . . opened the Charge against her, informs us, that the unfortunate Woman who had seemed unmoved at all the rest, could not bear a Hint which seemed to reflect on the Power of her Charms. It was insinuated that Miss Blandy's supposed Fortune of 10000 l.—might possibly be the chief Allurement to her Lover. She who could without Emotion hear herself accused of Want of Humanity, could not bear the least Hint of Want of Beauty; but the Fire kindled in her Eyes, and she discharged a Look at the Speaker, full of such Indignation and Contempt, that is inconceivable to any except those who beheld it." For more on Fielding and the Blandy case, see Susan Sage Heinzelman, "Guilty in Law, Implausible in Fiction: Jurisprudential and Literary Narratives in the Case of Mary Blandy, Parricide, 1752," in *Representing Women: Law, Literature and Feminism,* ed. Susan Heinzelman and Zipporah Batshaw Wiseman (Durham: Duke Univ. Press, 1994), 309–36. Lennard Davis suggests that in "classic novels" beauty is usually "a sign that . . . characters are admirable, worthy of imitation, and cultural paragons" and often "a sign of their social status." In Fielding's court, beautiful prostitutes clearly fail the social status test, but their beauty does seem overtly to carry for Fielding a promise of potential reformation and intrinsic goodness. Covertly, of course, the appeal is sexual and voyeuristic. See Lennard Davis, *Resisting Novels: Ideology and Fiction* (New York: Methuen, 1987), 123.

43. This entry is particularly interesting because it is followed by an italicized comment specifically identified as Brogden's: "*What doth that Wretch deserve, that was the Destroyer of an innocent lovely young Creature, who seems once to*

have so well merited Happiness herself and to have been so capable of bestowing it on an honest Man?" Fielding comments:"I was much pleased with this foregoing Observation of Mr. Brogden; who, tho' he hath drawn so many thousand Committments, is a Man of great Humanity."

44. Henry Fielding, *The History of Tom Jones, a Foundling,* ed. Fredson Bowers (Middletown: Wesleyan Univ. Press, 1975), 870. Further quotations cited parenthetically in the text.

45. *Amelia,* 200, 232. Further quotations cited parenthetically in the text.

46. *Have At You All: or, The Drury-Lane Journal* (London, 1752), 5. For Thornton's attacks on Fielding in *The Drury-Lane Journal,* see Lance Bertelsen, *The Nonsense Club: Literature and Popular Culture, 1749–1764* (Oxford: Clarendon Press, 1986), 19–28.

47. *The Covent-Garden Journal,* No. 51 (June 27, 1752). Fielding's objections to public (as opposed to private) executions are most completely presented in *An Enquiry into the Causes of the Late Increase of Robbers* (London, 1750/1). See also Battestin, *Fielding,* 517–19.

48. J. Paul Hunter, *Occasional Form: Henry Fielding and the Chains of Circumstance* (Baltimore: Johns Hopkins Univ. Press, 1975), 45.

49. Bertrand Goldgar, *Walpole and the Wits: The Relation of Politics to Literature, 1722–1742* (Lincoln: Univ. of Nebraska Press, 1976), 98–115, passim; Robert D. Hume, *Henry Fielding and the London Theatre 1728–1737* (Oxford: Clarendon, 1988), 251–55, passim.

50. Thomas Lockwood, "Fielding and the Licensing Act," *Huntington Library Quarterly* 50 (1987): 389. Battestin, on the basis of essays he attributes to Fielding that appeared in the *Craftsman* during this period, suggests that Lockwood's assessment is inaccurate. See Battestin and Michael Farrington, *New Essays by Henry Fielding* (Charlottesville: Univ. of Virginia Press, 1989), xxvi-vii; Battestin, *Fielding,* 650n. 412. On the other hand, the editorial decision not to include the essays in the Wesleyan edition of Fielding's works calls the attributions into question and would seem to support Lockwood's interpretation of Fielding's behavior following the Licensing Act.

51. Goldgar, "Whores," 272.

52. The frequent appearance of aggressive women in this catalogue of domestic altercations—and Fielding/Brogden's emphasis on their capacity for violence—would seem to modify John Zomchick's argument that eighteenth-century novels and trial reports worked to enforce a feminine role on women. See Zomchick, "'A Penetration Which Nothing Can Deceive': Gender and Juridical Discourse in Some Eighteenth-Century Narratives," *Studies in English Literature* 29 (1989): 535–61. Likewise, Susan Staves's description of Fielding's comic "reversal of gender roles that casts a woman as the big, strong person capable of physically controlling another" may in fact emerge as less of a "reversal" in light of the evidence from Bow Street. See Susan Staves, "Fielding and the Comedy of Attempted Rape," in *History, Gender & Eighteenth-Century Literature,* ed.

Beth Tobin (Athens: Univ. of Georgia Press, 1994), 94. Peter Earle's argument that the emergent mentality of the middle-class family of the early eighteenth century "was a sensibility that sees the beginning of 'Victorian' attitudes toward 'home'" might likewise be modified by a closer look at domestic violence during the period. See Peter Earle, *The Making of the English Middle Class: Business Society, and Family Life in London 1660–1730* (London: Methuen, 1989), 336.

53. Obviously this is an anachronistic comparison, for the judicial ethics of eighteenth-century England were not those of twentieth-century America (though the advent of "People's Court" and "Court TV" gives one pause). But it does serve to illustrate, in broad strokes, Fielding's compromised ethical position somewhere between the official world of the Bow Street Magistrate's Office, the journalistic world of *The Covent-Garden Journal,* and the commercial world of its sponsor, the Universal Register Office.

54. It is interesting to speculate whether Fielding might have been thinking about the Partridge scene when writing this one. There is at least one other verbal similarity: Bewley's niece declares the crime one "she would not tamely submit to while she had a Drop of Blood left in her Body"; Partridge's accusers declare that "if their Husbands should lift their Hands against them, they would have their Heart's Bloods out of their Bodies" (*Tom Jones,* 90).

55. For a similar case, in which a young women is charged with beating up an old one for allegedly stealing her husband, and then beats her again in front of Fielding, see Goldgar, *CGJ,* 414.

56. On the ambiguous portrayal of rape and attempted rape in eighteenth-century law and Fielding's fictions, see Staves, "Fielding and the Comedy of Attempted Rape," 86–112. Staves finds Fielding's attitudes toward women rather less enlightened than Angela Smallwood proposes in *Fielding and the Woman Question: The Novels of Henry Fielding and Feminist Debate 1700–1750* (Hemel Hempstead: Harvester Wheatsheaf, 1989), commenting that he "was both closer to normative masculine ideas of the period and more complicit in developing new ideals of dependent femininity than Smallwood is prepared to acknowledge," but acknowledging herself that "despite the crude state of criminal law doctrine during the period of Fielding's legal education and practice, his fictional plots productively explore fact situations that were to emerge as doctrinal cruxes" (89). Staves's mixed feelings extend to Fielding's performance as a magistrate as recorded in the Covent Garden columns, which she mistakenly confuses with the "Modern History" columns (106–7).

57. The charge of marital rape recurs in the Covent Garden columns. On May 15, 1752, for example, in a detail-filled episode, a woman charges that a staymaker took her "to his Brother's at Lambeth . . . took her up Stairs . . . kept her there all Night, and the next Day and Night . . . assaulted and ravished her against her Will and consent, and repeated the Ravishment several Times." But when the staymaker comes before Fielding, he reminds

the woman that they "'were married on Monday Morning at the Fleet'":
"Upon which she burst into Tears, and confessed it to be true; alledging as
an Excuse for what she had done, that she had been over persuaded to it.
The good Man presently forgave the Offence, and they departed very lov-
ingly together." Who or what "over persuaded" the woman we are never
told. On January 24, 1752, in another elaborate episode, a Mr. Labrosse is
charged by a female servant with having "ravished her and given her a bad
Distemper." But the girl is subsequently examined by Fielding and found
to have "been before notoriously guilty of Incontinency." Eventually
Labrosse's man-servant "declared himself that he had unfortunately and ignorantly given the Girl that Distemper of which she complained . . . by
which means Mr. Labrosse, who is a Person of very good Character, was
saved from long Imprisonment." On eighteenth-century judicial practice
with regard to rape, see Beattie, *Crime,* 124–32.

58. Battestin, *Fielding,* 556. Battestin (n. 296) corrects earlier accounts, including Goldgar, *CGJ,* xxxvii, which assign this proposition to January 8, 1752,
the date of the Smith case.

59. Battestin, *Fielding,* 556, citing *OBSP* (Jan. 1752, No. 89). As Battestin notes,
something must have happened during the hearing January 8 to offend
Hill because the next day the "Inspector" revealed Fielding's literary
proposition and accused him of "an insolent Deceit." On the continuing
paper war, see Goldgar, *CGJ,* xxxvii–li, and Betty Rizzo, "Notes on the War
between Henry Fielding and John Hill, 1752–53," *The Library,* 6th ser. vii
(1985): 338–53.

60. As Goldgar points out, the "'Court of Censorial Enquiry' . . . closely resembles both the mock-court set up in the *Champion* . . . and the 'Court of
Criticism' established in the *Jacobite's Journal.*" See Goldgar, *CGJ,* xxxi–xxxii.

61. Arlene Wilner, "The Mythology of History, the Truth of Fiction: Henry
Fielding and the Cases of Bosavern Penlez and Elizabeth Canning," *The
Journal of Narrative Technique* 21 (1991): 197.

62. Wilner, "Mythology," 198. In arguing that because of its genre Fielding's
fiction provided "far more complex social and epistemological paradigms"
than did the legal writing, Wilner seems to work against Barbara Shapiro's
sense that "Interpretation . . . has always been central to literary and hu-
manistic endeavors, but has taken on a growing importance for law as belief *in literature as a unique variety of text has eroded* (my emphasis). See
Barbara Shapiro, "Circumstantial Evidence: of Law, Literature, and Culture," *Yale Journal of Law and the Humanities* 5 (1992): 301. The dynamics of
generic contamination might usefully inform a more contextualized consideration of the supposedly "legal" writing of the pamphlets—a hodge-
podge of exemplar history, law citations, depositions, conversations, and
moralizing that, despite its cumulative ideological thrust, seems fundamen-
tally transgressive at the level of its published vehicle, a commercial pamphlet purchased probably as much for its entertainment value as for any
"truth" it might contain. Because of their material status as printed prod-

ucts in a retail market, the pamphlets (to a lesser degree) and *The Covent-Garden Journal* (to a greater one) seem always already to have relinquished the autonomy and authority of Bow Street to the potential audience and commercial imperatives of that *other* street. As Hugh Amory writes of *The Covent-Garden Journal*, Fielding may have "upheld at once the truth and the impotence of authority." See Amory, "Magistrate or Censor? The Problem of Authority in Fielding's Later Writings," *Studies in English Literature* 12 (1972): 515.

63. The interpretation of the eighteenth century as representing the triumph of progressive rationalism is familiar both to readers of Whig history and to students of Foucault. See, for example, Peter Stallybrass and Allon White, *The Politics and Poetics of Transgression* (London: Methuen, 1986), 21–22.

Chapter 2

1. Christopher Smart, *The Midwife; or the Old Woman's Magazine* (London, 1751–53), 1: 225–228.

2. Henry Fielding, *A Plan of the Universal Register-Office,* in *The Covent-Garden Journal and A Plan of the Universal Register-Office,* ed. Bertrand Goldgar (Middletown, CT: Wesleyan Univ. Press, 1988), 5.

3. Goldgar, *CGJ,* 6.

4. Smart, *Midwife,* title page.

5. Ibid., 2:130.

6. Ibid., 3:74–75.

7. In light of this critical history, my attempt to problematize Fielding's relations with his register office clientele may seem unduly negative; but I hope it will be taken as an attempt to restore balance to what has been a relatively one-sided argument. For the development of register offices, see M. D. George, "The Early History of Registry Offices," *Economic Journal: Economic History Supplement* 1 (1926–29): 570–90.

8. Pat Rogers, *Henry Fielding: A Biography* (London: Paul Elek, 1979), 176.

9. Martin C. Battestin with Ruthe R. Battestin, *Henry Fielding: A Life* (London: Routledge, 1989), 498.

10. Goldgar, *CGJ,* xx.

11. The Universal Register Office had opened a year earlier on February 19, 1749/50.

12. *Plan,* in Goldgar, *CGJ,* 8.

13. Ibid., 5.

14. For the Glastonbury waters dispute, see Rogers, *Henry Fielding,* 176–79; Battestin, *Fielding,* 525–27.

15. Wilbur L. Cross, *The History of Henry Fielding,* 3 vols. (New Haven: Yale Univ. Press, 1918), 2:402; F. Homes Dudden, *Henry Fielding: His Life, Works, and Times,* 2 vols. (Oxford: Clarendon Press, 1952), 2:888–89; cf. *The Covent-Garden Journal,* ed. Gerard Jensen, 2 vols. (New Haven: Yale Univ. Press, 1915), 1:32–33.

16. Goldgar, *CGJ*, xxv.

17. *The London Daily Advertiser*, November 4, 1751.

18. Ibid., November 6, 1751.

19. Structurally there are also differences: Fielding philosophizes at length at the beginning; D'Halluin a little at the end. But the lists of services are quite similar.

20. "Z.Z." in *The London Daily Advertiser*, June 3, 1751.

21. The simultaneously rationalized and paternalistic practice of the Universal seems to combine in interesting ways the "three competing economies" of the eighteenth and early nineteenth centuries that Beth Tobin summarizes: "a corrupt version of the older aristocratic economy of privilege and display that had been tempered with obligation and is now deformed by the forces of commercial enterprise and consumerism; the new bourgeois economy of surveillance and self-regulation; and the old economy of expenditure that is organized around hierarchies of service and obligation." See Beth Tobin, *Superintending the Poor: Charitable Ladies and Paternal Landlords in British Fiction 1770–1860* (New Haven: Yale Univ. Press, 1993), 93. As the Fieldings' behavior implies, these three seemingly distinct economies were more often than not mixed in practice.

22. Henry Fielding, *An Enquiry into the Causes of the late Increase of Robbers*, in *An Enquiry into the Causes of the Late Increase of Robbers and Related Writings*, ed. Malvin Zirker (Middletown, CT: Wesleyan Univ. Press, 1988), 111–13. Hereafter cited as *Enquiry and Related Writings*.

23. Zirker, *Enquiry and Related Writings*, 173.

24. *The London Daily Advertiser*, November 23, 1751.

25. On the general movement from the traditional "familial" or "paternal" relationship between master and worker to a relationship defined by contract between employee and employer, with salient examples from a servant memoir, see George Boulukos, "Memoirs of the Life and Travels of Thomas Hammond: An Edition for Readers," M.A. Report, University of Texas at Austin, 1994; cf. J. J. Hecht, *The Domestic Servant Class in Eighteenth-Century England* (London: Routledge, 1956). For analysis of literary renditions of servants, see Bruce Robbins, *The Servant's Hand: English Fiction from Below* (New York: Columbia Univ. Press, 1986); John Richetti, "Representing an Under Class: Servants and Proletarians in Fielding and Smollett," in *The New Eighteenth-Century*, ed. Laura Brown and Felicity Nussbaum (New York: Methuen, 1987), 84–98.

26. It is interesting to note that D'Halluin, a foreigner himself, makes a special appeal to foreigners to apply to the office where "they will meet with Gentlemen qualified to give them the most punctual Information in any Particular whatsoever" (See Appendix II). In general, the tolerance of D'Halluin's "Plan" seems to highlight the elitism and xenophobia of the Fieldings.

27. *The London Daily Advertiser*, November 6, 1751.

28. Ibid., November 4, 1751.

29. This version of the Universal Register Office's advertisement first appears in *The Covent-Garden Journal*, No. 3 (January 11, 1752): 4. Of tangential interest here is the reference to servants "lying out of Place at their own Expence," which would seem to indicate that instead of a servant shortage, as Pat Rogers contends (*Henry Fielding,* 176), there was a servant surplus. Patty Seleski makes a convincing case for widespread voluntary or temporary unemployment among female servants, again indicating a servant surplus; see Seleski, "Women, Work and Cultural Change in Eighteenth- and Early Nineteenth-Century London," in *Popular Culture in England, c. 1500–1850,* ed. Tim Harris (New York: St. Martin's Press, 1995), 143–67. However, Hecht contends that the demand for servants was on the rise at mid-century (77–78). See also D. A. Kent, "Ubiquitous but Invisible: Female Domestic Servants in Mid-Eighteenth Century London," *History Workshop Journal* 28 (Autumn 1989): 111–28; and John Fielding's important assessment in n. 52 below.

30. Goldgar, *CGJ,* xxvi.

31. *The Covent-Garden Journal* is called "A Paper of Entertainment."

32. Goldgar, *CGJ,* xxxiv & 16.

33. After destroying two armies, Drawcansir proclaims:

> Others may boast a single man to kill;
>> But I, the blood of thousands daily spill.
>> Let petty Kings the names of Parties know:
>> Where e'er I come, I slay both friend and foe.

See George Villiers, Duke of Buckingham, *The Rehearsal,* 3rd. ed. (London, 1675) Act V, sc. i, ll. 275–78. It is perhaps to this bit of dialogue that Thornton is responding when he calls his journal *Have At You All.*

34. That Fielding understood the potentially beneficial effects of a paper war (as an advertising and sales technique) is confirmed by his having asked John Hill to engage him in a mock paper war—an offer Hill refused (see above). But Hill soon joined in the real one.

35. Dudden, for example, calls Bonnell Thornton "a scurrilous hack-writer" (*Fielding,* 2:889); Battestin characterizes Fielding's opponents as "the Goths and Vandals of Grub Street" (*Fielding,* 555); cf. Gerard Jensen, *The Covent-Garden Journal,* 1:5, passim. Goldgar, *CGJ,* xxvii–liv, is the most balanced account. For a summary of the paper war, see Chapter 4 below.

36. William Kenrick, *Fun: A Parodi-tragical-comical Satire* (London, 1752), 32.

37. Bonnell Thornton, *Have At You All: or, The Drury-Lane Journal* (London, 1752), 25; further references cited parenthetically in the text.

38. Lance Bertelsen, "Journalism, Carnival, and *Jubilate Agno,*" *ELH* 59 (1992): 364–65. On the political resistance and resentment associated with women authors in the late seventeenth and early eighteenth centuries, see Paula McDowell, *Women of Grub Street: Press, Politics and Gender in the London Literary Marketplace* (Oxford: Clarendon Press, 1998), 63–90, 180–87, passim.

At mid-century, despite an actual decline in "impolite" women authors, the irreverence and rebelliousness attributed to them is found in residual form in the work of male authors masquerading as women.

39. Morris Golden, *Fielding's Moral Psychology* (Amherst: Univ. of Massachusetts Press, 1966), 25–26.

40. James Ralph, "The Case of Authors by Profession or Trade" (Gainsville: Scholar's Facsimiles & Reprints, 1966), 8.

41. Bertrand Goldgar is certainly correct in asserting that moral commentary, rather than literary criticism, forms *The Covent-Garden Journal*'s primary matter, but it is morality applied to exciting and often sordid topical subjects. See Goldgar, *CGJ*, xl. Goldgar also notes that *The Covent-Garden Journal*'s world is "not of Johnsonian reflection but of Hogarthian bustle" (xxxiii).

42. Goldgar, *CGJ*, 451, notes that "Fielding's hand is clearly present" in all the comments "signed 'C.'"

43. Goldgar, *CGJ*, lii.

44. The most famous example of the crime-business equation is, of course, Gay's *The Beggar's Opera*. On Wild's *modus operandi*, see Gerald Howson, *Thief-Taker General: The Rise and Fall of Jonathan Wild* (London: Hutchinson, 1970).

45. *The Covent-Garden Journal*, No. 7 (January 25, 1752); Goldgar, *CGJ*, 55.

46. *The London Daily Advertiser*, June 3, 1751.

47. On curiosity, observation, and possession, see Barbara Benedict, "The 'Curious Attitude' in Eighteenth-Century Britain: Observing and Owning," *Eighteenth-Century Life* 14 (1990): 59–98. "Curiosity" and "curious" were often terms used to encode the conjunction of visual and sexual interest (89–93).

48. Of this and a later letter signed "Z.Z.," Goldgar writes, "both were attributed to Fielding by his nineteenth-century biographers, although neither bear the slightest trace of his style" (Goldgar, *CGJ*, xxiii), and cites Cross as his source. Cross, for his part, says simply, "The identification of Henry Fielding with 'Z.Z.' is very doubtful. So far as one can judge from the style of the anonymous gentleman, he was the novelist's brother John" (*The History of Henry Fielding*, 2:361). But Cross refers only to the letter on Glastonbury waters of August 31, 1751, and in fact does not explain on what criteria he judges even that letter to be in John Fielding's "style." Both letters fail the famous "hath" test, but my suggestion is merely that Henry contributed visual and theatrical ideas to the June 3 letter, not that he authored it himself.

49. John Fielding had been completely blind since the age of 19, and before that had "suffered from weakness of vision" (Battestin, *Fielding*, 271). On spectating and theater, see Kristina Straub, *Sexual Suspects: Eighteenth-Century Players and Sexual Ideology* (Princeton: Princeton Univ. Press, 1992), 3–6, et passim.

50. *Plan*, in Goldgar, *CGJ*, 8.

51. *The London Daily Advertiser,* January 9, 1752.
52. *The London Chronicle,* April 6, 1758. M. Dorothy George partially transcribes this passage in *London Life in the 18th-Century,* 3rd ed. (London:
Kegan Paul, 1925; reprint, London: London School of Economics, 1951),
112–13, but in a note (p. 355 n.10) unaccountably adds to *The London
Chronicle* citation the parenthetical phrase "written in 1753." I have no idea
about the source of this information, but the text of the letter seems to
confute it, for Fielding writes of "the streets and shops of this metropolis,
in the years 1755 and 1756." John Fielding also adds significant information to the debate concerning the shortage or surplus of servants (see n. 29
above) when he notes that "there is always in London an amazing number
of women servants out of place: notwithstanding which, the useful house-
wifery servants, commonly called maids of all work, are not sufficiently numerous to supply the wants of the families in town." In other words, there
was a shortage of maids of all work, but a surplus of chambermaids or
maids in an upper station.
53. The widely accepted idea that maid servants were not only fair game but
sexually willing emerges most clearly in the Pamela–Antipamela debates
that swirled around Richardson's novel. Fielding's attitude on this matter
is memorably expressed in *Shamela*—a work that while ostensibly an attack on the hypocritical morals of Richardson's heroine seems to indicate that Fielding felt sexual laxity was the norm for females of the
servant class. For an illuminating discussion of this problem, see Scarlett
Bowen, "'A Sawce-box and Boldface Indeed': Refiguring the Female
Servant in the Pamela-Anti-Pamela Debate," *Studies in Eighteenth-Century Culture,* vol. 28 (Baltimore: The Johns Hopkins Univ. Press, 1999).
Bridgit Hill argues convincingly that many maid servants "voluntarily
entered into sexual liaisons"; see Hill, *Servants: English Domestics in the
Eighteenth Century* (Oxford: Clarendon Press, 1996), 62–63. For the gen-
eral sexual experience of eighteenth-century working women, see
Bridgit Hill, *Women, Work & Sexual Politics in Eighteenth-Century England*
(Montreal: McGill Univ. Press, 1994), and Anna Clark, *The Struggle for the
Breeches: Gender and the Making of the British Working Class* (Berkeley:
Univ. of California Press, 1995).
54. Robert Wark, *Drawings by Thomas Rowlandson in the Huntington Collection*
(San Marino: Huntington Library, 1975), 6.
55. While there is no hard evidence (such as an advertisement) that the Universal Register Office held organized "show days," Z.Z.'s letter describing
the clientele and inviting the "Curious" to visit clearly indicates that in-
person inspection was encouraged, and perhaps encodes the potentially
sexual nature of viewing. Benedict notes that caricaturists exploded the
"claim that curious people . . . look at naked figures to see only art not
sex" ("Curious," 92). Of course, several of Rowlandson's caricatures show
male "connoisseurs" inspecting naked female models. In a print relevant to
the gender reversal in "The Registry Office," a 1772 print, "The Female

Connoiseur," [*sic*] shows a woman gazing at the picture of a naked man (reproduced in Benedict, "Curious," 90, pl. 14).

56. See William Cleland, *Memoirs of a Woman of Pleasure,* ed. Peter Sabor (Oxford: Oxford Univ. Press, 1985), 4–7.

57. Joseph Reed, *The Register Office: A Farce,* new ed. (London 1771), 7. Although my text is a later edition, the play was originally performed in 1761. In the performed version, the Licenser excised passages containing profanity and double entendre that had originally appeared in an unlicensed version entitled *The Universal Register Office* (see Larpent MS 189 and 196, The Huntington Library). *The London Stage 1660–1800,* pt. 4, ed. George Winchester Stone (Carbondale: Southern Illinois Univ. Press, 1962), 861.

58. Reed, 36. In Reed's play, spectation turns to attempted rape as the Lord eventually assaults Maria, who is rescued by her former master who has come to London in search of her.

59. Cleland, 4–7.

60. "Philanthropos," *An Appeal to the Public Against the Growing Evil of Universal Register-Offices* (London, 1757), 22.

61. Ibid., 22. Both works praise the original idea behind the Fieldings' establishment while deploring its corruption over time. The *Appeal* (by "Philanthropos") concentrates primarily on loan-sharking and false advertisement (an activity also touched upon in Reed's farce—"What a crowd of deluded females have flocked here within these three hours, in expectation of the imaginary place we have advertised!") but also deplores the "vast number of offices" that have grown up over the last several years. Seleski notes that "pamphlet writers and even playwrights portrayed register offices as manufacturing good characters for dishonest servants" (154), but makes no mention of their connection with prostitution.

62. Cf. Staves, 86–88.

63. Cf. Janet Todd, "Pamela: Or the Bliss of Servitude," *British Journal for Eighteenth-Century Studies* 6 (1983): 135–48; Richard Gooding, "*Pamela, Shamela,* and the Politics of the *Pamela* Vogue," *Eighteenth-Century Fiction* 7.2 (1995): 109–30.

64. Laura Mandell argues that in Mandeville's *A Modest Defence of Publick STEWS* whores are figured as "filthy embodiments of and containers for the kind of pleasure that one must deny one gets from profit-intensive business management" and thus the pleasures of business are distinguished from the business of pleasure. But in the register offices it is possible that while an overt separation is argued (i.e., the employment office saves women from prostitution by finding them places as servants), a collapsing of categories is what actually occurs (i.e., the employment office provides servant/mistresses). See Mandell, "Bawds and Merchants: Engendering Capitalist Desires," *ELH* 59 (1992): 116.

65. H. W. Bleackley, *Ladies Fair and Frail: Sketches of the Demi-Monde During the Eighteenth Century* (New York: Dodd, Mead, 1926), 14.

66. James Boswell, *Boswell's London Journal 1762–1763,* ed. Frederick Pottle (New York: McGraw-Hill, 1950), 263–64.

67. On the issue of public and private responses to prostitutes, see Verne Bullough, "Prostitution and Reform in Eighteenth-Century England," *Eighteenth-Century Life* 9 n.s., 3 (May 1985): 61–74.

68. See, for example, James Grantham Turner, "Novel Panic: Picture and Performance in the Reception of Richardson's *Pamela,*" *Representations* 48 (1994): 70–96, on the cultural struggle over "alluring fiction versus improving didacticism" (73) and "media that express or draw forth the private, inward *sentiment* of the character . . . but do so in spectatorial forms that place the consumer securely in control" (90–91).

69. *Harris's List of Covent-Garden Ladies* (London, 1764). Samuel Derrick, who later became master-of-ceremonies at Bath, launched the published version of *Harris's List* in 1760.

70. Ibid., 14–15.

71. An inconsistent attitude toward female servants and their masters is evident throughout Fielding's life and work. His ridicule of Richardson's *Pamela* reveals at the very least a temporary dismissal, for the purposes of entertainment and profit, of the dangers actually faced by maid servants in an upper station; yet *Shamela's* ostensive thesis that female servants hypocritically employ their sexual allure to get ahead seems itself contradicted by Fielding's own marriage, in 1747, to his housekeeper, Mary Daniel.

72. *Old England,* December 21, 1751, in *Henry Fielding: The Critical Heritage,* ed. Ronald Paulson and Thomas Lockwood (London: Routledge & Kegan Paul, 1969), 286.

73. Henry Fielding, *Amelia,* ed. Martin Battestin (Middletown, CT: Wesleyan Univ. Press, 1983), 3.

74. This passage appeared at the end of bk. V, ch. 9 of the first edition; see *Amelia,* 571. It was deleted in later editions. On the question whether this deletion was made by Fielding himself, see Hugh Amory, "What Murphy Knew: His Interpolations in Fielding's *Works* (1762), and Fielding's Revision of *Amelia,*" *Papers of the Bibliographical Society of America* 77 (1983): 153–54, passim.

75. *The London Daily Advertiser,* November 23, 1751; see Appendix II. Is it possible that D'Halluin, or more likely his ally Thornton, had seen *Amelia* in manuscript or somehow caught wind of this puff for the Universal Register Office?

Chapter 3

1. Henry Fielding, *Amelia,* ed. Martin Battestin (Middletown, CT: Wesleyan Univ. Press, 1983), 17–38.

2. Andrew Wright comments that "one wonders why Booth's tale must be told to Miss Matthews [*sic*] rather than to the reader. To be sure, the various interruptions *en route* keep reminding the reader of Miss Matthews's

amorous hopes and seductive intent, and thus they throw light on the perhaps excessively obliging or overgallant aspect of Booth's character. But is it necessary?" See Andrew Wright, *Henry Fielding: Mask and Feast* (Berkeley: Univ. of California Press, 1965), 110.

3. Throughout this chapter I will generally use the name "Fielding" to denote the narrator of the novel although I recognize that the person and the authorial voice are not necessarily always congruent. Nevertheless, as the title page of *Amelia* explicitly states that it is "by Henry Fielding, Esq," his name seems as accurate a signifier as any.

4. On the relationship of Booth, Fielding, and Fielding's father, see, for example, Battestin, *Fielding*, 540–42.

5. Rawson points out that the vignette also recalls an episode in the *Enquiry into the Causes of the Late Increase in Robbers* (1751) in which Fielding mentions a squalid but pretty girl, "one of the prettiest . . . I had ever seen"; see Claude Rawson, *Henry Fielding and the Augustan Ideal under Stress* (London: Routledge, 1972), 75.

6. Rawson interprets the elision of the pretty girl's oaths as indicative of Fielding's "pained recoil" at the event: "The shock resides . . . in a quality of cruel surprise which Fielding has deliberately staged or heightened by his otherwise gratuitous emphasis on the girl's beauty and innocent countenance" (75). I agree that Fielding has "staged or heightened" the event, but I don't think he is a bit surprised or disconcerted by it—he, after all, constructs the scene precisely to emphasize the pretty girl's depravity.

7. James Boswell, *Boswell's London Journal 1762–1763,* ed. Frederick Pottle (New York: McGraw-Hill, 1950), 160.

8. Wright notes that "Booth's story . . . is neither domestic nor realistic: it is operatic and sentimental" (110).

9. Morris Golden, *Fielding's Moral Psychology* (Amherst: Univ. of Massachusetts Press, 1966),70.

10. Robert Alter, *Fielding and the Nature of the Novel* (Cambridge, MA: Harvard Univ. Press, 1968), 174.

11. Alter, *Fielding,* 175. Cf. Morris Golden: "Miss Matthews developed her passion when she heard Booth talk of his wife, and Mrs. Bennet married the sergeant because his adoration of Amelia demonstrated a great capacity for love and therefore the possession of many other virtues. Both of these women, one slightly tainted and the other corrupt, are partly exploiting love, seeking to transfer to themselves the love aroused by another whose nature deserves it" (89).

12. Alter, *Fielding,* 175.

13. Zomchick suggests that "instead of seeing public and private as two mutually exclusive spheres, they must be viewed simultaneously as connected and separate," but does not grant this complexity to the novel's characters, particularly Miss Mathews whom he reductively calls "the narrative's archvillainess." See John P. Zomchick, *Family and the Law in Eighteenth-Century Fiction: Public Conscience in the Private Sphere* (Cambridge: Cambridge Univ.

Press, 1993) 132, 150. Zomchick's overly conceptual approach seems to me to ignore the tonal and contextual subtleties that arise from and lead back to the material and emotional circumstances of its author—and that determine the experience of reading the novel.

14. Since December 1748 Fielding had had to deal with street robberies by sailor gangs as well as with the more general riotous behavior caused by demobilization. See Battestin, 461–64. On the cultural valence of sailors, see Peter Linebaugh, *The London Hanged: Crime and Civil Society in the Eighteenth Century* (Cambridge: Cambridge Univ. Press, 1992), 123–42.

15. Fielding was out of town when the riots began, but returned on July 3 and immediately took steps to restore peace. The most complete (but controversial) account of the Penlez incident is found in Peter Linebaugh, "The Tyburn Riot Against the Surgeons," in *Albion's Fatal Tree: Crime and Society in Eighteenth-Century England,* ed. Douglas Hay et al. (New York: Pantheon, 1975), 89–100.

16. Battestin dates the composition of *Amelia* from late autumn 1749. See *Amelia,* xlii–xliii.

17. A. L. Beier, *Masterless Men: The Vagrancy Problem in England, 1560–1640* (London: Methuen, 1985); Paul Slack, "Vagrants and Vagrancy in England, 1598–1664," *Economic History Review,* 2nd series, 37 (1974): 360–79. Slack and Beier both identify demobilized soldiers and sailors as a chief source of masterless men. Thanks to Jo Anne Shea for these references.

18. Jill Campbell contrasts Booth, "a half-pay officer in search of a regiment," to Serjeant Atkinson, who is "actively employed on duty in London"; but then generalizes inaccurately: "Apparently, military service offers a feasible form of employment for a working-class man, who labors at it as at any other job, but survives only as a 'broken' vestige of a past 'constitution' for the gentleman." Clearly, Fielding's experience would have led him to far different conclusions about the rank and file, who were as frequently unemployed and usually more riotous than their officers. My point is that the chaotic potential of all classes of unemployed military men is fictionally addressed in the behavior of Booth, Bath, and James. Serjeant Atkinson's virtues as a military man surely reflect more his personal virtue than any valorization of the non-commissioned ranks. See Jill Campbell, *Natural Masques: Gender and Identity in Fielding's Plays and Novels* (Stanford: Stanford Univ. Press, 1995), 219.

19. Battestin, *Fielding,* 474; Linebaugh, "Tyburn," 95; cf. Pat Rogers, *Henry Fielding: A Biography* (London: Paul Elek, 1979), 183–84.

20. Linebaugh, "Tyburn," 96.

21. Battestin, *Fielding,* 709.

22. Bertrand Goldgar, "Fielding and the Whores of London," *Philological Quarterly* 64 (1985): 267.

23. *Old England* (July 15, 1749); quoted in Battestin, *Fielding,* 475.

24. Campbell, summing up a long tradition of criticism, notes that Booth "repeatedly encounters ethical and interpretive impasses that leave him

stymied about how to act or how to explain others' actions to himself"
(*Natural Masques,* 206).

25. Andrew Elfenbein traces the difficulties of coherently understanding Mrs.
James's behavior in "Mysteries of Conduct: Gender and Narrative Structure in Fielding's *Amelia,*" Department of English, University of Min-
nesota; cited by Campbell, *Natural Masques,* 226–27.

26. John Coolidge, "Fielding and 'Conservation of Character,'" *Modern Philology* 57 (1960): 250. On Fielding's willingness throughout his fiction to sustain "unresolved dualities," see Henry Knight Miller, *Essays on Fielding's
Miscellanies. A Commentary on Volume One* (Princeton: Princeton Univ.
Press, 1961), 269; and Campbell, *Natural Masques,* 107.

27. See "Interested" in *The Oxford English Dictionary,* ed. James A. H. Murray
et al., 1st ed., 12 vols. (Oxford: Clarendon Press, 1888–1928).

28. Battestin, *Fielding,* 447.

29. Campbell, *Natural Masques,* 228–29. I use "clientage" rather than the usual
"patronage" because the former denotes the client's point of view—the
view from below.

30. Straub, examining the "issues of gender and power that are often implicit
in Foucault's 'pleasures' of spectatorship,'" remarks that a "consciousness
that the spectator's gaze is enacted within a power differential between the
watcher and the watched is at least as old as the seventeenth century. The
subject-object dichotomy of seventeenth-century psychology brings into
discourse an uneasiness about the moral implications of watching and the
power relations between the one who watches and the one who is
watched"; see Kristina Straub, *Sexual Suspects: Eighteenth-Century Players
and Sexual Ideology* (Princeton: Princeton Univ. Press, 1992), 5.

31. Variations on the first formulation are widespread; I quote Campbell, 240.
For the "post of domestic 'angel,'" see Campbell, *Natural Masques,* 206.
Many critics assign Amelia completely to the passive private sphere. Cynthia Griffin Wolff, for example, argues that "Amelia's virtue is private, and
its influence can be felt only in personal interaction" without understanding that in the world of clientage and connection "personal interaction" is
often already a public event with public consequences and rewards. See
"Fielding's *Amelia:* Private Virtue and Public Good," *Texas Studies in Language and Literature* 10 (1968): 54.

32. Terry Castle, *Masquerade and Civilization: The Carnivalesque in Eighteenth-
Century English Culture and Fiction* (Stanford: Stanford Univ. Press, 1986),
241–42.

33. Alison Conway, "Fielding's *Amelia* and the Aesthetic of Virtue," in Albert J.
Rivero, ed., *Critical Essays on Henry Fielding* (New York: G. K. Hall & Co.,
1998), 204–205.

34. On "hysterical excesses" in *Amelia,* see Glen Colburn, "'Struggling Manfully' through Henry Fielding's *Amelia:* Hysteria, Medicine, and the Novel
in Eighteenth-Century England," *Studies in Eighteenth-Century Culture,* vol.
26 (Baltimore: Johns Hopkins Univ. Press, 1998), 87–123. Colburn, how-

ever, does not include excesses of gratitude among the "abrupt emotional shifts" and "incoherencies" afflicting the feminized (though not exclusively female) characters of the novel.

35. Quoted by Battestin, *Fielding,* 506. The rhetoric and tone of this letter are representative of Fielding's style in writing to the great. As Malvin Zirker charitably remarks, "'Fielding's letters to Bedford, Hardwicke, and Lyttelton are extremely polite and deferential, and certainly do not read like an exchange between peers." See Malvin Zirker, *Fielding's Social Pamphlets* (Berkeley: Univ. of California Press, 1966), 37–38. Maaja Stewart has argued that in *Tom Jones* Fielding attempted to rehabilitate the Renaissance conception of gratitude as an all–encompassing relationship ("the servant was grateful to his master for protection and nurture and the master was grateful to his servant for service, and all—masters and servants—were grateful to God for his bountiful and unpayable gifts") at a time when the masculinity and economic agency were being redefined in terms of "independence." See Maaja Stewart, "Ingratitude in *Tom Jones*," *Journal of English and Germanic Philology* 89 (1990): 512–32. Certainly for someone who begged and thanked as often as Fielding such a rehabilitation would have been psychologically convenient. In *Amelia,* however, gratitude seems explicitly feminized. Particularly when the grateful character is a man (for example, Booth or Bennet), gratitude is so often misdirected and so often accompanied by loss of emotional control that it seems precisely the opposite of the "manly virtues . . . of possession and self-possession" that Stewart sees as central to the ideology of independence.

36. Interestingly, Amelia's conversation with Harrison concerns how to refuse Colonel James's offer that she live with him without making Booth suspect that James desires her. Clearly she *would* be thinking about the power of her beauty and ways to control it during, as she puts it, "the difficult Game I have to play" (376).

37. Raymond Williams, *Keywords: A Vocabulary of Culture and Society,* rev. ed. (New York: Oxford Univ. Press, 1983), 172; cf. *Oxford English Dictionary,* "Interest" and "Interested."

38. Williams, *Keywords,* 172.

39. Alter, *Fielding,* 149.

40. Ibid., 157; cf. Tiffany Potter, *Honest Sins: Georgian Libertinism and the Plays and Novels of Henry Fielding* (Montreal: McGill-Queen's Univ. Press, 1999), 151–54.

41. The text of the first edition is taken from Appendix II of *Amelia,* ed. Battestin.

42. *The London Daily Advertiser,* June 3, 1751.

43. *Amelia,* lx; cf. John Bender, *Imagining the Penitentiary: Fiction and the Architecture of the Mind in Eighteenth-Century England* (Chicago: Univ. of Chicago Press, 1987), 189–90.

44. Indeed, Hugh Amory argues that these revisions were made by Arthur Murphy after Fielding's death. See Hugh Amory, "What Murphy Knew:

His Interpolations in Fielding's *Works* (1762), and Fielding's Revision of *Amelia*," *Papers of the Bibliographical Society of America* 77 (1983): 133–66.

45. *The London Daily Advertiser*, June 3, 1751.

46. Bk.V, ch. 9 of the first edition; see *Amelia*, 571.

47. One has to wonder what Mr. Bennet's (and Fielding's) response would have been had the Lord accepted his friendship but in the long run offered him nothing material. Would this have constituted "ingratitude"?

48. *Amelia*, xxxix. For Fielding's praise of Dodington, see *Amelia*, 462–63.

49. *Amelia*, xxxix.

50. In an analysis of Elizabethan suitor's letters, Frank Whigham notes that the "oiliness of these letters reveal social conditions of pressure and anxiety" (866): social conditions in which a suitor's excessive gratitude had "the force of imposing on the patron the mantle of generosity, the refusal of which disconfirmed the patron's status, not the petitioner's" (874). He remarks of such letters' potential to become "self-defeatingly excessive" that "Renaissance readers may have begun to respond to these letters as lay readers do today to legal or governmental documents: we skim for the essentials, dismissing the highly wrought style as irrelevant information about a bureaucratic author" (877). See Whigham, "The Rhetoric of Elizabethan Suitor's Letters," *Publications of the Modern Language Association* 96 (1981): 864–82. Following Whigham's line of thought, I think it probable that in the eighteenth century the rhetorical excesses of gratitude and appreciation were well recognized, but nevertheless obligatory for the self-interested: something like the common deployment of the term "brilliant" in academic recommendations and reviews.

51. Although the incidents recorded in the Covent Garden columns are from a slightly later date, they surely represent the kind of cases that came before Fielding throughout his tenure as magistrate.

52. Goldgar, *CGJ*, 430–31. In the Covent Garden columns, instances of wife-beating occur with about the same frequency as instances of husband-beating. It is important to point out here that the so-called "rule of thumb," at least with regard to the legality of wife-beating (but not approximate measurement in carpentry), is a completely erroneous notion deriving from a series of scholarly and interpretive mistakes. As Christina Sommers demonstrates in *Who Stole Feminism?* (New York: Simon and Schuster, 1994), there never was a law that a women could be legally beaten by her husband as long as he used a rod no thicker than his thumb. Yet, after decades in the making, the myth achieved something like canonical status when in 1982 "a group of scholars and lawyers . . . prepared a report on wife abuse for the United States Commission on Civil Rights" (203) called *Under the Rule of Thumb*.

53. Even Dr. Harrison is caught up in the game when he is flattered excessively by a young clergyman's father, only to have him later explain his motivations to his son, "He hath given away above half his Fortune to Lord knows who. I believe I have had above 200l. of him, first and last; and

would you lose such a Milch-cow as this for Want of a few Compliments? Indeed, Tom, thou art as great a Simpleton as himself. How do you expect to rise in the Church, if you can't temporize, and give into the Opinion of your Superiors?'" (404).

54. For an extended reading of this scene, see Castle, *Masquerade*, 177–252.

55. See, for example, Brian McCrea, *Henry Fielding and the Politics of Mid-Eighteen-Century England* (Athens: Univ. of Georgia, 1981), 184–87; Thomas R. Cleary, *Henry Fielding: Political Writer* (Waterloo, Ontario: Wilfrid Laurier Univ. Press, 1984), 289–90; Alter, *Fielding*, 147–48.

56. Battestin notes this argument was central to Dodington's political crusade for the reformation of the patronage system. See *Amelia*, 457 n.1.

57. Bender argues that Dr. Harrison is "a figure who comes as close as a fictional character can to speaking for his creator" (185)—a statement I would extend to his blindness to his own contradictions. Indeed, this particular kind of contradictory context was not unfamiliar to the novelist. In the world outside the novel, Fielding on August 29, 1749, wrote to Lyttelton to solicit a position for a young man named Edward Moore. After buttering him up with a little moral philosophy—"there is a great Pleasure in Gratitude tho it is second I believe to that of Benevolence: for of all the Delights upon Earth none can equal the Raptures which a good Mind feels in conferring Happiness"— Fielding solicited the position for Moore, and then closed with a fawning, self-aggrandizing, and merit-based justification of his own solicitation: "In this Fault then you must indulge me: for should I ever see you as high in Power, as I wish, and as it is perhaps more my Interest than your own that you should be, I shall be guilty of the like as often as I find a Man in whom I can, after much Intimacy discover no Want." See Battestin, *Fielding*, 482–83.

58. James Thompson argues that in *Amelia* prostitution is "domesticity's contradiction"—a formulation based on a "central contrast" between Amelia as "the good wife . . . who protects her virtue at all costs and Mrs. Trent"; see James Thompson, *Models of Value: Eighteenth-Century Political Economy and the Novel* (Durham: Duke Univ. Press, 1996), 155. But as I have tried to show, during her interested flirtation with the Noble Lord, Amelia does not protect her virtue and in fact indulges emotionally (and, to a degree, physically) in something similar to domestic prostitution. Moreover, Thompson's formulation seems to ignore other contexts in which financially or sexually motivated marriages were considered to make wives whores even if there were no domestic infidelity. See, for example, Daniel Defoe, *Conjugal Lewdness, or Matrimonial Whoredom* (London, 1727; reprint, Gainsville: Scholars' Facsimiles & Reprints, 1967).

59. Another notable aspect of Trent's history is its style. Fielding drops the somewhat rambling, maudlin, and naive (not to say dull) voice that characterizes most of *Amelia* and writes with a detached irony more reminiscent of *Jonathan Wild* and parts of *Tom Jones*. Because all the parties can be presented as unproblematic opportunists (though "sensible," "genteel," and "bold" as well), Fielding seems to have less difficulty laughing at their

desires and tactics when they engage each other in chicanery. Thus, for example, we are told that after some years of marriage, Trent's "Wife, though one of the prettiest Women in Town, was the last Subject that he would have chose for any amorous Dalliance":

> Many other Persons however, greatly differed from him in this Opinion. Amongst the rest was the illustrious Peer of amorous Memory. This noble Peer having therefore got a View of Mrs. *Trent* one Day in the Street, did, by Means of an Emissary then with him, make himself acquainted with her Lodging, to which he immediately laid Siege in Form, setting himself down in a Lodging directly opposite her, from whence the Battery of Ogles began to play the next Morning. (469)

The amused treatment of vice ("illustrious Peer of amorous Memory") and the amorous visual artillery seem more appropriate to the Inn at Upton than to Amelia's apprehensive world. Freed momentarily from the necessity of portraying impossible ethical dilemmas, Fielding seems still capable of light-heartedness.

60. Thompson, *Models,* 145.
61. See J. G. A. Pocock, *Virtue, Commerce, and History* (Cambridge: Cambridge Univ. Press, 1985), 114, for one of the earlier statements of what has now become a critical commonplace.
62. The classic essays on moral economy and paternalism are E. P Thompson, "The Patricians and the Plebs" and "The Moral Economy of the English Crowd in the Eighteenth Century," in *Customs in Common: Studies in Traditional Popular Culture* (New York: New Press, 1993), 16–56, 185–254.
63. Roy Porter, *English Society in the Eighteenth Century,* 2nd. ed. (Harmondsworth, UK: Penguin, 1990), 113.
64. Harold Perkin, *The Origins of Modern English Society 1780–1880* (London: Routledge & Kegan Paul, 1972), 49.
65. Douglas Hay makes a notable (though controversial) case for such a recasting of judicial discretion as "mercy" in "Property, Authority, and the Criminal Law," *Albion's Fatal Tree: Crime and Society in Eighteenth-Century England,* ed. Douglas Hay et al. (New York: Pantheon, 1975), 17–64.
66. John Brewer, "Commercialization and Politics," in *The Birth of a Consumer Society: The Commercialization of Eighteenth-Century England,* ed. Neil McKendrick (Bloomington: Indiana Univ. Press, 1982), 198.
67. Zomchick, however, argues that this episode marks "the emergence of the reinvigorated patriarch, now aligned with the law." See *Family and the Law,* 149–50.
68. Cf. *Amelia,* 521 n.1.
69. Zirker, *Fielding's Social Pamphlets,* 61–2.
70. *A Proposal for Making an Effectual Provision for the Poor* in *An Enquiry into the Causes of the Late Increase of Robbers and Related Writings,* ed. Malvin Zirker (Middletown, CT: Wesleyan Univ. Press, 1988), 242.

71. Battestin notes that from March 6, 1752 to November 6, 1753 Fielding's "signature appears in eighty-one vouchers" authorizing payment for expenses incurred removing vagrants from London. See *Amelia,* xxv n.1.

Chapter 4

1. Fielding, *A Clear State of the Case of Elizabeth Canning* in *An Enquiry into the Causes of the Late Increase of Robbers and Related Writings,* ed. Malvin Zirker (Middletown, CT: Wesleyan Univ. Press, 1988), 287. Further quotations cited parenthetically in the text. My quotations are from Fielding's slightly revised redaction of Canning's actual deposition, which is printed complete later in *Elizabeth Canning.* His listing of articles stolen recalls the descriptions in the Covent Garden columns.

2. *The Daily Advertiser,* January 6, 1753, cited in John Hill, *The Story of Elizabeth Canning Considered* (London, 1752), 14; Lord, *State Trials,* 19: 491 & 479, cited in Judith Moore, *The Appearance of Truth: The Story of Elizabeth Canning and Eighteenth-Century Narrative* (Newark, DE: Univ. of Delaware Press, 1994), 13–14.

3. *Genuine and Impartial Memoirs of Elizabeth Canning* (London, 1754), v. Hereafter cited as *Genuine Memoirs.*

4. See Lillian Bueno McCue, "Elizabeth Canning in Print," *University of Colorado Studies,* series B, Studies in the Humanities 2.4 (October 1945): 223–34.

5. On the war, see *The Covent-Garden Journal,* ed. Gerard Jensen, 2 vols. (New Haven: Yale Univ. Press, 1915), 1:5, passim; *The Covent-Garden Journal and A Plan of the Universal Register-Office,* ed. Bertrand Goldgar (Middletown, CT: Wesleyan Univ. Press, 1988), xxvii–liv; Betty Rizzo, "Notes on the War between Henry Fielding and John Hill, 1752–53," *The Library,* 6th ser. vii (1985): 338–53; Lance Bertelsen, "'Neutral Nonsense, neither false nor true': Christopher Smart and the Paper War(s) of 1752–53," *Christopher Smart and the Enlightenment,* ed. Clement Hawes (New York: St. Martin's Press, 1999), 135–52.

6. William Kenrick, *Fun: A Parodi-tragical-comical Satire* (London, 1752), ii.

7. Ibid., 7. For Smart's disavowal, see *The London Daily Advertiser,* February 13, 1752.

8. Charles Macklin, *The Covent Garden Theatre, or Pasquin Turn'd Drawcansir* (1752), Larpent MS. 96, Augustan Reprint Society, no. 116, ed. Jean Kern (Los Angeles: William Andrews Clark Memorial Library, 1965), 3–4. Fielding advertised the play repeatedly in *The Covent-Garden Journal* (March 14, 17, 21, and 28, 1752).

9. Martin C. Battestin with Ruthe R. Battestin, *Henry Fielding: A Life* (London: Routledge, 1989), 557.

10. For other responses to Hill, see Goldgar, *CGJ,* 325 n.2.

11. "The Inspector" No. 422 (July 17, 1752).

12. *The Spring-Garden Journal* (London, 1752), title page.

13. Ibid., 5.

14. Ibid., 7.

15. Jensen, *The Covent-Garden Journal,* 1:84 n.5, records Fitzpatrick's name as "Richard."

16. Notes by Richard Cross, Drury-Lane prompter, in *The London Stage 1660–1800,* part 4: 1747–1776, ed. George Winchester Stone (Carbondale: Southern Illinois Univ. Press, 1962), 329–31.

17. Rizzo, "Notes," 344–45.

18. "The Inspector," December 7, 1752.

19. Jesse Foot, *Life of Arthur Murphy* (London, 1811), 106. For Fielding's possible contributions, see Rizzo, "Notes," 348–53.

20. *The London Daily Advertiser,* January 31, 1752.

21. The best short account of the Canning case is found in Zirker's "General Introduction" to *Elizabeth Canning* in *Enquiry and Related Writings,* although he consistently refers to the *Public Advertiser* as "Publick Advertiser"—spelling that, as far as I can determine, never appeared on the paper's masthead.

22. *Genuine Memoirs,* 13–14.

23. Canning's place of captivity—"up an old pair of stairs" in "a back room like a hayloft"—seems almost a quotation from the story Thornton (writing as Smart's Midnight) told of visiting Thornton's persona, the ex-bawd Roxana Termagant, "up a pair of rotten worm-eaten stairs . . . into a little room, which you could scarce stand upright in, because the raftors that hung just as if they were going to drop upon your head"—much like the ceiling that had in fact fallen on Elizabeth Canning's head, making her subject to fits. See Bonnell Thornton, *Have At You All: or, The Drury-Lane Journal* (London, 1752), 60.

24. Moore, *Appearance,* 65–66, suggests that there is confusion about the date on which Hall was initially examined, some sources suggesting that the examination took place as late as February 14. A notice in *The Public Advertiser* of February 10, 1753, however, states that on "Thursday Evening [i.e., February 8] a Girl who lived in the House, and who was apprehended by a Warrant from the Justice, was brought before him, and was under Examination from Six till Twelve at Night; when, after many hard Struggles and stout Denials of the Truth, she at length confessed the whole." Moore includes only a partial quotation ascribed to "*The Public Advertiser* of Friday, 9 February." The correct date is Saturday, February 10; and the original quotation appears above. Moreover, the description from the *Public Advertiser* was later used against Fielding by Gascoyne as proof that he has intimidated Hall. See *Enquiry and Related Writings,* 301 n.1.

25. *The Gazetteer,* February 16, 1753. The report also notes that "a certain Gentleman present took an exact Drawing of the Physiognomy of this infamous Gypsy, with a Copperplate Print of which we are informed the Publick will soon be obliged."

26. For the trial, see Moore, *Appearance,* 72–78.

27. For an overview of various interpretations, see Moore, *Appearance,* 176–239.

28. *Canning's Magazine: or, a review of the Whole Evidence that has been hitherto offered for, or against Elizabeth Canning, and Mary Squires* (London, 1753), iii–iv.

29. Ibid., 5.

30. Ibid., 13.

31. *The Account of Canning and Squires fairly ballanc'd* (London, 1753), 4, 10; *The Inspector,* No. 623, March 9, 1753. Zirker conjectures that the *Account* "must have been one of the first to appear, for it does not mention either Fielding's or Hill's pamphlet" (ciii), but the first advertisement for it (under a somewhat different title) appears in the *Public Advertiser* on May 3, 1753.

32. *The Account of Canning and Squires fairly ballanc'd,* 11.

33. As marginal notes by Bonnell Thornton to Charles Churchill's *Independence* reveal, it was a common practice in reviewing to write the review in the margins next to passages marked for extraction. See Lance Bertelsen, *The Nonsense Club: Literature and Popular Culture, 1749–1764* (Oxford: Clarendon Press, 1986), 246.

34. *The Account of Canning and Squires fairly ballanc'd,* 23–24.

35. Another interesting aspect of the *Account* is that it was first advertised in *The Public Advertiser* of May 3, 1753 as *An Impartial Review of the Case of Elizabeth Canning and Mary Squires* "By a disinterested Bystander" with the imprint of "R. Baldwin, at the Rose in Pater-noster Row." But on May 8, 1753, it was advertised with the title found on all extant copies, *The Account of Canning and Squires fairly ballanc'd,* with the imprint "W. Bizet, at the Golden Ball in St. Clements Churchyard." Baldwin had just published what Hugh Amory calls an "unauthorized abridgement" of Fielding's *Elizabeth Canning* under the title *An Impartial Review.* See Amory, *The Virgin and the Witch: an exhibition at the Harvard Law School Library of materials from the Hyde Collection and Harvard Libraries on the celebrated trial of Elizabeth Canning* (Cambridge, MA: Harvard Univ. Press, 1987), n.p. Is it possible that Baldwin's publishing two pieces with such similar titles, only to have the second almost immediately re-appear with a different title and imprint, indicates that the abridgement was perhaps *not* unauthorized and that, to seem even more "disinterested," the "bystander" of the second pamphlet had it retitled and published by a different bookseller?

36. Sir Crisp Gascoyne, *An Address to the Liverymen of the City of London* (London, 1754), 4–5.

37. Catalogue numbers refer to the *Catalogue of Prints and Drawings in the British Museum: Division I. Political and Personal Satires,* ed. F. G. Stephens, et al., 4 vols. (London, 1883). The significance of "witch" association is recognized by Hugh Amory in his entitling a Harvard exhibition and catalogue of Canning materials, *The Virgin and the Witch* (1987).

38. Christopher Smart, *The Midwife; or the Old Woman's Magazine* (London, 1751–53), 2:147; Kenrick, *Fun,* 7; *Canning's Magazine,* appendices 10 and 12.

39. Robert A. Erickson, *Mother Midnight: Birth, Sex, and Fate in Eighteenth-Century Fiction* (New York: AMS Press, 1986), 18. For more on witches, midwives, and Grub Street, see Lance Bertelsen, "Journalism, Carnival, and *Jubilate Agno*," *ELH* 59 (1992): 365

40. *Genuine Memoirs*, 6; cf. Moore, *Appearance*, 25.

41. *Enquiry and Related Writings*, c.

42. E. P. Thompson, *Whigs and Hunters: The Origin of the Black Act* (New York: Pantheon, 1975), 256–57.

43. Moore, *Appearance*, 39. Moore notes that the pro-Squires pamphlet, *The Controverted Hard Case of Mary Squires* (London, 1753), argues that "tho' Squires has been all along represented as one of the Clan and Fraternity of Gipseys, it is certain she never did belong to them" (13; quoted Moore, 39).

44. See T. W. Perry, *Public Opinion, Propaganda, and Politics in Eighteenth-Century England: A Study of the Jew Bill of 1753* (Cambridge, MA: Harvard Univ. Press, 1962).

45. One alderman says, "Why faith any Friend to tell you true/ for a good bribe, I'd Ene turn Jew."

46. On the "solidarities" of the lower classes, see Peter Linebaugh, "The Tyburn Riot Against the Surgeons," in *Albion's Fatal Tree: Crime and Society in Eighteenth-Century England,* ed. Douglas Hay, et al. (New York: Pantheon, 1975), 79–88.

47. For a useful summary of Fielding's strategy of argumentation, see Arlene Wilner, "The Mythology of History, the Truth of Fiction: Henry Fielding and the Cases of Bosavern Penlez and Elizabeth Canning," *The Journal of Narrative Technique* 21 (1991): 194–95.

48. Interestingly, the absurdly universal promises of the full title recall both Smart's parodic title page for *The Midwife, or the Old Woman's Magazine* ("*Containing* all *the* WIT, *and* all *the* HUMOUR, *and* all *the* LEARNING, *and* all *the* JUDGEMENT, *that has* ever been, *or* ever will be *inserted in* all *the other* Magazines, *or the* Magazine of Magazines, *or the* Grand Magazine of Magazines, *or any other Book whatsoever*") and Fielding's more serious claim for the Universal Register Office, where the "Curious will be supplied with every thing which it is in the Power of Art to produce."

49. *The Imposture Detected* (London, 1753), quoted in John Treherne, *The Canning Enigma* (London: Jonathan Cape, 1989), 79. The "rabbit-woman" is, of course, Mary Toft. The most complete account of her celebrated affair is found in Dennis Todd, *Imagining Monsters: Miscreations of the Self in Eighteenth-Century England* (Chicago: Univ. of Chicago Press, 1995), 1–139. Fielding mentions the affair in his burlesque history of the reign of George II that appeared in *The Covent-Garden Journal*, No. 12 (February 11, 1752). The "adventure of the quart-bottle" is also described by Fielding in this burlesque history: "A certain Juggler placed a common Quart-Bottle on a Table, on the Stage of a public Theatre, and in the Sight of several Hundreds of People, conveyed himself into the Bottle, where he remained a decent Time; after which he again returned out of his Place of Confinement,

in the same Manner as he had gone into it." Goldgar summarizes the actual event:"Someone advertised that on the night of 16 Jan. 1749 he would place himself in a tavern quart bottle on the stage of the Haymarket Theatre. . . . A great crowd assembled, waited half an hour, and became impatient; when a voice in the pit called out, 'For double the price the conjuror will go into a pint bottle,' the crowd rioted and set the theatre on fire." See Goldgar, *CGJ,* 90 n.2.

50. James Dodd, *A Physical Account of the Case of Elizabeth Canning, With an Enquiry into the Probability of her subsisting in the Manner therein asserted, and her Ability to Escape after her suppos'd ill Usage* (London, 1753), title page.

51. Daniel Cox, *An Appeal to the Public, in Behalf of Elizabeth Canning, In which the material Facts of her Story are fairly stated, and shown to be true, on the Foundations of Evidence* (London, 1753), 23–24. For a more complete review of this pamphlet, see Moore, *Appearance,* 119–21.

52. For Fielding's relationship with the hospital, see Goldgar, *CGJ,* 251 n.3. The Covent Garden column for January 10, 1752, noted that "eleven married Women, all big with Child, appeared before the said Justice, at one and the same Time, to receive their Certificates for the Lying-In Hospital in Brownlow Street. A Sight highly pleasing to a good Mind, and a Charity which doth great Honour to those who first planned it, and to those who contribute to it." The editorial comment seems to have been added by Fielding.

53. See Hill, *The Story of Elizabeth Canning Considered,* 22.

54. The term "discursive hysteria" is used by Glen Colburn to describe the rhetoric of medical writers on hysteria: rhetoric characterized by "self-contradictions, which arise from the writers' attempts to conflate deductive, moral truths and inductive, physiological truths" and which tend "to blur the distinction between medical and moral inquiries"; see Glen Colburn, "'Struggling Manfully' through Henry Fielding's *Amelia:* Hysteria, Medicine, and the Novel in Eighteenth-Century England," *Studies in Eighteenth-Century Culture,* vol. 26 (Baltimore: Johns Hopkins Univ. Press, 1998), 98. He suggestively compares such rhetoric to "Fielding's blurring of the distinction between literary and empirical agendas in the opening chapter of *Amelia,*" but I find it equally relevant to the rhetoric of Canning's story about her kidnapping and to the rhetoric of Fielding's pamphlet about Canning's story. The linkage of medicine and literary endeavor may account as well for an oddly coincidental occurrence of about this time (after Hill's *Inspector* columns rejecting Canning's story, but before his overt repudiation of her medical condition above), which possibly marks the final fertilization of the Fielding-Hill matrix by the Canning publishing paroxysm. On March 20, 1753, the very day that Fielding's *Elizabeth Canning* was published, Garrick staged Fielding's old play, *The Mock-Doctor,* as the afterpiece for Henry Woodward's benefit, with Woodward in the title role mimicking "Dr." Hill—"his foppish dress, his smirk, his waddle of a walk" (Battestin, 564). The "Prologue," which wittily pointed up Hill as the

new Mock Doctor, was contributed by Christopher Smart. Not only was Hill held up to ridicule as a medical fake, the play surely brought to mind Hill's own medical and media troubles, when in the wake of the Brown affair he had reported regularly on his supposed injuries in *The London Daily Advertiser,* describing himself at one point as losing "the Stream of Life" (May 9, 1752), and at another as in danger of developing an "Empyema" in his side (May 11, 1752). Such reports made Hill the butt of literary London. (See *CGJ,* 325 n.2.) In reviving *The Mock Doctor* on the day that Fielding's *Elizabeth Canning* appeared, Garrick presented a play by Hill's chief literary enemy, acted by Hill's new theatrical enemy, as a satire on Hill's claims to medical authority (or, for that matter, any authority), with a prologue (though in fact it was never performed) by another of his tormentors, Christopher Smart.

55. Treherne, *Canning Enigma,* 9.
56. Pat Rogers, *Grub Street: Studies in a Subculture* (London: Methuen, 1972), 40.
57. Ibid., 43–44.
58. Alexander Pope, *The Dunciad Variorum,* in *The Poems of Alexander Pope,* ed. John Butt (New Haven: Yale Univ. Press, 1963).
59. It is instructive to walk this route, which takes about 25 minutes, today. It begins in Cable Street at the site of Wells Close Square and proceeds west along what becomes Royal Mint street, passing between new housing developments to the south and railway lines to the north. Turning northwest onto The Minories, which turns into Houndsditch Street, it curves through the heart of the City's opulent business development, toward the Barbican and the Museum of London.
60. The accounts of Canning's attack vary in detail but seem to indicate that she was seized on London Wall street just east of Bethlehem Hospital (which backed onto that street and faced the open walks of Moorfields) and dragged around its eastern end down the gravel walk that led toward the central gate to the hospital. Somewhere along this walk she was struck in the head.
61. Rogers, *Grub Street,* 50.
62. Dennis Todd discusses the relationship of Mary Toft and Dulness in terms that suggest the simultaneous popular interest in Canning's bodily and imaginative productions: "Both Dulness and Mary Toft are feminine forces who possess the terrifying power to subvert language, civilization, and the very structures of thought. Presiding over a process of corporealization, they dissolve distinctions, blur boundaries, and precipitate the mind into a giddy whirl of confusion that descends into chaos and the body and ends in parody. Their power of destruction is located, paradoxically, in their monstrous activity" (*Monsters,* 209).
63. Catherine Ingrassia, "Women Writing/Writing Women: Pope, Dulness, and "Feminization" in the *Dunciad,*" *Eighteenth-Century Life* 14 (1990): 44.
64. See Pocock, *Virtue, Commerce, and History* (Cambridge: Cambridge Univ. Press, 1985), 114; Bertelsen, "Journalism," 357–61; Ingrassia, "Women," 40–45.

65. My categories are based on Stallybrass and White's well-known interpretation of Bakhtin's vocabulary of "grotesque" and "classical": "the grotesque body . . . was usually multiple,. teeming, always already part of a throng. By contrast, the classical statue is the radiant center of transcendent individualism, 'put on a pedestal.'" Stallybrass and White, of course, famously connect "The Grotesque Body and the Smithfield Muse." See *The Politics and Poetics of Transgression*, 21–22, 80–124. For an interesting reading of the "statuesque" versus the carnivalesque in eighteenth-century theater, see Denise Sechelski, "Garrick's Body and the Labor of Art in Eighteenth-Century Theater," *Eighteenth-Century Studies* 29 (1996): 373–77.

66. Treherne, *Canning Enigma*, 79.

67. *Genuine Memoirs*, 48.

68. Hill, *The Story of Elizabeth Canning Considered*, 29.

69. *Enquiry and Related Writings*, xcii–xciii.

70. Ibid., 180.

71. The word "Fool" here also serves as a topical allusion to his old antagonist "The Fool," author of a regular essay series in *The Daily Gazetteer.* See *Enquiry and Related Writings*, 292 n.7.

72. Jonathan Swift, *A Tale of a Tub, The Prose Works of Jonathan Swift*, ed. Herbert Davis, 14 vols. (Oxford: Basil Blackwell, 1939–68), 1:109.

73. The reference may be to Anne Killigrew, the poet, painter, and subject of Dryden's famous elegy (whose uncle was a theater manager), although this allusion would seem quite dated in 1753.

74. See Battestin, *Fielding*, ix–x.

75. See, for example, Ronald Paulson, *Hogarth*, 3 vols. (New Brunswick, NJ: Rutgers Univ. Press, 1993), 3:31. James Basire engraved the portrait in 1762, but it seems reasonable to believe that the notation "AEtatis XLVIII" on the frame comes from Hogarth's original drawing. It should be noted, however, that Fielding was 47 not 48 when he died.

76. Battestin, *Fielding*, ix–x.

Chapter 5

1. Henry Fielding, *The Journal of a Voyage to Lisbon*, ed. Tom Keymer (Harmondsworth, UK: Penguin, 1996), 83–91. Further quotations cited parenthetically in the text. Albert J. Rivero compares Fielding's *Journal* to *A Tale of a Tub:* "a book whose diversity figures forth, not a capacious self, but the random consciousness and broken body of an author whose last known address is Bedlam." He also compares Fielding to Montaigne—"His *Essais,* obeying no apparent order, perfectly embody a various self"—but neglects the more radical, if sometimes tongue-in-cheek, manifestations of literary reflexivity in Fielding's contemporary milieu. See "Figurations of the Dying: Reading Fielding's *The Journal of a Voyage to Lisbon*," *Journal of English and Germanic Philology* 93 (1994): 521.

2. Charles Churchill, *The Ghost, Book IV,* ll. 813–18, *The Poetical Works of Charles Churchill,* ed. Douglas Grant (Oxford: Clarendon, 1956).

3. On reflexive process poetry, see T. E. Blom, "Eighteenth-Century Reflexive Process Poetry," *Eighteenth-Century Studies* 10 (1976): 59, passim. On the aesthetic of spontaneity, see Lance Bertelsen, *The Nonsense Club: Literature and Popular Culture, 1749–1764* (Oxford: Clarendon Press, 1986), 106–111, passim.

4. Christopher Smart, *The Poetical Works of Christopher Smart,* ed. Karina Williamson et al., 4 vols. (Oxford: Clarendon, 1980–87), 1: B. 243.

5. *The Public Advertiser,* March 11, 1754. On the temple of luxury, see William W. Appleton, *Charles Macklin: An Actor's Life* (Cambridge, MA: Harvard Univ. Press, 1960), 98–102.

6. *The Public Advertiser,* November 21, 1754. Walpole to Richard Bentley, December 24, 1754, in *Correspondence,* vol. 35, ed. W. S. Lewis (New Haven: Yale Univ. Press, 1973), 200. See also Appleton, *Macklin,* 103–108.

7. Jonathan Swift, *The Prose Works of Jonathan Swift,* ed. Herbert Davis, 14 vols. (Oxford: Basil Blackwell, 1939–68), 1:73; Alexander Pope, *The Dunciad in Four Books,* in *The Poems of Alexander Pope,* ed. John Butt (New Haven: Yale Univ. Press, 1963), 794–95.

8. On the potential for appropriated forms—particularly chaotic ones—to reappropriate the author, see Clement Hawes, *Mania and Literary Style: The Rhetoric of Enthusiasm from the Ranters to Christopher Smart* (Cambridge: Cambridge Univ. Press, 1996), 122–23.

9. On Smart and hybridization, see Lance Bertelsen, "Journalism, Carnival, and *Jubilate Agno,*" *ELH* 59 (1992): 375.

10. Tom Keymer, "*The Journal of a Voyage to Lisbon:* Body, City, Jest," in *Critical Essays on Henry Fielding,* ed. Albert J. Rivero (New York: G. K. Hall & Co., 1998), 229–31, 237.

11. Henry Fielding, *The Journal of a Voyage to Lisbon,* ed. Harold E. Pagliaro (New York: Nardon Press, 1963), 9.

12. Claude Rawson, *Henry Fielding and the Augustan Ideal Under Stress* (London: Routledge, 1972), 96.

13. On inclusiveness in Smart's *Jubilate Agno,* see Bertelsen, "Journalism," 374–75; see also Hawes, *Mania and Literary Style,* ch. 8. On inclusiveness in Churchill's poetry, see Bertelsen, *The Nonsense Club,* 226–28. For the phrase, "anti-encyclopedic," I am indebted to Fraser Easton, "Christopher Smart's Anti-Encyclopedia," paper delivered at the American Society for Eighteenth-Century Studies annual meeting, New Orleans, 1989.

14. Fielding's *Enquiry into the Causes of Late Increase of Robbers* also has a dedication, preface, and introduction, although the introduction is included in the main body of the text, and I do not consider the *Enquiry* to be primarily an entertainment. The *Journal's* dedication was not written by Fielding but probably by Arthur Murphy; nevertheless, Fielding almost always dedicated his works and had he lived we would expect to find a dedication in this position.

15. Keymer, "Body, City," 231–32.
16. Swift, *Prose Works*, 1: 27.
17. Terence N. Bowers, "Tropes of Nationhood: Body, Body Politic, and Nation-State in Fielding's *Journal of a Voyage to Lisbon*," *ELH* 62 (1995): 603.
18. Battestin notes that *The Mock Doctor's* Dedication to Misaubin parodies the dedication of a contemporary translation of Moliere's *L'Avare* to Mead. See Martin C. Battestin with Ruthe R. Battestin, *Henry Fielding: A Life* (London: Routledge, 1989), 138.
19. Henry Fielding, *The Covent-Garden Journal and A Plan of the Universal Register Office*, ed. Bertrand Goldgar (Middletown, CT: Wesleyan Univ. Press, 1988), 9.
20. Rivero ("Figurations," 525) notes Fielding's interest in "conveyance," but ignores the satirical treatment of the topic.
21. Philip Edwards, *The Story of the Voyage: Sea Narratives in Eighteenth-Century England* (Cambridge: Cambridge Univ. Press, 1994), 177.
22. Simon Varey notes the pattern of using a "rather minor incident as a starting point for a digression" but declines to speculate about its significance. See Simon Varey, *Henry Fielding* (Cambridge: Cambridge Univ. Press, 1986), 139.
23. William Cowper, "An Epistle to Robert Lloyd, Esqr.," in *The Poems of William Cowper*, ed. John D. Baird and Charles Ryskamp, 2 vols. (Oxford: Clarendon Press, 1980), 1: 56–57.
24. Robert Lloyd, "The Author: An Epistle to C. Churchill," in *The Poetical Works of Robert Lloyd, A.M.*, ed. William Kenrick, 2 vols. (London, 1774; reprint, Farnborough, UK: Gregg, 1969), 2:18.
25. Battestin, *Fielding*, 589.
26. In bestowing "'honorary' Scriblerian status" on Fielding, Brean Hammond neglects the more problematic aesthetic of the later works and, perhaps because his study terminates at 1750, mentions *The Covent-Garden Journal, Amelia*, and *The Journal of a Voyage to Lisbon* not at all. See Brean S. Hammond, *Professional Imaginative Writing in England 1670–1740: 'Hackney for Bread'* (Oxford: Clarendon Press, 1997), 239, 275–86. On the transition from "Dulness" to "Progress," see Bertelsen, "Journalism," 357–60 n. 17; cf. Paula McDowell, *Women of Grub Street: Press, Politics and Gender in the London Literary Marketplace* (Oxford: Clarendon Press, 1998), 10.
27. Battestin, *Fielding*, 590.
28. *The Monthly Review*, 28 (June 1763), 479. Interestingly, Kenrick is reviewing Bonnell Thornton's burlesque ode on St. Caecilia's Day.
29. James Boswell, *Boswell's London Journal 1762–1763*, ed. Frederick Pottle (New York: McGraw-Hill, 1950), 266; George Colman, *Prose on Several Occasions*, 3 vols. (London, 1787), 1:11–12.
30. Swift, *Prose Works*, 1:29.
31. Ibid., 1:24.
32. Henry Fielding, *The True Patriot and Related Writings*, ed. W. B. Coley (Middletown, CT: Wesleyan Univ. Press, 1987), 219–20.

33. Richardson writes in his Preface to *Clarissa* that many readers "were of the opinion that in all works of this, and of the dramatic kind, *story* or *amusement* should be considered as little more than the vehicle to the more necessary *instruction*." See Richardson, *Clarissa or The History of a Young Lady*, ed. Angus Ross (Harmondsworth, UK: Penguin, 1985), 36.

34. Interestingly, in *The Covent-Garden Journal* No. 12, Fielding cites his persona, in a mock history, as someone who also had achieved a "thorough Reformation" of society, "which, according to the best Chronologists, happened in the Year 1753, brought about by one General DRAWGAND-SIR, who *at the Head of a vast Army*, set up his Standard in Common Gardens, and with a certain Weapon called Ridicule, or Ridicle, or as one conjectures a Wry-Sickle, brought the People by main Force to better Manners." See Goldgar, *CGJ*, 90.

35. A reference, presumably, to Alexander the Great and dueling. For Fielding's mixed views on Alexander the Great, see Rawson, *Henry Fielding and the Augustan Ideal*, 119–20, 149–50, 208–10.

36. George Villiers, *The Rehearsal* (London, 1675), Act IV, sc. i, ll. 190–91.

37. Battestin, *Fielding*, 577.

38. Dexter Marks, "A Death in Lisbon" (MASECS Conference, Toledo, October 1992), "traces the influence that the Voyage has had on later biographers, who have downplayed or dismissed Fielding's eating and drinking excesses"; cited by Bowers, "Tropes," 600 n.20.

39. Bowers, "Tropes," 582.

40. Keymer, "Body, City," 226.

41. Rivero, "Figurations," 532.

42. Henry Fielding, *The Author's Farce*, ed. Charles B. Woods (Lincoln: Univ. of Nebraska Press, 1966), 53.

43. *The St. James's Chronicle*, 29 April–1 May 1762. See also Ronald Paulson, *Popular and Polite Art in the Age of Hogarth and Fielding* (Notre Dame, IN: Univ. of Notre Dame Press, 1979), 40.

44. Robert D. Hume, *Henry Fielding and the London Theatre 1728–1737* (Oxford: Clarendon Press, 1988), 63–66.

45. Goldgar, *CGJ*, 214–15. Writing as "Nobody," Fielding answers this letter in *CGJ* No. 41.

46. Friedrich Nietzche, *The Geneaology of Morals* (1:10), quoted in Fredric Jameson, *The Political Unconscious* (Ithaca: Cornell Univ. Press, 1981), 201.

47. Peter Stallybrass and Allon White, *The Politics and Poetics of Transgression* (London: Methuen, 1986), 9, 22.

48. I am grateful to Elizabeth Burow Flak for this observation.

49. *The St. James's Chronicle*, 29 April–1 May 1762. The use of transformative body metaphors for cultural mixing and hybridizing was, of course, common in the eighteenth-century and derives in part from scientific and popular interest in the breeding of mixed species, i.e., "monsters." See, for example, Barbara Stafford, *Body Criticism: Imaging the Unseen in Enlightenment Art and Medicine* (Cambridge, MA.: MIT Press, 1993), 254–66, passim.

50. See William J. Burling, "'Merit Infinitely Short of Service': Fielding's Pleas in the *Journal of a Voyage to Lisbon,*" *English Studies* 70 (1989): 53–62.

51. The anti-gang campaign waged by Fielding appears to have been remarkably successful and to have provided a real basis for his last request. Fielding writes that "In this entire freedom from street-robberies, during the dark months, no man will, I believe, scruple to acknowledge, that the winter of 1753 stands unrival'd, during the course of many years" (*Journal,* 14).

52. Keymer ("Body, City," 229–30) notes as well the emotional incongruity of "Burnet's insouciance as he informs a poor man that his neck is to be snapped, on behalf of the horse-owning classes, as an edifying piece of theatre" and the inappropriateness of the Blenheim reference, given Marlborough's arraignment for peculation.

53. Letter to Samuel Richardson, May 28, 1755, in Ronald Paulson and Thomas Lockwood, eds., *Henry Fielding: The Critical Heritage* (London: Routledge & Kegan Paul, 1969), 393.

54. Arthur Murphy, "An Essay on the Life and Genius of Henry Fielding, Esq.," in *The Works of Henry Fielding, Esq.,* 2nd. ed., 8 vols. (London, 1762), 1:46.

55. Peter Linebaugh, *The London Hanged: Crime and Civil Society in the Eighteenth Century* (Cambridge: Cambridge Univ. Press, 1992), 89–90.

Conclusion

1. See "Convenient" in *The Oxford English Dictionary,* ed. James A.H. Murray et al., 1st ed., 12 vols. (Oxford: Clarendon Press, 1888–1928).

2. On Fielding's latitudinarian sympathies, see Martin C. Battestin with Ruthe R. Battestin, *Henry Fielding: A Life* (London: Routledge, 1989), 332–35, passim.

3. Robert D. Hume, *Henry Fielding and the London Theatre 1728–1737* (Oxford: Clarendon, 1988), 52.

4. Thomas Lockwood, "Fielding and the Licensing Act," *Huntington Library Quarterly* 50 (1987): 382, 385.

5. Sandra Sherman, *Finance and Fictionality in the Early Eighteenth-Century: Accounting for Defoe* (Cambridge: Cambridge Univ. Press, 1996), 2.

6. "Disembarking, the Trojans gain the welcome beach" (*Aeneid,* I, 172); Henry Fielding, *The Journal of a Voyage to Lisbon,* ed. Tom Keymer (Harmondsworth, UK: Penguin, 1996), 142.

7. "This is the end of the story and the journey" (adapting Horace, *Satires,* I, v, 104); *Journal,* 142.

Bibliography

The Account of Canning and Squires fairly ballanc'd. London, 1753.

Alter, Robert. *Fielding and the Nature of the Novel.* Cambridge: Harvard Univ. Press, 1968.

Amory, Hugh. "Magistrate or Censor? The Problem of Authority in Fielding's Later Writings." *Studies in English Literature* 12 (1972): 503–18.

———. "Preliminary Census of Henry Fielding's Legal Manuscripts." *Papers of the Bibliographical Society of America* 62 (1968): 587–601.

———. *The Virgin and the Witch: an exhibition at the Harvard Law School Library of materials from the Hyde Collection and Harvard Libraries on the celebrated trial of Elizabeth Canning.* Cambridge, MA: Harvard Univ. Press, 1987.

———. "What Murphy Knew: His Interpolations in Fielding's *Works* (1762), and Fielding's Revision of *Amelia.*" *Papers of the Bibliographical Society of America* 77 (1983): 133–66.

Appleton, William W. *Charles Macklin: An Actor's Life.* Cambridge, MA: Harvard Univ. Press, 1960.

Arendt, Hannah. *Between Past and Future: Six Exercises in Political Thought.* New York: Viking Press, 1961.

Armitage, Gilbert. *The History of the Bow Street Runners.* London: Wishart, 1932.

Armstrong, Nancy. *Desire and Domestic Fiction: A Political History of the Novel.* New York: Oxford Univ. Press, 1987.

Barthes, Roland. *S/Z.* Paris: Sueil, 1970.

Battestin, Martin C. with Ruthe R. Battestin, *Henry Fielding: A Life.* London: Routledge, 1989.

Battestin, Martin C. and Michael Farrington, eds. *New Essays by Henry Fielding.* Charlottesville: Univ. of Virginia Press, 1989.

Beattie, J. M. "The Criminality of Women." *Journal of Social History* 8 (1975): 80–116.

———. *Crime and the Courts in England, 1660 - 1800.* Princeton: Princeton Univ. Press, 1986.

Beier, A. L. *Masterless Men: The Vagrancy Problem in England, 1560 - 1640.* London: Methuen, 1985.

Bender, John. *Imagining the Penitentiary: Fiction and the Architecture of the Mind in Eighteenth-Century England.* Chicago: Univ. of Chicago Press, 1987.

Benedict, Barbara. "The 'Curious Attitude' in Eighteenth-Century Britain: Observing and Owning." *Eighteenth-Century Life* 14 (1990): 59–98.

Bertelsen, Lance. *The Nonsense Club: Literature and Popular Culture, 1749 - 1764.* Oxford: Clarendon Press, 1986.

———. "Journalism, Carnival, and Jubilate Agno." *ELH* 59 (1992): 357–84.

———. "Committed by Justice Fielding: Judicial and Journalistic Representation in the Bow Street Magistrate's Office, January 3–November 24, 1752." *Eighteenth-Century Studies* 30 (1997): 337–63.

———. "'Neutral Nonsense, neither false nor true': Christopher Smart and the Paper War(s) of 1752–53." *Christopher Smart and the Enlightenment.* Ed. Clement Hawes. New York: St. Martin's Press, 1999.

Bleackley, H. W. *Ladies Fair and Frail: Sketches of the Demi-Monde during the Eighteenth Century.* New York: Dodd, Mead, 1926.

Blom, T. E. "Eighteenth-Century Reflexive Process Poetry." *Eighteenth-Century Studies* 10 (1976): 52–72.

Boswell, James. *Boswell's London Journal 1762–1763.* Ed. Frederick Pottle. New York: McGraw-Hill, 1950.

Bowen, Scarlett. "'A Sawce-box and Boldface Indeed': Refiguring the Female Servant in the Pamela-Anti-Pamela Debate." *Studies in Eighteenth-Century Culture.* Vol. 28. Baltimore: Johns Hopkins Univ. Press, 1999.

Bowers, Terence N. "Tropes of Nationhood: Body, Body Politic, and Nation-State in Fielding's Journal of a Voyage to Lisbon." *ELH* 62 (1995): 575–602.

Boulukos, George. "Memoirs of the Life and Travels of Thomas Hammond: An Edition for Readers." M.A. Report. University of Texas at Austin, 1994.

Brewer, John. "Commercialization and Politics." *The Birth of a Consumer Society: The Commercialization of Eighteenth-Century England.* Ed. Neil McKendrick. Bloomington: Indiana Univ. Press, 1982.

Brewer, John and John Styles, eds. *An Ungovernable People: The English and Their Law in the Seventeenth and Eighteenth Centuries.* New Brunswick: Rutgers Univ. Press, 1980.

Bullough, Verne. "Prostitution and Reform in Eighteenth-Century England." *Eighteenth-Century Life* 9 n.s., 3 (May 1985): 61–74.

Burling, William J. "'Merit Infinitely Short of Service': Fielding's Pleas in the Journal of a Voyage to Lisbon." *English Studies* 70 (1989): 53–62.

Campbell, Jill. *Natural Masques: Gender and Identity in Fielding's Plays and Novels.* Stanford: Stanford Univ. Press, 1995.

Canning's Magazine: or, a review of the Whole Evidence that has been hitherto offered for, or against Elizabeth Canning, and Mary Squires. London 1753.

Castle, Terry. *Masquerade and Civilization: The Carnivalesque in Eighteenth-Century English Culture and Fiction.* Stanford: Stanford Univ. Press, 1986.

Catalogue of Prints and Drawings in the British Museum: Division I. Political and Personal Satires. Ed. F. G. Stephens et al. 4 vols. London, 1883.

Cheek, Pamela. "Prostitutes of 'Political Institution.'" *Eighteenth-Century Studies* 28 (1994–95): 193–219.

Churchill, Charles. *The Poetical Works of Charles Churchill.* Ed. Douglas Grant. Oxford: Clarendon Press, 1956.

Clark, Anna. *The Struggle for the Breeches: Gender and the Making of the British Working Class.* Berkeley: Univ. of California Press, 1995.

Cleary, Thomas R. *Henry Fielding: Political Writer.* Waterloo, Ontario: Wilfrid Laurier Univ. Press, 1984.

Cleland, William. *Memoirs of a Woman of Pleasure.* Ed. Peter Sabor. Oxford: Oxford Univ. Press, 1985.

Cody, Lisa Forman. "The Politics of Reproduction: From Midwives' Alternative Public Sphere to the Public Spectacle of Man-Midwifery." *Eighteenth-Century Studies* 32 (1998): 477–96.

Colburn, Glen. "'Struggling Manfully' through Henry Fielding's Amelia: Hysteria, Medicine, and the Novel in Eighteenth-Century England." *Studies in Eighteenth-Century Culture.* Vol. 26. Baltimore: Johns Hopkins Univ. Press, 1998.

Coley, W. B. "Fielding's Two Appointments to the Magistracy." *Modern Philology* 63 (1965): 144–49.

Colman, George. *Prose on Several Occasions.* 3 vols. London, 1787.

The Controverted Hard Case of Mary Squires. London, 1753.

Conway, Alison. "Fielding's Amelia and the Aesthetic of Virtue." *Critical Essays On Henry Fielding.* Ed. Albert J. Rivero. New York: G. K. Hall & Co., 1998.

Coolidge, John. "Fielding and 'Conservation of Character.'" *Modern Philology* 57 (1960): 245–59.

Cowper, William. *The Poems of William Cowper.* Ed. John D. Baird and Charles Ryskamp. 2 vols. Oxford: Clarendon Press, 1980-.

Cox, Daniel. *An Appeal to the Public, in Behalf of Elizabeth Canning, In which the material Facts of her Story are fairly stated, and shown to be true, on the Foundations of Evidence.* London, 1753.

Cross, Wilbur L. *The History of Henry Fielding.* 3 vols. New Haven: Yale Univ. Press, 1918.

The Daily Advertiser. London, 1751–53.

Damrosch, Leo. *Fictions of Reality in the Age of Hume and Johnson.* Madison: Univ. of Wisconsin Press, 1989.

Davis, Lennard. *Resisting Novels: Ideology and Fiction.* New York: Methuen, 1987.

Defoe, Daniel. *Conjugal Lewdness, or Matrimonial Whoredom.* London, 1727. Reprint, Gainsville: Scholars' Facsimiles & Reprints, 1967.

Dobson, Austin. *Henry Fielding: A Memoir.* Rev. ed. New York: Dodd, Mead, 1900.

Dodd, James. *A Physical Account of the Case of Elizabeth Canning, With an Enquiry into the Probability of her subsisting in the Manner therein asserted, and her Ability to Escape after her suppos'd ill Usage.* London, 1753.

Donoghue, Frank. *The Fame Machine: Book Reviewing and Literary Careers.* Stanford: Stanford Univ. Press, 1996.

Dudden, F. Homes. *Henry Fielding: His Life, Works, and Times.* 2 vols. Oxford: Clarendon Press, 1952.

Earle, Peter. *The Making of the English Middle Class: Business, Society, and Family Life in London 1660–1730.* London: Methuen, 1989.

Edwards, Philip. *The Story of the Voyage: Sea Narratives in Eighteenth-Century England.* Cambridge: Cambridge Univ. Press, 1994.

Erickson, Robert A. *Mother Midnight: Birth, Sex, and Fate in Eighteenth-Century Fiction.* New York: AMS Press, 1986.

Fielding, Henry. *The Covent-Garden Journal. London, 1752.*
————. *The Covent-Garden Journal.* Ed. Gerard Jensen. 2 vols. New Haven: Yale Univ. Press, 1915.
————. *The Journal of a Voyage to Lisbon.* Ed. Harold E. Pagliaro. New York: Nardon Press, 1963.
————. *The Author's Farce.* Ed. Charles B. Woods. Lincoln: Univ. of Nebraska Press, 1966.
————. *The History of Tom Jones, a Foundling.* Ed. Fredson Bowers. Middletown: Wesleyan Univ. Press, 1975.
————. *Amelia.* Ed. Martin Battestin. Middletown, CT: Wesleyan Univ. Press, 1983.
————. *The True Patriot and Related Writings.* Ed. W. B. Coley. Middletown, CT: Wesleyan Univ. Press, 1987.
————. *The Covent-Garden Journal and A Plan of the Universal Register Office.* Ed. Bertrand Goldgar. Middletown, CT: Wesleyan Univ. Press, 1988.
————. *An Enquiry into the Causes of the Late Increase of Robbers and Related Writings.* Ed. Malvin Zirker. Middletown, CT: Wesleyan Univ. Press, 1988.
————. *The Journal of a Voyage to Lisbon.* Ed. Tom Keymer. Harmondsworth, UK: Penguin, 1996.
Foot, Jesse. *Life of Arthur Murphy.* London, 1811.
Foucault, Michel. *Discipline and Punish: The Birth of the Prison.* New York: Vintage, 1979.
Gascoyne, Sir Crisp. *An Address to the Liverymen of the City of London.* London, 1754.
Gatrell, V. A. C. *The Hanging Tree: Execution and the English People 1790–1868.* Oxford: Oxford Univ. Press, 1994.
The Gazetteer. London, 1753.
The Gentleman's Magazine. Vol. 22. London, 1752.
Genuine and Impartial Memoirs of Elizabeth Canning. London, 1754.
George, M. D. *"The Early History of Registry Offices."* Economic Journal: Economic History Supplement 1 (1926–29): 570–90.
————. *London Life in the 18th-Century.* 3rd ed. London: Kegan Paul, 1925. Reprint, London School of Economics, 1951.
Golden, Morris. *Fielding's Moral Psychology.* Amherst: Univ. of Massachusetts Press, 1966.
Goldgar, Bertrand. *Walpole and the Wits: The Relation of Politics to Literature, 1722–1742.* Lincoln: Univ. of Nebraska Press, 1976.
————. "Fielding and the Whores of London." *Philological Quarterly* 64 (1985): 265–73.
Gooding, Richard. "Pamela, Shamela, and the Politics of the Pamela Vogue." *Eighteenth-Century Fiction* 7.2 (1995): 109–30.
Habermas, Jürgen. *The Structural Transformation of the Public Sphere: An Inquiry into a Category of Bourgeois Society.* Trans. Thomas Burger. Cambridge, MA: MIT Press, 1991.
Hall, Stuart. "Encoding/decoding." *Culture, Media, Language.* Ed. Stuart Hall et al. London: Hutchinson, 1980.

Hammond, Brean S. *Professional Imaginative Writing in England 1670–1740: 'Hackney for Bread'*. Oxford: Clarendon Press, 1997.

Harris's List of Covent-Garden Ladies. London, 1764.

Hawes, Clement. *Mania and Literary Style: The Rhetoric of Enthusiasm from the Ranters to Christopher Smart*. Cambridge: Cambridge Univ. Press, 1996.

———. "Introduction" and "The Utopian Public Sphere: Intersubjectivity in Jubilate Agno." *Christopher Smart and the Enlightenment*. Ed. Clement Hawes. New York: St. Martin's Press, 1999.

Hay, Douglas. "Property, Authority, and the Criminal Law." *Albion's Fatal Tree: Crime and Society in Eighteenth-Century England*. Ed. Douglas Hay et al. New York: Pantheon, 1975.

Hecht, J. J. *The Domestic Servant Class in Eighteenth-Century England*. London: Routledge, 1956.

Heck, Marina Camargo. "The ideological dimension of media messages." *Culture, Media, Language*. Ed. Stuart Hall et al. London: Hutchinson, 1980.

Heinzelman, Susan Sage. "Guilty in Law, Implausible in Fiction: Jurisprudential and Literary Narratives in the Case of Mary Blandy, Parricide, 1752." *Representing Women: Law, Literature and Feminism*. Ed. Susan Heinzelman and Zipporah Batshaw Wiseman. Durham: Duke Univ. Press, 1994.

Hill, Bridgit. *Women, Work & Sexual Politics in Eighteenth-Century England*. Montreal: McGill Univ. Press, 1994.

———. *Servants: English Domestics in the Eighteenth Century*. Oxford: Clarendon Press, 1996.

Hill, John. *The Story of Elizabeth Canning Considered*. London, 1752.

Howson, Gerald. *Thief-Taker General: The Rise and Fall of Jonathan Wild*. London: Hutchinson, 1970.

Hume, Robert. *Henry Fielding and the London Theatre 1728–1737*. Oxford: Clarendon Press, 1988.

———. *Reconstructing Contexts: The Aims and Principles of Archaeo-Historicism*. New York: Oxford Univ. Press, 1999.

Hunter, J. Paul. *Occasional Form: Henry Fielding and the Chains of Circumstance*. Baltimore: Johns Hopkins Univ. Press, 1975.

Ingrassia, Catherine. "Women Writing/Writing Women: Pope, Dulness, and 'Feminization' in the Dunciad." *Eighteenth-Century Life* 14 (1990): 41–55.

———. *Authorship, Commerce, and Gender in Early Eighteenth-Century England: A Culture of Paper Credit*. Cambridge: Cambridge Univ. Press, 1998.

Innes, Joanna and John Styles. "The Crime Wave: Recent Writing on Crime and Criminal Justice in Eighteenth-Century England." *Journal of British Studies* 25 (1986): 380–435.

Jones, B. M. *Henry Fielding: Novelist and Magistrate*. London: George Allen & Unwin, 1933.

Kenrick, William. *Fun: A Parodi-tragical-comical Satire*. London, 1752.

Keymer, Tom. "The Journal of a Voyage to Lisbon: Body, City, Jest." *Critical Essays On Henry Fielding*. Ed. Albert J. Rivero. New York: G. K. Hall & Co., 1998.

Landau, Norma. *The Justices of the Peace, 1679–1760*. Berkeley: Univ. of California Press, 1984.

Langbein, John H. "Albion's Fatal Flaws." *Past and Present* 98 (1983): 96–120.

———. "Shaping the Eighteenth-Century Criminal Trial: A View from the Ryder Sources." *University of Chicago Law Review* 50 (1983): 1–137.

Linebaugh, Peter. "The Tyburn Riot against the Surgeons." *Albion's Fatal Tree: Crime and Society in Eighteenth-Century England*. Ed. Douglas Hay et al. New York: Pantheon, 1975.

———. *The London Hanged: Crime and Civil Society in the Eighteenth Century*. Cambridge: Cambridge Univ. Press, 1992.

Lloyd, Robert. *The Poetical Works of Robert Lloyd, A.M.* Ed. William Kenrick. 2 vols. London, 1774. Reprint, Farnborough, UK: Gregg, 1969.

Lockwood, Thomas. "Fielding and the Licensing Act." *Huntington Library Quarterly* 50 (1987): 379–93.

The London Chronicle. London, 1758.

The London Daily Advertiser. London, 1751–54.

The London Stage 1660–1800. Pt. 4. Ed. George Winchester Stone. Carbondale: Southern Illinois Univ. Press, 1962.

Low, David. "Mr. Fielding of Bow Street." *Henry Fielding: Justice Observed*. Ed. K. G. Simpson. London: Vision, 1985.

Macklin, Charles. *The Covent Garden Theatre, or Pasquin Turn'd Drawcansir* (1752). Larpent MS. 96. Augustan Reprint Society. No. 116. Ed. Jean Kern. Los Angeles: William Andrews Clark Memorial Library, 1965.

Mandell, Laura. "Bawds and Merchants: Engendering Capitalist Desires." *ELH* 59 (1992): 107–23.

McCrea, Brian. *Henry Fielding and the Politics of Mid-Eighteen-Century England*. Athens: Univ. of Georgia, 1981.

McCue, Lillian Bueno. "Elizabeth Canning in Print." *University of Colorado Studies. Series B. Studies in the Humanities* 2.4 (October 1945): 223–34.

McDowell, Paula. *Women of Grub Street: Press, Politics and Gender in the London Literary Marketplace*. Oxford: Clarendon Press, 1998.

Miller, Henry Knight. *Essays on Fielding's Miscellanies: A Commentary on Volume One*. Princeton: Princeton Univ. Press, 1961.

Moi, Toril. *Sexual/Textual Politics: Feminist Literary Theory*. London: Routledge, 1991.

The Monthly Review. London, 1763.

Moore, Judith. *The Appearance of Truth: The Story of Elizabeth Canning and Eighteenth-Century Narrative*. Newark, DE: Univ. of Delaware Press, 1994.

Murphy, Arthur. *The Works of Henry Fielding, Esq*. 2nd. ed. 8 vols. London, 1762.

Nicholson, Colin. *Writing and the Rise of Finance: Capital Satires of the Early Eighteenth Century*. Cambridge: Cambridge Univ. Press, 1994.

O'Brien, John. "Union Jack: Amnesia and the Law in Daniel Defoe's Colonel Jack." *Eighteenth-Century Studies* 32 (1998): 65–82

Paulson, Ronald, ed. *Fielding: A Collection of Critical Essays*. Englewood Cliffs, NJ: Prentice-Hall, 1962.

———. *Popular and Polite Art in the Age of Hogarth and Fielding.* Notre Dame, IN: Univ. of Notre Dame Press, 1979.

———. *Hogarth.* 3 vols. New Brunswick, NJ: Rutgers Univ. Press, 1993.

Paulson, Ronald and Thomas Lockwood, eds. *Henry Fielding: The Critical Heritage.* London: Routledge & Kegan Paul, 1969.

Perkin, Harold. *The Origins of Modern English Society 1780–1880.* London: Routledge & Kegan Paul, 1972.

Perry, T. W. *Public Opinion, Propaganda, and Politics in Eighteenth-Century England: A Study of the Jew Bill of 1753.* Cambridge, MA: Harvard Univ. Press, 1962.

Pettit, Alexander. *Illusory Consensus: Bolingbroke and the Polemical Response to Walpole, 1730–1737.* Newark, DE: Univ. of Delaware Press, 1997.

"Philanthropos." *An Appeal to the Public Against the Growing Evil of Universal Register-Offices.* London, 1757.

Pocock, J. G. A. *Politics, Language, and Time: Essays on Political Thought and History.* New York: Atheneum, 1973.

———. *Virtue, Commerce, and History.* Cambridge: Cambridge Univ. Press, 1985.

Pope, Alexander. *The Poems of Alexander Pope.* Ed. John Butt. New Haven: Yale Univ. Press, 1963.

Porter, Roy. *English Society in the Eighteenth Century.* 2nd. ed. Harmondsworth, UK: Penguin, 1990.

Potter, Tiffany. *Honest Sins: Georgian Libertinism and the Plays and Novels of Henry Fielding.* Montreal: McGill-Queen's Univ. Press, 1999.

The Public Advertiser. London, 1753–54.

Ralph, James. "The Case of Authors by Profession or Trade." London, 1758: Reprint, Gainsville: Scholar's Facsimiles & Reprints, 1966.

Rawson, Claude. *Henry Fielding and the Augustan Ideal under Stress.* London: Routledge & Kegan Paul, 1972.

Reed, Joseph. *The Register Office: A Farce.* New ed. London, 1771.

———. *The Universal Register Office (1761).* Larpent MS 189 and 196. Huntington Library.

Richardson, Samuel. *Clarissa or The History of a Young Lady.* Ed. Angus Ross. Harmondsworth: Penguin, 1985.

Richetti, John. "Representing an Under Class: Servants and Proletarians in Fielding and Smollett." *The New Eighteenth-Century.* Ed. Laura Brown and Felicity Nussbaum. New York: Methuen, 1987.

Rivero, Albert J. "Figurations of the Dying: Reading Fielding's The Journal of a Voyage to Lisbon." *Journal of English and Germanic Philology* 93 (1994): 520–33.

———. "Introduction." *Critical Essays on Henry Fielding.* Ed. Albert J. Rivero. New York: G. K. Hall & Co., 1998.

Rizzo, Betty. "Notes on the War between Henry Fielding and John Hill, 1752–53." *The Library,* 6th ser., vii (1985): 338–53.

Robbins, Bruce. *The Servant's Hand: English Fiction from Below.* New York: Columbia Univ. Press, 1986.

Rogers, Pat. *Grub Street: Studies in a Subculture.* London: Methuen, 1972.

———. *Henry Fielding: A Biography.* London: Paul Elek, 1979.

Rumrich, John P. *Milton Unbound*. Cambridge: Cambridge Univ. Press, 1996.

The St. James's Chronicle. London, 1762.

Sechelski, Denise. "Garrick's Body and the Labor of Art in Eighteenth-Century Theater." *Eighteenth-Century Studies* 29 (1996): 369–89.

Seleski, Patty. "Women, Work and Cultural Change in Eighteenth-and Early Nineteenth-Century London." *Popular Culture in England, c. 1500–1850*. Ed. Tim Harris. New York: St. Martin's Press, 1995.

Shapiro, Barbara. "Circumstantial Evidence: of Law, Literature, and Culture." *Yale Journal of Law and the Humanities* 5 (1992): 301–24.

Shepperson, Archibald Bolling. "Additions and Corrections to Facts about Fielding." *Modern Philology* 51 (1954): 217–24.

Sherman, Sandra. *Finance and Fictionality in the Early Eighteenth-Century: Accounting for Defoe*. Cambridge: Cambridge Univ. Press, 1996.

Slack, Paul. "Vagrants and Vagrancy in England, 1598–1664." *Economic History Review*. 2nd series, 37 (1974): 360–79.

Smallwood, Angela J. *Fielding and the Woman Question: The Novels of Henry Fielding and Feminist Debate 1700–1750*. Hemel Hempstead. UK: Harvester Wheatsheaf, 1989.

Smart, Christopher. *The Midwife; or the Old Woman's Magazine*. 3 vols. London, 1751–53.

———. *The Poetical Works of Christopher Smart*. Ed. Karina Williamson et al. 4 vols. Oxford: Clarendon Press, 1980–87.

Sommers, Christina. *Who Stole Feminism?* New York: Simon and Schuster, 1994.

Stafford, Barbara. *Body Criticism: Imaging the Unseen in Enlightenment Art and Medicine*. Cambridge, MA: MIT Press, 1993.

Stallybrass, Peter and Allon White. *The Politics and Poetics of Transgression*. London: Methuen, 1986.

Stewart, Maaja. "Ingratitude in *Tom Jones*." *Journal of English and Germanic Philology* 89 (1990): 512–32.

Staves, Susan. "Fielding and the Comedy of Attempted Rape." *History, Gender & Eighteenth-Century Literature*. Ed. Beth Tobin. Athens: Univ. of Georgia Press, 1994.

Straub, Kristina. *Sexual Suspects: Eighteenth-Century Players and Sexual Ideology*. Princeton: Princeton Univ. Press, 1992.

Swift, Jonathan. *The Prose Works of Jonathan Swift*. Ed. Herbert Davis. 14 vols. Oxford: Basil Blackwell, 1939–68.

Thompson, E. P. *Whigs and Hunters: The Origin of the Black Act*. New York: Pantheon, 1975.

———. *Customs in Common: Studies in Traditional Popular Culture*. New York: New Press, 1993.

Thompson, James. *Models of Value: Eighteenth-Century Political Economy and the Novel*. Durham: Duke Univ. Press, 1996.

[Thornton, Bonnell]. *Have At You All: or, The Drury-Lane Journal*. London, 1752.

———. *The Spring-Garden Journal*. London, 1752.

Tobin, Beth. *Superintending the Poor: Charitable Ladies and Paternal Landlords in British Fiction 1770–1860*. New Haven: Yale Univ. Press, 1993.

Todd, Dennis. *Imagining Monsters: Miscreations of the Self in Eighteenth-Century England.* Chicago: Univ. of Chicago Press, 1995.

Todd, Janet. "Pamela: Or the Bliss of Servitude." *British Journal for Eighteenth-Century Studies* 6 (1983): 135–48.

Treherne, John. *The Canning Enigma.* London: Jonathan Cape, 1989.

Turner, James Grantham. "Novel Panic: Picture and Performance in the Reception of Richardson's Pamela." *Representations* 48 (1994): 70–96.

Varey, Simon. *Henry Fielding.* Cambridge: Cambridge Univ. Press, 1986.

Villiers, George. *The Rehearsal.* 3rd ed. London, 1675.

Walpole, Horace. *Correspondence.* Vol. 35. Ed. W. S. Lewis. New Haven: Yale Univ. Press, 1973.

Wark, Robert. *Drawings by Thomas Rowlandson in the Huntington Collection.* San Marino: Huntington Library, 1975.

Welsh, Alexander. *Strong Representations: Narrative and Circumstantial Evidence in England.* Baltimore: Johns Hopkins Univ. Press, 1992.

Whigham, Frank. "The Rhetoric of Elizabethan Suitor's Letters." *Publications of the Modern Language Association* 96 (1981): 864–82.

Williams, Raymond. *Marxism and Literature.* Oxford: Oxford Univ. Press, 1977.

———. *Keywords: A Vocabulary of Culture and Society.* Rev. ed. New York: Oxford Univ. Press, 1983.

Wilner, Arlene. "The Mythology of History, the Truth of Fiction: Henry Fielding and the Cases of Bosavern Penlez and Elizabeth Canning." *The Journal of Narrative Technique* 21 (1991): 185–202.

Wilson, Kathleen. *The Sense of the People: Politics, Culture and Imperialism in England, 1715–1785.* Cambridge: Cambridge Univ. Press, 1995.

Wolff, Cynthia Griffin. "Fielding's Amelia: Private Virtue and Public Good." *Texas Studies in Language and Literature* 10 (1968): 37–55.

Wright, Andrew. *Henry Fielding: Mask and Feast.* Berkeley: Univ. of California Press, 1965.

Zirker, Malvin. *Fielding's Social Pamphlets.* Berkeley: Univ. of California Press, 1966.

Zomchick, John P. "'A Penetration Which Nothing Can Deceive': Gender and Juridical Discourse in Some Eighteenth-Century Narratives." *Studies in English Literature* 29 (1989): 535–61.

———. *Family and the Law in Eighteenth-Century Fiction: Public Conscience in the Private Sphere.* Cambridge: Cambridge Univ. Press, 1993.

Index